The *What PC?* Guide to your PC

The *What PC?* Guide to your PC

Rob Young

1999 Edition

PRENTICE HALL EUROPE

London New York Toronto Sydney Tokyo
Singapore Madrid Mexico City Munich Paris

First edition published 1990
This edition published 1999
by Prentice Hall Europe
Campus 400, Maylands Avenue
Hemel Hempstead
Hertfordshire, HP2 7EZ
A division of Simon & Schuster International Group

© Prentice Hall Europe 1999

Typeset by Pantek Arts, Maidstone, Kent

Printed and bound by Redwood Books, Trowbridge, Wiltshire

Library of Congress Cataloging-in-Publication Data

Available from the publisher

British Library Cataloguing-in-Publication Data

A catalogue record for this book is available from
the British Library

ISBN 0-13-997073-8

---

1 2 3 4 5   03 02 01 00 99

Contents

Acknowledgements

I get the enjoyable stuff all to myself: I do the writing. When it comes to the real hard work, a team of people steps in to sort it all out. If that sounds like a slice of heaven already, you should meet 'my team'.

Jason Dunne, my commissioning editor since day one, the man who starts the ball rolling with a good idea, and keeps it rolling with more good ideas. If my name appears on the front of a book, Jason's should appear on every page.

Lizzy Gray, the editorial assistant. Lizzy a sorts out all the problems that inevitably crop up, and makes it possible for the rest of us to do what we're supposed to be doing.

David Hemsley, the production editor, saddled with the task of turning my heap of scribbles into a book. David's a new arrival on the team, and I'm looking forward to doing many more books together.

Maria Catt & Maggie Macleod head up the marketing team. We love Maria and Maggie — without them, we'd all be looking for new jobs!

Jo Prentice at **Pantek Arts** for lending us their superb design and editorial skills.

Caroline Ellerby, the copy editor, who translates from Gibberish to English, and corrects all my speeling miskates.

These people, along with the much bigger team of people who support them, all earn my deepest admiration and thanks for doing so much so well.

About this Book

Many people are having to deal with PCs from a standing start. Perhaps you've suddenly found yourself grappling with a PC at work, or your kids are using PCs at school and blinding you with technical gibberish. Maybe you want to work faster, organize your business or connect to the Internet.

In *The What PC? Guide to your PC, 1999 Edition* you'll find clear explanations and advice to help you decide what you need, buy with confidence, and start getting results from your PC. But instead of just leaving you to muddle through alone, *The What PC? Guide to your PC* will help you graduate from 'nervous novice' status by acting as a comprehensive reference whenever you want to buy new hardware and software, solve a problem, or become more expert at using Windows.

How to Use this Book

Although you *can* read this book from cover to cover you probably won't want to, or indeed need to. For this reason, *The What PC? Guide to your PC* makes it easy to casually 'dip in' and find what you need, whether you're buying, learning, troubleshooting or looking for a few practical tips. You can use the Contents pages or the Index to locate what you need, or just flick through until you see something you'd like to know more about. Here's a thumbnail description of what you'll find in each part of the book:

Part 1 looks at the PC itself: its internal bits and pieces such as memory and disks, external devices like mouse and keyboard, and optional add-on gadgets such as a printer or a scanner. What are all these things? What do they do to each other when they get together? What should you have in your PC?

Part 2 gives you all the details you'll need to work with Windows 95 and Windows 98. Learn how to open, save, edit and print files, switch between programs, customize Windows to suit your way of working, and keep the system running smoothly.

Part 3 examines the types of program you can use on your PC to accomplish different tasks, and the most popular titles in each category. With plenty of tips and clear advice on what to buy, you'll learn how to install and uninstall software and start getting results from the programs you choose.

Part 4 tells you how to get connected to the Internet, and what to do once you're online. Find out what software you need and where to get it, and learn how to send and receive email, browse the World Wide Web, and chat to other Internet users all over the world.

The **Directory** gives you an indispensable collection of contact details for companies and stores that sell computer software and hardware, provide access to the Internet, or offer other computer-related services. If you decide to connect to the Internet, you'll also find a useful list of companies' Web sites from where you can download software or find answers to problems.

Licensing Agreement

This book comes with a CD software package. By opening this package, you are agreeing to be bound by the following:

The software contained on this CD is, in many cases, copyrighted, and all rights are reserved by the individual licensing agreements associated with each piece of software contained on the CD. This software is provided free of charge, as is, and without warranty of any kind, either expressed or implied, including, but not limited to, the implied warranties of merchantability and fitness for a particular purpose. Neither the book publisher nor its dealers and its distributors assumes any liability for any alleged or actual damages arising from the use of this software.

Introduction

Consider the VCR. The Video Cassette Recorder was *the* gadget of the 1980s. Resistance was useless: sooner or later you just had to have one. And so began the ritual 'new toy' combination of button-pushing and swearing. In desperation, perhaps, you read the manual. Eventually you admitted defeat, and asked the nearest eight-year-old for a clue. Within a week, you'd probably achieved the ultimate goal of taping the programme you hoped you were taping, and the rest was history.

The VCR is a type of computer. But, with apologies to anyone still struggling to use theirs, it's a pretty basic one – it handles just one task after all – so choosing a VCR is a relatively simple process of weighing up price, ease-of-use and appearance. There's no jargon involved, no add-on bits and pieces to buy, no need to read books about it before buying.

Choosing a PC is a whole different ball-game. The PC is capable of handling a vast number of tasks, but this capability isn't actually *built into* the machine. What your computer can do depends almost entirely on your choice of hardware and software, and each separate element comes complete with its own set of jargon and techno-speak. To make matters more confusing still, the computer is one of the few items you buy inside-out! All the internal organs of a computer are proudly listed in its advertisements to let you poke around and decide what you want in yours.

The importance point to understand is that this is *good!* Although a little daunting at first, it's all this choice that makes the PC so much more versatile than the VCR. And it's the reason why the PC is able to earn its keep in almost any environment: multinational company; school; small business; child's bedroom; film or music studio...

At this stage, of course, the 'daunting' aspect is going to win every time, but don't be put off by all the acronyms, abbreviations and technical twaddle that crop up in any discussion of computers. You don't *have* to know how it all works to buy it or use it, and you certainly don't have to memorize it all!

Part One

Buying & Upgrading your PC

In This Part...

Chapter 1

What is a PC?

In This Chapter...

What is this thing we call a PC?

Meet the five major pieces that make up a computer

Choose your PC – desktop, notebook or miniature

What is a PC?

What's a computer?

In its most basic terms, the computer is a device that accepts some form of input (you punch in a number, for example), processes it in some way (adds it to a number you'd punched in previously), and produces an output or result (gives you the answer to its piece of addition).

Obviously we're talking calculators here. The pocket-calculator is a non-technical, non-frightening example, but it has all the basic attributes of the modern computer: it has buttons for input, a processor to do the calculations, a small amount of memory to let it remember one number while dealing with another, and a screen to display its output. The major difference is that the calculator knows only one trick, and it isn't likely to learn any new ones. In fact, the very first home-computers back in the mid-1970s were little more than glorified adding machines, but they had one extra vital ingredient: ambition!

JARGON BUSTER

Hardware

Hardware is a blanket term that describes all the electronic compenents of a computer: a piece of hardware could be anything from a mains-plug to a monitor. Think of it this way: would it break if you dropped it from the top of a building? If it would, it's hardware.

So what's a PC?

PC is simply an abbreviation of personal computer. This general term could be applied to any moderately small computer containing all the hardware and software it needs to 'compute' by itself. The idea behind a computer being 'personal' is that it should be cheap enough that each user should be able to have his or her own machine rather than sharing it with the entire office, and small enough that it fits on a desktop or sits on your lap.

This general definition could encompass a vast range of computers manufactured by companies such as Apple-Macintosh, Atari, Amiga and Acorn. In recent years, however, the term has taken on a new *generic* meaning, and now refers specifically to a computer that is IBM Personal Computer-compatible – the type of computer made by Dell, Gateway, Viglen, Packard-Bell, and thousands of others.

Software

The general term that describes a computer program (or a set of computer programs) that tells the computer to do particular things according to the input you provide. Common software you're likely to need would be a word-processing program (to write letters and reports), and a graphics program (to draw and edit pictures and photographs).

What's in the box?

The odd thing about PCs is that they tend to be bought in pieces. You'll almost certainly want to add extra capabilities to your machine somewhere down the road, and perhaps replace some of its internal organs for bigger, better, or faster versions. All those separate pieces of computer are available straight off the shelf, and we'll take a closer look at them later in this part of the book.

New computers are bought in just the same way. You decide what you need, wander into your local computer store or pick up the phone, and say: 'It's got to have one of these, and one of those, and I want a built-in thingummy and a couple of wossnames.' The retailer will put all this together for you, check it works, and present you with a large cardboard box. But apart from a year's supply of polystyrene, what will that box contain?

There are five basic elements to a computer, and these vary in description depending on your choice of desktop or notebook machine (covered on the next few pages). We'll look at each element in greater detail later on, but here's a thumbnail view:

System unit

This is the largest component, and is the case which houses the computer itself. In here, should you choose to look, you'll find the motherboard: this is a large circuit board containing the processor, memory chips, and expansion slots. In the drive bays towards the front of the unit you should spot a hard-disk drive and a floppy-disk drive. Looking at the outside of the unit, the floppy-disk drive is a little more obvious, with a slot to insert the disk and a light to indicate when the drive is busy. You should also find a power switch, a reset switch, and varying numbers of coloured lights (some manufacturers seem to be frustrated disc jockeys!).

Drive bays

A drive bay is a slot in the front of the system unit where more disk drives can be installed. Drive bays are two different sizes, $5^1/_4$-inch and $3^1/_2$-inch, to accept different-sized drives. CD-ROM drives are $5^1/_4$ inches wide, floppy-disk and tape drives are usually $3^1/_2$ inches. Most new PCs will offer at least three bays, one of which will already have a floppy-disk drive fitted.

Monitor

This is the large item that looks a lot like a TV screen. In the computer's Input/Process/Output sequence, the monitor represents the main output device, which lets you see the results of your input and the computer's processing. The monitor is connected to the system unit by two cables: one is a power cable drawing current from the system unit's power supply; the other connects to a circuit board, called the display adapter, which tells the monitor what to display.

Keyboard

The keyboard is one of the two ubiquitous input devices that pass on what you type into the system unit for processing by means of a single cable. This cable also provides a tiny power supply to the keyboard.

Mouse

Not the small furry thing that chews through your cables, but the second of the two input devices. Movement of the mouse around a small àrea of your desk controls the movement of an arrow-shaped pointer on the monitor screen. By itself this doesn't accomplish much, but the mouse also has two or three buttons: clicking these buttons will make the computer do different things depending upon what you're 'pointing' at when you 'click'.

Software

Okay, this is a bit of a sly one. You might find a small amount of software in the box (most deals on new computers include a few games or product samplers that you can install or ignore as you wish) but the most important software should be already installed on the hard-disk and ready to use.

Fundamentally, this should be an operating system, a collection of software programs that handles the vital task of interpreting your input and telling the rest of the system what to do to make you happy. Unless you've been living down a hole for the last few years, you've probably heard of Windows, the most popular operating system for PCs. Depending on the deal offered by the computer store, and/or what software you specifically asked for, other software might also be included. Stores will almost always install the software for you, and make sure it all runs correctly: if they didn't, they'd risk the expense of sending someone out to help if you got into difficulties!

Three flavours of PC

Of course, with each of these elements there are choices to be made when buying, and they usually come down to a balance between what you like and what you need to do. So let's round off this first look at the PC by addressing one of the basic choices you'll have to make before you buy: desktop, notebook or handheld?

The desktop PC

The desktop PC has long been the established standard, and it's probably what you picture when you think of a computer. As its name suggests, it's designed to sit on your desk and stay there. One big difference between this and the notebook PC is size: the system unit has a mass of free space inside, allowing extra components to be fitted that will increase the power and flexibility of your machine. Once installed, these new accessories are instantly available every time you switch on your PC. Similarly, it's usually easy to replace existing components with newer, more powerful ones (known as upgrading) if the need arises.

Despite its name, the desktop PC's system unit no longer needs to be on the desk. Traditionally, the unit sat behind your keyboard and you plonked the monitor on top of it. In response to demand, a little rejigging of layout has resulted in a system unit with a tower case: in a small room, this has the great advantage that you can stow the unit out of the way under your desk and still be able to pop a disk into its floppy-disk drive without too many physical contortions.

The second major difference between the desktop and the notebook is price. The technical difficulties involved in building all this power into a smaller box mean that a notebook PC is always more expensive than a desktop with the same specifications.

The notebook PC

The notebook PC has been known by quite a variety of names over the years: to begin with it was called the 'portable' – a term which required a slight stretch of the imagination when trying to carry one any distance. The portable gradually became smaller and lighter and today these early portables tend to be known as 'luggables' for obvious reasons. Further downward shifts in scale gave us the 'laptop', and now finally the notebook, so called because of its similarity in size to a sheet of A4 paper (apart from being about two inches thicker, of course!).

It isn't easy to make a PC portable. It must have similar capabilities to the desktop variety in a much smaller case, which obviously involves removing a few components and making a number of others more compact. Nevertheless, the fundamentals are all there: the monitor is housed in the hinged lid, which flips up to reveal the keyboard; the mouse is replaced by a trackball or a touch-sensitive pad, which requires less room to manoeuvre; and the hard disk sits beneath the keyboard together with the slot-in rechargeable battery.

As with the desktop PC, extra accessories can be added to the notebook, but due to the constraints of size they can't be fitted permanently. The solution is the addition of slots in the side of the case so that the extras (in the form of credit card-sized devices known as PC Cards) can be plugged in when needed. Another constraint upon notebook-users is that upgrading internal components can be difficult, expensive and, in some cases, impossible, so it becomes all the more important to choose your machine carefully.

The miniature PC

The third type of PC is the 'everything else' category. If you've decided you need a computer, the odds are that you need either the desktop or the notebook variety and you won't need to consider the remaining options. Miniature PCs vary in their power and capability, but what they have in common is that they make significant compromises to bring you something that looks and acts rather like a PC in a much smaller case.

The first of these types is the **sub-notebook**, a device that looks a lot like a notebook PC but is roughly half the size and weight. This means that the screen and keyboard are half the size as well, which may make the PC uncomfortable to use for long periods, but many sub-notebooks are as powerful and capable as a full-sized notebook computer. One of the most popular sub-notebooks is the Toshiba Libretto.

Scaling down even further, there's the **handheld PC** (HPC, sometimes called a Personal Digital Assistant or PDA). The HPC is small enough to hold in your hand, at around 7 inches across by 4 inches deep. Despite its diminutive size, it still has a screen and tiny keyboard, along with enough storage capacity to hold a bundle of useful programs and files you create yourself. Until recently, the HPC market has been ruled by the US Robotics PalmPilot and the Psion series, which were essentially electronic organizers rather than computers, but a new range of handhelds has arrived that uses a cut-down version of the Windows operating system called Windows CE. Windows CE enables the HPC to do some of the things a desktop or notebook PC can do, but its main role is still to act as a pocket organizer and scratch pad for times when you're away from your desktop PC. Popular HPCs are Hewlett-Packard's HP320/HP360 series and the Philips Velo 1.

Finally there's the **Palm PC**, a still smaller device that also uses Windows CE. The keyboard appears as a picture on its tiny screen and letters are 'typed' by touching the screen. This little unit can record voice messages and recognize your handwriting when you write on its screen with a stylus. Like the sub-notebook and handheld PCs, you can connect this to your main PC to transfer files back and forth between the two.

Chapter 2

Ins & Outs
of the PC

In This Chapter...

The computer: it works like you do!

Three vital PC functions: processing, memory and storage

Counting in kilobytes and megabytes

The difference between programs and documents

Ins & Outs
of the PC

If you've never used a computer before, there's no escaping the fact that you're about to expand your vocabulary with words like 'processor', 'megabyte', 'files' and 'hard disk'. You might not be able to throw them casually into everyday conversation, but they'll crop up whenever you want to buy computer hardware or software. So, before we get down to the task of choosing a PC, let's take the mystery out of some of these words.

What's going on in there?

The basic principles of how the computer operates are pretty straightforward – the PC works very much like you do:

- Your brain receives input from your ears, eyes, and so on; the computer receives input from the keyboard and the mouse (and, perhaps, one or two other optional devices you've connected).

- You have a brain for working things out; the computer has a processor.

- You have various methods of outputting the results of your brainwork, such as writing or speaking; the computer can output results by displaying them on the monitor, printing on paper, or saving on to a disk.

- As you try to think out a tricky problem, you keep as many of the details in your mind as you can; the computer has its own forms of memory to do a similar job.

- If a job comes in that suddenly requires your full attention, you make notes about the first job on a piece of paper so that you can come back to it later; the modern PC is able to empty its memory enough to handle a different task and then 'read' this same information back in when it wants to use it again.

- You probably have a filing cabinet or a drawer where you keep your important files and documents; the computer contains a disk for the same purpose.

The brains behind the operation

In the internal workings of the human being, nothing at all can happen without the active participation of the brain. The same is true of the computer, but the 'brain' in question is a small microchip called a central processing unit (CPU) or processor. Because the processor plays a vital part in everything the computer does, it's constantly working behind the scenes and juggling a large number of tasks in blindingly quick succession. Exactly how fast it can handle each task is one of the main yardsticks used in determining that subjective factor, the power of the computer. To a large extent, the faster your processor, the more powerful your PC.

JARGON BUSTER

Data

Data is a sort of synonym for 'information'. While the computer is storing it or working with it, it's data – a meaningless stream of numbers to you and me. When some sense has been made of it all and it's presented on screen or paper, it's information.

Ins & outs

To continue the 'brain' analogy just a little longer, the processor sends data to most parts of the PC's 'body', and receives data back from most of them. But not every part of the system will receive data, and not every part will send it. The computer is made up of three types of hardware component: input devices, output devices, and combined input/output devices.

- An **input** device sends data to the processor but doesn't need to receive anything in return: the mouse is a good example of an input-only device.

- An **output** device receives data from the processor and presents it to us in some way; examples of output devices are the monitor and the printer.

- An **input/output** device exchanges data back and forth with the processor. The archetypal input/output device is the hard disk: sometimes the processor will send data to the disk to be stored, and at other times it will retrieve data from the disk to be used.

Bits & PCs

As you can tell from the brief outline above, there's a lot going on, and data is endlessly being passed around the system. But what is this data? What form does it take?

Computers work only with binary numbers. The binary system is a method of counting in 'base two', which involves using combinations of the numbers 0 and 1, equating to 'off' and 'on'. On the surface this may seem limiting, but if the processor only has to distinguish between these two possible states it can therefore handle immense streams of these digits (generically known as data) in a very short space of time. Each of these 0s and 1s is called a bit, which is short for BInary digiT.

Because a single bit by itself can't convey much information, bits are grouped into sets of eight called bytes. A byte is far more meaningful, offering 256 different combinations of 0s and 1s, so a single byte can communicate numbers from 0 to 255. As a point of interest, one byte is equivalent to a single typed character.

Kilobytes & megabytes

Bits and bytes are terms used to count quantities of data, but they're pretty small measures and computers have to deal with much larger chunks of data. For example, a small word-processor program with fairly limited features could be around 200,000 bytes in size. Because we're dealing with numbers of this order most of the time, two additional terms are used: the kilobyte (abbreviated to K), which equals 1,024 bytes, and the megabyte (abbreviated to Mb), which equals 1,024 kilobytes or 1,048,576 bytes. Another term being encountered more frequently as technology progresses is the gigabyte (Gb), which is equal to 1,024 megabytes.

These terms are used most frequently when discussing the capacities of two particular types of computer hardware: memory and hard disk.

Programs and operating systems are getting bigger all the time (for example, Windows 98 will typically take a minimum of 150Mb of space on your hard disk), so the greater the capacity of the hard disk, the better.

Memory & storage

The computer, as we know, deals with huge amounts of data. However, at any one time only a comparatively tiny amount is actually being processed, and a small amount is travelling between the various components. So where's all the rest of it?

By far the largest amount of data is stored ready for use whenever it's needed (which could be in a couple of minutes' time, or even next year!) and the main storage medium is the hard disk. This is a magnetic disk inside the computer on which all your programs are kept, together with the documents you create when using those programs, and all the other software required to control the computer itself.

Memory is a type of short-term storage, and the modern PC has several types of memory at its disposal. The most important of these is called RAM (Random Access Memory) which comes in the form of small modules on cards that slot into the computer's motherboard. Every program and document that you use (including the operating system) is read from the hard disk and loaded into the computer's RAM. When the RAM gets full, the computer has to find alternative places to put some of this data temporarily. These alternatives do exist, but they can't send back the data as quickly as RAM when it's next needed, which results in the whole computer slowing down. The bottom line here is that there's no such thing as too much RAM!

Motherboard

A large circuit board inside the system unit on which most of the computer's major components are situated. The design of the board ensures that everything attached to it (including any devices you add later) will be able to communicate wth everything else.

Files, programs & documents

Returning once again to the 'human body' analogy, data is the 'blood' of the computer, being passed around its major organs all the time and keeping the whole thing working. Although all this data moves around as a stream of bits, it needs to be grouped and stored in a more organized way to let you find what you need quickly and easily. These groups of related data are called **files**, and a file will be either of two types: a program or a document.

A program is a file containing a specific set of instructions or commands to the computer. Some of these programs will be run automatically when your computer starts to make the computer work as it should. These are part of the operating system. Other programs you will run yourself when you need to use them – for example a word-processing application when you want to write a letter, or a graphics application when you want to draw a picture.

Application

An application is a type of program that is used to create something – a drawing, a table, a database, and so on – as distinct from a program that provides entertainment (such as a game) or lets you change system settings or dial a phone number.

A document file is something you create yourself. When you run your word-processing application and write a letter, this letter is being stored in the short-term memory (RAM) while you're working on it. When it's finished and sitting on the screen in front of you, you can choose what to do with it. You might want to print it out on paper ready to send to someone, then close down the application and forget it – if you do this, the RAM will forget it too. Or you can save the letter as a file that you can look at and edit in the future; in effect, this means you're moving your letter from the short-term memory to the permanent store (the hard disk). Files that you create in this way, which contain meaningful information, are called documents.

Chapter 3

Under the Hood – The Important Stuff

In This Chapter...

Choose the best processor for your needs

Hard disk and memory – you can't have too much!

Make sure you've got room for future expansion

Find out where everything plugs in

Under the Hood – The Important Stuff

Of all the hundreds of possible bits and pieces that could make up your PC system, some are vital, some are desirable, and many more are optional add-ons that one user would regard as essentials and another would consider to be frivolous luxuries. In the next few chapters we'll look at what's available and how to choose the devices you need, whether you're buying a completely new system or upgrading your current machine. And where better to start than inside the system unit, home of the indispensable parts that make your computer 'compute'!

The processor – brain & brawn

The processor is the 'brain' of the computer – the chip that makes all the calculations and produces the results – so it's one of the most important parts of the machine despite its diminutive size – about one-and-a-half inches square. You'll sometimes see it referred to as a microprocessor or a CPU (Central Processing Unit), but these names all refer to the same thing. Because of its essential nature, the type of processor included is used to describe the computer and distinguish it from other PCs: when people say they have a powerful computer, what they really mean is that they have a computer with a powerful processor.

What does it do?

Just like the human brain, the processor does a vast number of things: it obeys instructions one at a time, but so quickly that they all appear to be happening at the same time. In any given fraction of a second, the processor will take a look at the keyboard input socket to see if you've typed anything, and at the mouse input to see if you've moved or clicked the mouse; it might send more data to be displayed on the monitor, and read data from the computer's memory store or hard disk. If you have other devices attached to your computer, such as a printer or a modem, it will be watching these for incoming data and/or sending data to them.

So, however calm and unflustered it all seems on the surface, the processor is actually going like crazy underneath! And it follows that whatever you do and whenever you do it, you're going to interrupt its well-organized routine. Just as the human brain is adept at swapping back and forth between different tasks, the processor uses the computer's memory chips (RAM) to keep track of what it was doing before you interrupted.

What do you need?

If you've looked at advertisements for PCs, you've probably noticed that they prominently feature a line that looks something like this:

Pentium II 350MHz

This is one of the most important things to check in any computer advertisement. The first part of the line (Pentium) refers to the type of processor chip, and the second refers to the chip's speed in megahertz:

The **type** of chip might be a Pentium or a Pentium II. Older types of chips were called the 386 (long since defunct) and the 486 (recently defunct).

The **speed** is given in megahertz (pronounced 'megga-hurts') and measures how fast the processor works. In general, the higher the speed, the less time you'll have to wait for the computer to do what you're asking.

The standard buy is the Intel Pentium II processor at a speed of around 333MHz. If you're looking for a budget machine, go for a Pentium II at 233MHz or a Pentium at 200MHz. Any of these will comfortably run the Windows 95 or Windows 98 operating systems, but a Pentium II processor will give an extra turn of speed to any operating system you use, and is the better bet if you opt to use the heavyweight Windows NT operating system. If you're working with large graphics such as photographs or computer-aided design (CAD), or with very large databases, spreadsheets and desktop-publishing, a fast processor is essential. You can expect to see Pentium II processors with speeds of up to 600MHz appearing during 1999. Alternatives to the Pentium and Pentium II processors come in the form of the Intel Celeron, a cheap and low-powered device, and the powerful Intel Xeon, aimed at demanding network environments rather than the typical home or small office user.

You may have heard the term 'MMX', which stands for 'multimedia extensions', or seen the advertisements for processors with MMX on television. Although MMX has been hyped out of all reality, a processor with MMX is better than one without. If you choose a machine with a Pentium processor, try to pick one that includes the 'MMX' tag to get slightly better performance from graphics, games, sound and video. Pentium II processors all have MMX, so don't worry if the PII computer you're looking at doesn't explicitly mention MMX.

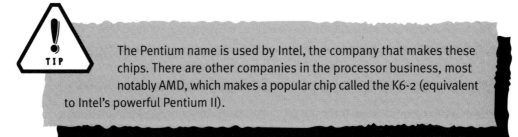

The Pentium name is used by Intel, the company that makes these chips. There are other companies in the processor business, most notably AMD, which makes a popular chip called the K6-2 (equivalent to Intel's powerful Pentium II).

Memory – the more the merrier

Memory is a short-term holding place for data that is currently in use, is about to be used, or has just been used. In fact, there are several holding places of different types that the PC uses in different situations, and they vary in speed and effectiveness. The most important of these is RAM (Random Access Memory): as long as your computer has enough RAM, all the files currently in use are held there, and your PC should respond quickly when you try to do something. But when the RAM is full, the computer starts using the much slower hard disk to supplement it. The more the hard disk needs to be used, the slower your machine will run.

The answer, of course, is to have enough RAM so that the computer rarely (or never) needs to use the hard disk as temporary memory. So how much is enough? Don't go for anything with less than 32Mb and regard 64Mb as being the optimum amount for most uses. Some new computers are still being sold with only 16Mb, but any retailer will be happy to slot in another 8 for a small amount of extra money.

TIP

RAM comes in different types. The 'ordinary' RAM is known as DRAM (pronounced 'dee-ram'), but look out for systems with EDO-RAM for a slight performance boost, or SDRAM for even more speedy operation.

A second type of memory is called the cache (pronounced 'cash'), which is a lightning-fast store that holds recently used data in case it's needed again. You'll sometimes see this referred to as 'external cache' or 'level 2 cache'. Pentium systems come with 256Kb of cache memory, but Pentium II systems and Pentiums with MMX often double this up to a punchier 512Kb.

Hard disk – the bigger the better

Think of your files (operating system, applications and documents) as a car: when you want to use your car you take it out on to the road, and drive about between Processorville, RAM City, and other nearby places. When you don't want to use it you park it somewhere. Once you've parked it, you can leave it there as long as you like. This could be for just a minute or two, or it could be for months or even years!

The disk is a car park for your files, known generically as a 'mass storage medium', and there are two different types: the hard disk and the floppy disk (sometimes referred to as a diskette). Of these two, the hard disk is by far the more important because it can hold much more data. Since the most significant consideration about any storage device is how much data you can store in it, hard disks are noted by their capacities in megabytes (Mb).

To put hard-disk size into some sort of perspective, when you take delivery of your new PC your hard disk will already have a Windows operating system installed, perhaps a suite of office applications such as Lotus SmartSuite (see Chapter 24), and a few other 'freebie' programs. At a rough estimate, 400Mb of your hard disk is already in use, and that's before you start adding the other programs you want to use, and storing the files you create yourself!

The intention with a hard disk isn't to fill it! If the disk has plenty of empty space, your PC will always be able to find somewhere on it to store data quickly and easily, and remain that much more responsive as a result.

If there's any budget-stretching to be done, a large hard-disk is the reason to do it. It isn't easy to replace the disk you've outgrown with a larger one and transfer all your data to it, and adding a second disk is a lot more expensive than buying a large one at the outset. Regard a 3.2Gb disk as the absolute minimum; something over 4Gb is a safer bet. Many systems now include a 6.4Gb disk as standard, and this is well worth stretching to if you can. Systems with hard disk capacities of over 9Gb are becoming increasingly common, and you might want to consider something of this size if you expect to put your computer to a number of different uses involving a number of different programs, or to work extensively with large files such as graphics, sounds, videos or desktop publishing.

A floppy-disk drive for sharing files

Now is a good time to clarify the word 'drive'. A disk is literally a circular magnetic piece of metal on which data is stored. The drive is the surrounding box that contains the disk and the various components that read data from it and write more data onto it.

The hard disk and its drive are bought as a single unit and hidden away inside your PC's system unit. The drive for floppy disks is a $3\frac{1}{2}$-inch wide unit installed at the front of your system unit with a slot for inserting disks and a button for ejecting them.

All new desktop computers come with a single $3\frac{1}{2}$-inch floppy-disk drive, and one is usually enough. A floppy disk holds up to 1.44Mb of data, which isn't really sufficient for day-to-day work with files, and computers read floppy disks much more slowly than they read from your hard disk. Floppy disks are mainly used to copy files onto in order to give them to someone else, or to keep safety copies of small files. The disks themselves are cheap (around 30p each).

Many notebook computers come with a floppy-disk drive, but the constraints of size mean that it may be a separate device that you plug in when you need it. In some notebooks you'll need to unplug the CD-ROM drive first (see Chapter 5) and plug the floppy drive in its place. If the notebook is going to be your only PC, try to find a system that lets you use both CD-ROM and floppy drives at the same time.

A BIOS to get things started

As with the floppy-disk drive, you don't need to ask specifically for a computer with a BIOS – it's definitely got one! 'BIOS' is an acronym for basic input/output system and, as its name suggests, it plays an important part in transferring your input (for example from the keyboard) to the processor, and transferring the processor's output to the monitor and other devices. As far as this goes, it's comforting to know that something is doing that, but it's not terribly interesting and we won't dwell on it. However, before the BIOS embarks on this full-time job, it has a sort of paper-round to take care of first: it has to get your system working.

The BIOS is a set of small programs stored on a special chip, the basic role of which is to tell your computer about itself. When you turn on your computer's power switch, the BIOS programs spring into action and start a sequence known as the POST (Power-On Self Test). Until the PC knows it has a hard drive, a floppy drive, memory, a keyboard, and so on, and that they're all properly connected and working, it can't start to use them. You'll see the BIOS details displayed briefly every time you turn on your PC.

When buying your PC, there are three things worth looking for in a BIOS, and the salesperson should be able to confirm these for you:

- A BIOS that's 'Plug and Play compatible' will make the installation and setup of new hardware an automatic process rather than a tedious and (sometimes) difficult one.

- An energy-saving BIOS can put your computer to sleep after a specified period if you go away and do something else, drawing just enough power to keep the contents of the RAM intact for when you return.

- A 'flash BIOS' can be upgraded to the latest version by installing special software instead of replacing the BIOS chip itself. This feature is seen less often than the two listed above; it certainly isn't vital, but it's an added bonus.

Holding it all together...

Everything we've mentioned in this chapter, and every other piece of hardware you want to add to your system, connects to the motherboard, which is a large circuit board inside the system unit that lets everything 'talk' to everything else. Generally speaking, the larger the motherboard, the more room there is for future expansion to increase the power or capability of your PC. The size of the motherboard is determined by the style of case it has to fit into, so let's start by looking at what's available.

Choose your case

The case of the desktop PC's system unit comes in three flavours, although each will vary in size and layout according to the manufacturer:

Desktop – the original case design, roughly 4 inches high and 15 inches wide, designed to sit behind the keyboard with the monitor on top.

Mini tower – looks like an up-ended desktop case, and stands on your desk beside the monitor.

Full tower – a larger version of the mini tower that sits on the floor beneath your desk.

Very often, the computer you've got your eye on will be available with a choice of case styles, so it doesn't hurt to ask if you can't see any mention of the style you want.

Counting the drive bays

Drive bays are slots in the front of the system unit into which additional drives can be installed. When you take delivery of your new PC, you'll probably find that two of these are in use already, holding the floppy disk drive and a CD-ROM drive. The remaining bays have plastic covers to protect them from your lunch until they're needed.

Drive bays come in two sizes and most modern PCs have at least two bays of each size. The $3\frac{1}{2}$-inch bay holds a standard floppy-disk drive and some types of backup drive (see Chapter 6). The larger $5\frac{1}{4}$-inch bay is for CD-ROM drives, backup drives, and an older type of floppy-disk drive now rarely used.

As with most things in the computer world, the more drive bays you have available, the better. This is going to depend to some degree on your choice of case: a full tower case might have a total of six or seven bays, whereas the desktop or mini tower might have just four. If you expect to use or copy floppy disks in any great quantity, a spare $3\frac{1}{2}$-inch slot will let you add a second floppy drive. Otherwise, $5\frac{1}{4}$-inch drives are the more plentiful, so a PC with a CD-ROM drive already installed, and one or more free bays of this size is ideal.

Memory & expansion slots

Hidden away in the dim recesses of the motherboard is a rack of expansion slots into which you can plug expansion cards that add new capabilities to your PC. These cards are 4 to 8 inches long and about 3 inches wide. If you were to look inside the system unit you'd see at least two of these cards: one is the graphics adapter that keeps the picture on your monitor updated (more on that in Chapter 4), and the other handles the task of moving data around between all the different pieces of your system. Other types of card might contain a modem to let you send faxes or connect to the Internet (see Chapter 6), or add sound capabilities (Chapter 5).

To complicate the issue a little, there are two types of slots and cards used in modern PCs:

ISA (Industry Standard Architecture) – an old technology that the computer industry can't seem to shake off.

PCI (Peripheral Component Interconnect) – a more recent format that lets cards handle data faster and with less involvement from the processor.

A new PC should have at least three of each type of slot, and you'd ideally want two of each to be empty unless your PC already has a soundcard and modem installed. Some types of.expansion card will be ISA and others will be PCI. A few devices can be bought in either format, but the PCI version will be more expensive. You don't need to know how these work but there's one important point to remember: try to keep track of how many free slots of each type you have – it's heartbreaking to come home with a new PCI card and find that all your PCI slots are full!

Some Pentium II systems also include a single **AGP** slot, which stands for Accelerated Graphics Port. This lets you use one of the latest and fastest AGP graphics cards (see Chapter 4) to give the best possible display of games, video and 3D graphics. If your PC has an AGP slot, the odds are that you've already got an AGP graphics card installed in it.

You might stumble across another format, VESA or (VL Bus). This was the forerunner to PCI, and any remaining computers using this format are best avoided.

A smaller set of slots in the motherboard holds the chips containing the RAM. These chips are called SIMMs or DIMMs (Single or Dual Inline Memory Modules), and a single chip might contain 8, 16, 32 or 64Mb of memory. SIMM chips must be fitted in pairs, whereas you can buy and install DIMM chips one at a time. You'll usually have at least four of these slots, but ideally no more than two should be in use when you take delivery of your computer: if your PC has 32Mb of RAM, you should have either one 32Mb DIMM chip or a pair of 16Mb SIMMs. At any time in the future, you can buy another DIMM or a pair of SIMMs to install in the free slots to increase your PC's total RAM.

Ports & sockets

The back of the system unit is where everything gets connected together, and you'll find a dazzling array of sockets (some of which, inexplicably, are known as 'ports'). On most systems each socket will be labelled, but here's a quick rundown of what you can expect to find:

Main power – a 3-pin male socket that powers the whole system and looks like an electric kettle connection.

Monitor power – a 3-pin female socket that powers the monitor.

Monitor display – a 15-pin female socket that sends the display signal to the monitor.

Keyboard – a 5-pin DIN (circular) socket to connect and power the keyboard.

Serial ports – two 25-pin male sockets called COM1 and COM2 (short for 'Communications') to which the mouse, external modem, and other devices can be connected. Some PCs and devices use a 9-pin socket or cable, but you can buy a cheap adapter to connect the two types.

Parallel port – a 25-pin female socket that could be labelled LPT1 or Printer Port, to which printers, scanners and other devices can be connected.

PS2 ports – one or more 6-pin female sockets, used for the mouse and keyboard. Few PCs have PS2 ports; instead they use the serial and keyboard sockets.

USB ports – a new type of port included in the latest PCs. Up to 127 separate devices can be connected to a single USB port, by linking them together in a chain. USB ports let you install a new device by simply adding it to the end of the chain; no complicated settings need to be made before you start using it, unlike devices that plug into expansion slots. The only catch is that the devices you buy must be built specifically for connecting to a USB port, and the range of compatible devices is still fairly limited.

Many of the expansion cards you install on your system will add extra sockets. These are fitted to one edge of the card, and this edge is visible at the back of the system unit when the card is installed. If you add a soundcard, for example, you'll have a speaker-output socket, a headphone socket, and a game port for plugging in a joystick.

Never connect or disconnect your mouse, keyboard or any other device while your computer is switched on: it's one of the surest ways to turn electronic technology into frazzled desktop ornaments.

Chapter 4

Three Essentials – Monitor, Mouse & Keyboard

In This Chapter...

Make sure your monitor is large enough

Improve the viewing experience with a quality graphics card

Rodent or not? Pick your pointing device

Choose a keyboard for comfort

Three Essentials – Monitor, Mouse & Keyboard

Although the system unit contains all the technical wizardry that *is* the computer, by itself it isn't much use. To actually work with the computer you need a monitor to see what's going on, and a keyboard and mouse to communicate with the system. In this chapter, we'll tell you what to look for and what to avoid, whether you're buying an entire system or just looking for a more comfortable keyboard.

Picture this – your ideal monitor

The most important thing to consider in a monitor is its size, and you'll see 14-inch, 15-inch and 17-inch monitors bundled with new computers (although larger sizes are available separately). The first piece of advice here is simple: don't buy a 14-inch monitor. Although the difference between 14-inch and 15-inch seems small, the larger size represents an extra 15 per cent of viewing area. If a 14-inch monitor is quoted in the price of a computer, ask what it costs to upgrade to a 15-inch – most companies will happily quote for this, and the small additional cost is money well spent.

The price jump to a 17-inch monitor is greater, but this is the recommended size, particularly if you'll be using your computer for more than a few hours a day. For particular uses, 17-inch or larger monitors are worth their weight in gold (which, admittedly, is what they seem to cost at the moment): if you'll be working with large spreadsheets, desktop publishing or artwork and graphics, you'll want to see as much information on screen at once as you possibly can. Remember that it's better to pay £150 extra for a large monitor now than to pay £400 upwards to replace your current monitor next year.

Size is important, but it isn't everything. You'll be spending many hours gazing at your monitor, so here are three extra features to check before buying:

● It must be an **SVGA** monitor (and it probably will be). This is a vast improvement over the old VGA type, displaying over 16 million colours (as opposed to just 16) with much greater clarity and definition.

● It must be **non-interlaced**. Interlaced monitors use a method of updating the screen that creates a constant flicker, making them very unpleasant to work with.

● It should have a **dot pitch** of 0.28mm or less. The dot pitch is the spacing between the tiny dots that make up the display: as a rule of thumb, the smaller the dot pitch, the greater the clarity.

There are many good makes of monitor available, but three of the best are ADI, Panasonic, and Iiyama.

You need a graphics card

The graphics card is the expansion card that controls what your monitor displays, and it's referred to by a number of different names including 'display adapter' or 'graphics accelerator'. For your monitor to display anything at all a graphics card is required, but a monitor can only be as good as the graphics card that drives it, so it pays to buy carefully.

Graphics cards come with their own built-in memory (RAM) modules, and the quantity of RAM on the card determines the maximum resolution and colour depth your monitor can display. The resolution refers to the number of dots per inch (dpi) that your monitor can display: you don't want to work at anything less than 800 × 600dpi, and the next largest resolution, 1,024 × 768dpi, allows much more information to be displayed at any one time. The colour depth refers to the number of colours used to draw what you see on the screen. You can choose from colour palettes containing a rather washed-out 16 colours up to a true-to-life 16.7 million colours.

Both of these settings need particular quantities of RAM on the card: if your card has insufficient RAM you might find that to use the True Colour palette (16.7 million colours), for example, you'll have to drop to a much lower screen resolution.

Refresh rate

The image on the monitor is updated a number of times every second, and the time interval between each update is called the refresh rate. If the rate is fast enough you won't be aware it's happening, but if it's too slow, the screen will appear to have a constant flicker.

For general use, go for a 64-bit graphics card with at least 2Mb RAM, and make sure that it can provide a refresh rate of 72MHz or higher at a resolution of 1,024 x 768dpi. These combined features will give a crisp, clear image and allow you to use the vibrant High Colour palette (65,500 colours) at 1,024 × 768dpi. If you're a fan of arcade-quality games, or plan to work extensively with graphics, you'll want an AGP card with at least 4Mb RAM. Most 2Mb cards allow more memory to be added, but you should make sure of this before you buy, and find out what the maximum is. Popular cards are the Matrox Millennium and Mystique, and the ATIXpert series.

Meet the mouse (& friends)

The original type of input device for a PC was the keyboard, which was ideal for the purpose because most of the original operating systems and programs were text-based. However, the arrival of Windows with its friendly buttons and icons required a more intuitive method of working, and the mouse became a ubiquitous feature of PCs, based largely upon a device called a trackball that was used in much earlier computer systems (and, in fact, still survives as a mouse-alternative). Most mice plug into one of your PC's serial ports (COM1 is recommended), although a few use a smaller PS2 port.

The mouse is a small plastic box sculpted to fit under your palm, with two or three buttons at the front and a cable (or tail!) leading to the PC's system unit. A ball in the base of the mouse enables it to roll around your desk, and sensors inside measure the direction and speed of travel. The movement of the mouse controls the movement of a small pointer on the monitor screen in a thoroughly intuitive way – move the mouse to the left and the pointer moves to the left, and so on.

Never swing the mouse around by its tail, tempting though it is. And if it stops working, don't flush down the toilet!

The movement of the mouse enables you to position the pointer wherever you want it, but doesn't actually achieve anything useful by itself. However, once the pointer is placed over an icon or button, pressing (or clicking) one of the mouse's buttons will perform some kind of action. Exactly what happens will depend upon the operating system, the object you're clicking on, and a variety of other things, but a mouse-click might run a program, display more details about the object in question, or present you with a list of options (a menu) to choose from, as shown in the screenshot below.

The bestselling mouse is made by Microsoft and revels in the exotic name of Microsoft Mouse. The newest version of this mouse adds a small wheel to the usual two-button set-up, which greatly increases the mouse's talents. Logitech is another manufacturer which is popular for its mice and other pointing devices.

The trackball

The trackball is like an upside-down mouse, with the ball on top. The design of trackballs can vary from the mundane to the eccentric, and the buttons can end up just about anywhere, but trackballs all have one thing in common – they're stationary. Instead of moving the whole device around your desk, your hand rests on it and moves the ball in its socket; one benefit of this approach is that no arm movement is required.

The light pen

This is a slightly unusual sort of device that seems to surface from time to time, fail entirely to catch on,

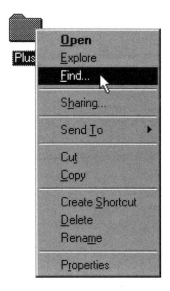

Clicking a mouse button on this icon produces a menu of options. Moving the pointer on to one of these options and clicking again will select that option.

and then vanish again. It looks a lot like a normal writing pen with an added cable to connect it to the computer, and it lets you 'draw' on the monitor screen. A tiny sensor in the tip of the pen detects where the pen is on the screen and sends this information back to the computer. Buttons on the side of the pen are used to click and double-click.

The light pen is a device the PC isn't used to working with, so an expansion card that can deal with it needs to be installed, unlike the other types of pointing device that can plug straight into one of the PC's serial ports. On the positive side, because the light pen is an expansion device you can still have a mouse or trackball connected as well.

One of the primary uses for the light pen is in artwork and graphics (an area to which the mouse isn't well suited) since you can hold it up to the screen and use it like a pen on paper. And therein lies the cause of its lack of success: the discomfort of holding your arm up for long periods soon makes you want your rodent back!

The graphics tablet

The tablet is a more popular alternative to the light pen. It features a touch-sensitive square pad that sits on your desk, and the movement of the onscreen pointer is controlled by the movement of your finger or an attached stylus over the pad's surface. Clicking may be carried out by tapping the pad or using buttons on the tablet's case, or a combination of the two. The larger-sized tablets give about the best input method for graphic design and artwork applications.

Meet the keyboard

The computer keyboard is remarkably similar to its typewriter counterpart, despite the much wider range of actions called for by a PC. For example, the same QWERTY layout is used, the Tab, Shift, and Caps Lock keys survive, and there's even the equivalent of a carriage-return lever called the Enter (or, sometimes, Return) key.

QWERTY keyboard

This is the standard UK keyboard layout, named after the first six keys on the top row. The QWERTY system was originally designed as a counter-intuitive layout to slow down typists who were reaching such great speeds that the typewriter keys kept getting stuck in a bunch. Obviously this can't happen on a computer keyboard, but by now we're all too used to it to change!

A few extra keys have been added to the computer keyboard, so let's take a look at them:

The standard 105-key computer keyboard

Function keys – A row of keys usually located at the top of the keyboard numbered F1, F2, and so on. Different operating systems and programs assign different commands to some of these keys, usually serving as alternatives to clicking an option with the mouse.

CTRL and ALT keys – These work rather like the Shift key, in that they're used in combination with other keys to produce a result. These key combinations are used mostly to select options from menus, once again as an alternative to using the mouse.

Arrow keys – These are four keys for Up/Down/Left/Right that are mainly used either for moving the cursor around a block of text, or for navigating through lists or groups of icons.

Page Up/Page Down keys – Because modern operating systems display each document in its own 'window' (a box on the screen), it may not be possible to view the whole of a long document at once. The Page keys provide one method of moving up and down the document a screenful at a time, rather like rolling a piece of paper backwards and forwards through a typewriter.

Home/End keys – These provide a quick method of moving the cursor to the beginning or end of a line, or to the top or bottom of a long document or window.

Del – Short for 'Delete', and not surprisingly used to erase the files or section of text you select in advance. On a word processor, it deletes the character immediately to the right of the current cursor position.

Backspace – On a word processor, this deletes the character immediately to the left of the current cursor position, moving the cursor back one step in the process.

Esc – Short for 'Escape', this key is commonly used to back out of something you've started and would rather not finish – a sort of Cancel button.

Numeric keypad – A group of keys on the right of the keyboard. This group contains copies of the numerical and arithmetical keys on a calculator (together with a second Enter key). These keys actually have dual-functionality: with the key marked Num Lock turned on they function as calculator keys; with Num Lock off they double as an extra set of Home/End/Page/Arrow keys.

Windows keys – Three extra keys specifically for use with Windows. There are two identical 'Win' keys with a small flag motif and one 'Menu' key which, between them, mean that you don't have to stop and reach for the mouse quite as often when typing.

The main factors to consider when buying a keyboard are key spacing and responsiveness – a good keyboard will have a slight spring in its action that cushions your fingers. The sound of a keyboard can make a difference too – most users like to hear a slight click as they press a key, but some keyboards give a very plastic, rattly noise which can grate on your nerves after a short time

Keyboard ergonomics

With business and industry moving increasingly to computers, and the computers being able to handle most of their needs, many people are spending their entire working day sitting at their PCs. As a result, some of the latest technical terms to hit computing are distinctly medical – RSI (Repetitive Strain Injury), upper-limb disorder, carpal-tunnel syndrome, and so on – and these have given PC manufacturers something new to think about. Ergonomics is an attention to designing equipment that's comfortable to use for long periods and less likely to result in stress, illness, or litigation.

> **TIP**
>
> Ergonomic or not, a keyboard is often more comfortable to use if you can lift the back of it and tilt it slightly towards you. Most keyboards have recessed legs for this purpose, but it's best to check before you buy.

Many manufacturers are producing ergonomically designed equipment, usually with radically different ideas about exactly what form it should take, but in the area of keyboards there seems to be some agreement. The most common features are wrist supports, a layout that slopes upwards towards the back, and a central split which divides the keys into two clear left-hand/right-hand groups. The split-keyboard feature has great ergonomic benefits, and ifs pretty easy to get to grips with for a touch-typist, but the two-finger typist will probably find themselves reduced to using just one, and be thwarted still further by the slight angling-apart of the halves in most designs.

Chapter 5

Getting Equipped for Multimedia

In This Chapter...

Software, music, games and more on CD-ROM

DVD – full-length feature films on disk

Play sounds and music, and control your PC by voice command

Enjoy built-in TV, video and radio

Getting Equipped for Multimedia

A couple of years ago you could buy a PC or you could buy a multimedia PC. The multimedia PC was the desirable, all-singing, all-dancing machine that supposedly elevated the dull office computer to the status of a complete entertainment centre by adding a soundcard, speakers, and a CD-ROM drive.

Today, the 'multimedia' tag has been all but dropped: you'd be hard put to find a PC that doesn't have these extras nowadays, and a whole host of extra goodies can be bought to extend your computer's entertainment capabilities. But, as in all areas of computing hardware and software, all that glitters isn't necessarily gold. In this chapter, we'll explore some of the multimedia add-ons available, and point you in the right direction.

JARGON BUSTER

Multimedia

A method of presenting information using a combination of sound, video, animation, graphics, and text, but the term is getting wider all the time as new media such as television are being added to the PC's capabilities. Although you can buy a 'multimedia kit' to add these features to your existing PC, this is something of a misnomer – the kit will usually include CD-ROM, soundcard, and speakers, but it won't include an MPEG card to improve video playback, or a microphone to let you record sound.

CD-ROM – music, games & more

The CD-ROM drive has become as fundamental to a PC as its hard-disk and far more useful than a floppy-disk drive. The main reason for this is the size of modern software applications. Two years ago it was common to buy a major software title and be presented with 30 floppy disks, making the whole process of installing the software painfully slow. Today, the latest version of the same program could easily fill 60 floppies. A single compact disk (CD) can hold 650Mb of data, and your PC can read that data from a CD much faster than it can read data from a floppy disk so the CD has become the preferred medium for selling most types of software.

It doesn't sound much like multimedia so far, though. Here's a quickfire list of rather more entertaining reasons to own a CD-ROM drive:

- With a soundcard and speakers (explained below), you can play ordinary audio CDs just as you do on your home hi-fi.

- The best arcade-style games with visual effects, sound, and fast-moving action, come on CD-ROM disks. Only a CD-ROM can hold all this data and play it quickly enough.

- Multimedia software titles such as interactive encyclopaedias and books can be bought only on CD-ROM.

CD-ROM drives are easy to buy: the only difference between drives is their speed. The slowest drive available is the 6-speed (sometimes noted as 6x), and the fastest at present is the 24-speed. Don't buy anything slower than a 12-speed, unless you're positive you'll never use it for anything but playing your Diana Ross CDs while you work. For gameplay, go for one of the faster drives (16-speed upwards). The faster the quoted speed of the drive, the faster it will read data from the disk making software installations more speedy, and video playback more smooth.

JARGON BUSTER

CD and CD-ROM

The two names refer to exactly the same type of disk, but the term 'CD' usually refers to an audio disk that you can play on your home stereo system, and 'CD-ROM' means a disk that contains computer data (definitely not for playing on your stereo!). The 'ROM' part stands for Read-Only Memory – data on the disk is stored permanently and can't be erased.

New technologies have brought drives called the CD-R (recordable CD-ROM), and the CD-RW (rewritable CD-ROM). Neither type of drive can read a disk as quickly as a plain CD-ROM drive, but they have other powerful features that we'll look at in Chapter 6. An emerging standard set to replace the CD-ROM entirely is the DVD-ROM drive, explained below.

An eye to the future – DVD-ROM

DVD stands for Digital Versatile Disk, and it expands on some of the best capabilities of the compact disk. The biggest improvement is in the capacity of these disks. At the moment, a DVD can store over 4.7Gb of data, and this will soon increase to an amazing 17Gb (roughly 3 times the capacity of the average hard disk). This means that a single disk can hold a full-length cinema movie and soundtrack, and you can watch these movies on your home computer. Another bonus is that a DVD-ROM drive can still play back your ordinary music CDs and data CD-ROMs.

Unfortunately, much of DVD's promise lies in the future. At the moment, you can't write your own data to these disks since no recordable drives are available, few titles are available on DVD, and there are already so many extensions and planned extensions to DVD that no real standard yet exists. But it's a safe bet that DVD-ROM drives will increasingly replace CD-ROM drives in computer systems, and more multimedia titles should appear on DVD disks as this happens. If you decide to go for a DVD-ROM drive, make sure that your PC has support for video playback (preferably in the form of an MPEG card) to make the most of it. But you may prefer just to stick with the cheaper CD-ROM drive until the dust has had a chance to settle around this new gadget.

Hear sounds & music with a soundcard

Your PC has a small internal speaker that enables it to beep indignantly at you if you do something it doesn't like. Without an expansion card called a soundcard that's the only sound your computer will ever make. These days, just about everything comes with its own soundtrack: computer games rely heavily on sound effects for realism, applications provide confirmatory audio feedback when you click a button or select an option, and a lot of new software now comes with a CD-ROM-based tutorial that literally talks you through the manual.

On a more musical level, connect your CD-ROM drive to your soundcard and you'll be able to play your audio CDs while you work. And if you have a creative leaning, you can use special software to record your own musical masterpieces.

The bog-standard soundcard is a 16-bit stereo card. Some types of music format will sound pretty atrocious, but this type of card is fine for playing back sound effects, speech, and audio CDs. For better quality sound, go for a 32-bit wavetable card, particularly if you play computer games or videos, or want to create your own music. If you opt for one of the latest DVD-ROM disk drives, mentioned earlier, video soundtracks will be far better handled by the 32-bit wavetable card. Finally, a full-duplex card will give better results than a half-duplex card when coupled with a microphone.

Pick of the crop in the field of wavetable soundcards are the Creative Labs AWE64 Cold, Yamaha DB50XG, and Terratec Maestro.

> **TIP** Whatever type or brand of soundcard you buy, check that it has SoundBlaster (SB) compatibility. Although the SoundBlaster is a brand of card, it quickly became extremely popular to the extent that most software and games expect your PC to be using a compatible card.

You'll need speakers too!

Well, of course you will. Among a little bundle of sockets which appear at the back of your system unit after the soundcard is installed, you'll find one labelled Speaker Out, or something similar. If your PC comes with a soundcard, you'll get speakers too, but some of these are hideously under-powered and too tinny for music playback. If the sound quality matters to you, there are several available options:

- Ask to upgrade to a 3-piece system that adds a subwoofer for better bass performance.

- Connect the Speaker Out to the CD or Tape input on your home stereo system instead.

- Connect the Speaker Out to a cheap amplifier and stereo hi-fi speakers (Tandy is a good place to look for these).

Get interactive with a microphone

Your soundcard will also provide you with a socket into which you can plug a microphone, and this is one of the cheapest peripheral devices you can buy, at around £10. Until recently, a microphone simply allowed you to record speech and other 'live' sounds into your PC, which has limited usefulness. Now the microphone has come into its own in two important respects.

The first of these is the ability to control your computer by voice commands: instead of clicking buttons with the mouse, or typing streams of text, you can select options by saying their names, and dictate text into your word processor. The software needs a little training before it can understand you, and word-recognition isn't yet perfect, but the technology is coming on in leaps and bounds.

> **!**
> **TIP**
>
> Make sure you get a full duplex soundcard to make best use of a microphone. A half-duplex card can record sound or play it back, but it can't do both at the same time, so using your microphone for phone calls is something like a walkie-talkie conversation: you need to turn it off to hear the other person talk (no good for arguments!). A full duplex card can record and play simultaneously, exactly mimicking the way you use a telephone.

The second great advantage of the microphone is that it works hand in hand with your modem (see Chapter 6). Not only can the microphone/modem partnership replace your telephone, but if you have a connection to the Internet you'll be able to make international phone calls for exactly the same price as a local call.

Gameplay with a joystick

The joystick is a device known and loved by computer-game fans and ignored by everybody else, but it has essentially the same features as a mouse: a handgrip for controlling the movements of objects on the screen, and a variety of buttons and triggers for wiping out all alien life-forms. If your PC has a soundcard, you'll probably find a game port on the card for plugging in the joystick. If your card doesn't have a game port, you'll either need to buy a dedicated gamecard or replace your soundcard with one that does. (And if you don't have a soundcard, buy one – most games use sound, so you'll kill two birds with one stone.)

Gameplay isn't a subject we're going to dwell on too much, so while we're here it's worth pointing out a few basic pros and cons. On the positive side, there's a huge number of games available for the PC, and the better ones (when you're lucky or informed enough to find them) can be every bit as good as their arcade counterparts. On the negative side, games more than anything test your PC to the limits with their need for a speedy processor, a good supply of RAM on the graphics card, a wavetable soundcard and a fast CD-ROM drive. To see the latest 3D games at their best, invest in a 3D video card – preferably an AGP card if your PC is recent enough to have an AGP slot. Ordinary graphics cards will display simpler and less engaging versions of a 3D game's graphics.

Full-screen video playback

Here's another little acronym for your collection: MPEG (pronounced 'emm-peg' and short for Moving Pictures Expert Group). An ordinary PC can play video clips, and it will do a bearable job if you have enough RAM on your graphics card and a fast enough processor. Nevertheless, the picture will be small, slightly jerky, and perhaps rather fuzzy.

For smooth video playback that fills your screen (like a television picture) you need an MPEG card, another of those slot-in expansion cards. Beware of computer deals that offer 'software MPEG': the difference that software can make to video playback is negligible, and only 'hardware MPEG' in the form of this add-on card will give good results. The advent of the DVD-ROM disk and drive should see a marked rise in the sales of MPEG cards as feature-length films become available on DVD disks.

TV & radio while you work

One of the few things the modern PC can't do is to lift you up gently and plonk you in front of the TV when you've finished for the day. While they work on that one, they have delivered the next best thing: as long as your PC is equipped with soundcard, speakers, and a reasonable graphics card, you can slot in a TV or radio card to watch television (full screen or in a small window) or listen to the radio while you work.

TIP   To receive a TV picture, remember that you'll need to connect the card to your main TV aerial – an indoor aerial won't give good results.

Although this is a new technology, it's improving all the time and combined radio and TV cards are starting to appear, saving you a valuable expansion slot. One of the best combined cards, which has the bonus of Teletext and requires a PCI slot, is Win/TV-Radio from ODT.

Once you have all these bits and pieces in place, you can use a Windows 98 feature called WebTV to set up your TV tuner card and retrieve program listings and other information from the Internet.

Chapter 6

Optional Extras – Luxury or Necessity?

In This Chapter...

Cool colour or the best black-and-white printing

Fax from your PC and get on the Internet with a modem

Scan, edit and store documents and photographs

Backup valuable files for security and archive rarely used files

Set up a simple network with two or more PCs

Optional Extras – Luxury or Necessity?

There are more peripheral devices available for your PC than you can shake a stick at, and new ones are arriving all the time. In this chapter, we take a look at some of the most popular add-ons, along with the choices you'll have to make and the pros and cons of each option.

Printers – the good, the bad & the ugly

The printer has been a mainstay in the peripherals market since the birth of the personal computer, so there's a vast amount of choice in this area, and prices range from about £150 to £8,000. Let's narrow it down a bit. You probably don't want a dot-matrix printer; this is a 'cheap and cheerless' printer that's fine if you just want to print something roughly for reference, but has very poor presentation. Its one redeeming feature is that it can be used to print NCR stationery such as invoices. (If you do buy a dot-matrix printer, choose a 24-pin rather than a 9-pin model for better definition.)

That leaves a choice of either an inkjet or a laser printer, and brings us to the basic decision you need to make: do you need to print in colour, or will a black-and-white printer do the job?

For colour printing, even a cheap laser printer will put a £4,000-sized hole in your pocket. Colour inkjet printers are slower, but they're much more affordable at between £200 and £500, and the results can be superb. Most colour inkjet printers use a system of two swappable cartridges – one contains black ink only, for use in non-colour work such as letters, and the other contains either three or four colours, which are mixed to create full colour output. The superior system is usually the one that uses the four-colour cartridge, but always look at a sample output before buying to make sure you're getting the quality you need. Inkjet printers worth looking at include Hewlett-Packard's DeskJet 890C, the Epson Stylus 800, and Canon's BJC series.

> Choose your paper carefully. For colour printing especially, special coated paper should be used to prevent colours bleeding or soaking through the page. This paper can be expensive if you use it all the time, but there's no reason not to use ordinary copy paper when printing drafts and reference copies.

For black-and-white printing, the inkjet printer has been all but vanquished by the arrival of budget-priced laser printers, at similar prices to the colour inkjet above. The laser printer produces output that can at least match the quality of the best inkjet, but it does so at a much speedier four to six pages per minute (compared to one to two pages per minute for an inkjet). Models to look for include the Brother HL760 and NEC 860 for everyday use, or the 12-pages-per-minute Hewlett-Packard LaserJet for heavy-duty printing.

Finally, here are a few points on the subject of printers worth checking:

● When inkjet printers claim a 'pages per minute' speed, these are optimistic approximations based on how much print an average page contains. Laser printer speeds can be trusted.

● Cheek the output quality, measured in dpi (dots per inch). The higher this figure, the better the quality: 600dpi is a good score for a budget laser printer; a colour inkjet should be able to manage 600 to 720dpi, and some can offer more than 1,000dpi.

● Make sure your printer comes with an auto sheet-feeder. If it doesn't, you'll have to insert each sheet of paper manually.

● Remember that printers have additional costs in their 'consumables' – special paper, replacement cartridges or refills for inkjets, toner and drum for laser printers. For heavy-duty printing, the difference in price in consumables for one printer model and another might add up to a tidy sum over a long period.

Fax & Internet with a modem

The surge in popularity of the Internet and the sudden rush to buy modems is more than coincidental; we'll look more closely at the Internet in Part Four, but if surfing the Net sounds like the thing for you, you'll need to join the queue at the modem counter.

Other uses include the capability to send and receive faxes from your computer instead of having a separate fax machine (the software you need for this will usually be included), and to dial the phone from your computer to save the exertion of all that button-pushing. Modems with voicemail ability will let you use your computer as an answerphone, storing incoming messages to hard disk (provided that you leave your computer running when you're away from your desk or out of the office). To record and playback voicemail messages you'll need to have a soundcard installed (see Chapter 5), but some voicemail-compatible modems include a basic soundcard in the package.

Keep your modem at least a few feet away from any fluorescent lights – they can cause interference, lost data, and even dropped connections if they're too close.

Unarguably the main use of a modem is for Internet connectivity, and this is where your choice of device becomes important. The job of a modem is to convert computer data into sound so that it can be sent down a telephone line, and to convert it back to data at the other end: the faster it can do this, the more you'll enjoy the multimedia-rich Internet experience. Modem speeds are measured in bps (bits per second), and the minimum buy is a 28,800bps device starting at around £50. For a similar price you can buy a slightly faster 33,600bps modem, but the best buy for the future is the latest 56,000bps device.

Decision number two is whether to go for an internal modem (which plugs into an expansion slot) or an external modem. The external modem is slightly more expensive and needs to be plugged into a power socket like any stand-alone electrical device, but it's simple to install and has the benefit of a panel of flashing lights that tells you what's going on. As internal devices, modems can be more complicated to install than some other expansion cards. If you'd prefer to have your modem tucked away inside the system unit, look for an internal modem with 'Plug and Play' compatibility to automate as much of the setting-up as possible.

Scanning for a paperless office

Okay, the truly paperless office will probably never happen, but the scanner is the device that makes it theoretically possible. A scanner works rather like a photocopier, but instead of producing a duplicate on paper, it copies the original into your PC. When scanning pictures, graphics, and photographs, this allows you to load the image into photo-editing software, remove scratches and colour defects, apply filters, and so on, and save or print the finished result. Text-based documents can be stored as image files for reference, but special OCR (Optical Character Recognition) software, which will usually be included with your scanner, can convert these documents into text that can be loaded into your word processor, edited, and saved as a much smaller text file.

Like most peripheral devices there are choices to be made, and scanners come in two flavours: the flatbed and the document scanner. The flatbed looks like a 4-inch high photocopier, slightly larger than an A4 sheet of paper, with a hinged lid. This is the more flexible of the two types, allowing easy scanning of photographs and documents along with open books and magazines. Some flatbed scanners include auto sheet-feeders for scanning multiple pages without any intervention. Budget flatbeds such as the Umax Astra and Agfa SnapScan start at less than £200.

JARGON BUSTER

OCR

This stands for Optical Character Recognition, a clever software trick that can recognize printed text and convert it into text that you can edit and save with your word processor, as if you'd typed it yourself.

The document scanner is a physically smaller machine – ideal if you're short of desk space – that will accept only single sheets fed between two rollers. These are as easy to use as the flatbed, but lack its flexibility. The undoubted king of document scanners is the Visioneer Paperport, which is as popular for the software it includes as for its scanning quality, and can also be found for less than £200. The excellent software, confusingly also known as Visioneer Paperport, can be bought separately and used with any scanner to organize, store and retrieve scanned documents.

A variant on the document scanner is the handheld device, which looks like a large mouse and has to be rolled slowly over the document to be scanned. The potential 'curse of the wobbly hand' means that handheld scanners are best avoided for OCR work but the results are pretty consistent in other areas, and clever software can stitch together large images that you scan in multiple strips. Scanners worth considering in this department include the Logitech Scanman Color, at around £100.

Here are a few points to consider when shopping for a scanner:

- Like printers, scanning quality is measured in dpi (dots per inch). For OCR work this measurement makes little difference, but 600dpi upwards is desirable when scanning photographs and graphics. Bear in mind that a 600dpi scan can still only be printed at 300dpi if you have a 300dpi printer.

- Not all scanners are colour models, so check what you're buying. Colour is unnecessary for OCR work, but you're likely to want to scan photographs in colour.

- A scanner that has TWAIN compatibility is useful as this allows you to scan straight into many different applications and start working with the results immediately.

- Many scanners are SCSI (pronounced 'skuzzy') devices (covered later in this chapter). If you don't have a SCSI expansion card, you'll need to buy and install one, or look for a scanner that plugs into the parallel port or a serial port instead.

Backup drives for safety & convenience

When you buy your PC it's a major purchase and a valuable asset. As time goes on you'll begin to realize that you're collecting a disk full of equally valuable (and in some cases irreplaceable) files. If your PC is damaged or stolen, or your hard disk stops working, what would you do? The odds are that your lost data would suddenly seem a lot more important than your lost computer.

For this reason, it's usual to keep backups (copies) of vital files on separate disks. One option is to regularly copy the files that matter to floppy disks, but for any serious quantity of data this could take a mountain of floppies and a full day's work. A better solution is to buy a dedicated backup drive, which uses removable tapes or disks capable of storing hundreds or even thousands of megabytes of data.

For true backup use (as opposed to archiving which we'll look at in a moment), speed and capacity are what matter most. A tape streamer is ideal for this. Tape streamers are drives that use low-priced magnetic tape cartridges, and each reusable cartridge can hold up to 750Mb of data. Popular manufacturers include Hewlett-Packard, with its Colorado series, and Connor.

TIP

Because magnetic tape is recognized as being a less than perfect medium, the software bundled with tape drives includes a Verify procedure that checks the data it has just stored against the original. It might double the start-to-finish time of the procedure, but it's a good idea to select this option, particularly if you reuse the same tape over and over (as you'd normally expect to).

Archiving is a similar process, but it's done for a different reason and so requires different hardware. Over time, your hard disk is likely to gather large files such as images or videos that you rarely need to use, but need to keep handy. Rather than have them wasting valuable hard-disk space, wouldn't it be useful if you could move them to a separate disk where they're still quickly accessible but not in the way? That's archiving.

Tape streamers don't make good archive drives due to the way they store data. Rather like listening to a music cassette, if you want something that's near the end of the tape you have to wait while the tape is wound forward. For archiving purposes you want high capacity, but easy retrieval, and the ideal devices for this are drives that use disks that look like the humble floppy (although they're more expensive, needless to say). The most popular of these is Iomega's ZIP drive, which takes 100Mb disks, and this is closely followed by its big brother, the Jaz drive, which can handle 1Gb. Another option is to replace your current floppy-disk drive with a SuperDisk Drive from Imation Corp, which can read and write ordinary floppy disks as well as its own 120Mb disks.

Finally, there are variations on the CD-ROM drive: CD-R (recordable CD) and CD-RW (rewritable CD). Both can hold up to 650Mb of computer data, or up to 75 minutes of stereo sound. CD-R drives start at around £250, and you can record data to them in up to 99 separate sessions until the disk is full. CD-RW allows data on a CD to be erased, making a far more flexible system with a higher price-tag. Both types of drive rely on speed and most require a SCSI adapter. One popular CD-R model available for both SCSI and parallel port connections is the Hewlett-Packard SureStore series. For CD-RW, look out for Ricoh and Nomai drives.

Recording to CD requires a constant stream of data to be sent from the PC to the CD drive. In the case of CD-R, if the data flow is interrupted, the disk will usually be ruined. A Pentium system and 16Mb RAM is a minimum specification.

SCSI – speed & expandability

SCSI ('skuzzy') provides a slightly different, but very fast, system for installing add-on hardware devices to your PC. A SCSI expansion card is fitted into one of your expansion slots, and then up to eight SCSI-compatible devices can be connected together in a chain linking back to the card. These are usually storage devices like hard disks and CD-ROM drives, which benefit from SCSI's lightning-fast speeds, but SCSI can control all sorts of devices. If you want to add even more devices (or you have compatibility problems with some of the devices), you can add a second SCSI controller.

SCSI cards can be bought to plug into an ISA slot or the more recent PCI slot. The PCI card is the better buy, but it's also more expensive.

Easy networking with an NIC

If you have two or more PCs in your office or home, it makes sense to connect them together so that you can get at data stored on one while working on the other. This is known as networking, and your group of connected computers is known as a LAN, or Local Area Network.

Connecting two or more Windows PCs is a reasonably hassle-free experience. First, each PC needs an NIC (Network Interface Card), which plugs into an expansion slot, with a cable joining the two computers. A Novell NE2000-compatible Ethernet card should cost no more than £35, and a Plug and Play compatible card will automate the setting-up that makes the two computers 'talk' to each other.

A detailed explanation of networking is beyond the scope of this book, but the basic principles are straightforward enough: to be able to use data on another computer (or a device connected to it, such as a printer) it needs to be 'shared'. In Windows you can opt to share a device or the contents of a folder by clicking it with the right mouse-button and selecting the **Sharing** option on the menu. Assign a memorable name to the item, choose whether it should be protected with a password, and Bob's your uncle. To access this item from elsewhere on the network is a simple case of referring to it by name.

Gadgets & gizmos

The PC has been around long enough for an endless array of gadgets and small, expensive plastic things to find their way into the stores. Here's a few of the presents you might want to buy for your computer:

Mouse mat – A rubber pad with a plastic or cloth covering that makes a better surface than a desktop for smooth mouse-control. These come in shapes, designs and colours – some have a built-in wrist support (another little extra you can also buy separately), or a tray for holding pens and other office bits and bobs.

Mouse house – A rodent residence designed to keep your mouse dust-free while you're not using it. There are several million cheaper ways of doing this, but none is quite as cute.

Keyboard cover – A fitted cover for your keyboard that keeps the crumbs and coffee out but still lets you tap away.

Computer covers – Separate plastic dust-covers are available for the monitor, system-unit and keyboard to keep them clean and dust-free while you're not using the PC. The monitor cover is an especially sensible buy.

Copy holder – A plastic arm that attaches to the side of your monitor with a clip to hold papers you need to refer to while working. A cheap and very useful accessory.

Anti-glare filter – A thin mesh that fits over the front of your monitor and cuts reflections from nearby lights and windows to prevent eye-strain. These filters can also increase your privacy by making the screen contents difficult to see from an angle.

Parallel port switchbox – Most PCs have a single parallel port labelled LPT1 to which the printer is connected. If you buy a scanner or backup drive that uses the parallel port, you should be able to plug your printer into a connector on this second device's cable. But what if you buy a parallel port scanner *and* a backup drive? The answer is to plug the switchbox into your parallel port, plug all your devices into the switchbox, and then flick the front panel switch to activate the device you want to use.

Chapter 7

The Notebook & Portable Add-ons

In This Chapter...

What to look for in a notebook PC

PC cards – pocket-sized add-ons

Mobile printing in full colour

Do you really need a desktop PC as well?

The Notebook & Portable Add-ons

When it comes to buying a notebook PC and choosing add-on hardware to use with it, there's good news and there's bad news. The good news is that the choices are much easier to make, but this is largely because of the bad news: there's a lot less to choose from. In this chapter we'll look at the issues to consider when buying the notebook itself, and what options are available for connecting extra devices.

Get it right first time!

When you buy a desktop PC, you've got some leeway to make mistakes. Not that you want to do that, of course, but if you're not happy with your keyboard or mouse, for example, you can buy replacements for as little as £20 each. Even the monitor, though expensive, can be replaced.

With a notebook PC, things aren't quite as simple. The monitor screen and keyboard are built into the machine, making replacement almost impossible, so the single most important thing to do before deciding what to buy is to spend time in a few computer stores trying out as many notebooks as you can get your hands on. Remember that keyboard and screen quality can vary immensely even between models from the same manufacturer.

The monitor is especially important, and the two things to check are size and clarity. Sizes currently vary between 10.4 inches and 13.3 inches, and the picture quality will tend to be determined by whether the monitor is dual-scan colour or a more expensive TFT screen. TFT screens are essential if you'll be using your notebook for work that relies on accurate colour representation (desktop publishing, graphics, and so on), and you might feel that the better quality is worth the extra expense even for non-graphics use, especially if this is to be your main PC. The TFT screen is recommended, but, as with anything else you buy, remember that there are good dual-scan screens and poor TFT screens.

Along with the comfort, spacing, and layout of the keyboard, the device used to replace the mouse is important. Some notebooks use a trackball – a small thumb-operated ball that sits just below the keyboard. Increasingly, however, new notebooks use a touch-sensitive glide-pad instead, generally making control of the onscreen pointer much easier. The size of this pad makes a difference (larger is usually better), and you'll want to be sure that the pad is responsive to a finger-tap or drag.

Here are a few additional features to check:

- The screen must be capable of displaying a resolution of at least 800 × 600 dpi.

- You'll need at least two Type II card slots for PC card devices, which together make one Type III slot (see below).

- Battery life can vary between one and five hours. Remember that the quoted battery life will always be slightly optimistic, and check the recharge time.

- Most notebooks come with a floppy-disk drive and a CD-ROM drive, but some allow you to use only one at a time. If the notebook is to be your main computer, you'll often want to access both at the same time.

TIP

When buying larger PC card devices such as CD-ROM drives, make sure the cable between the card and the drive itself is long enough: a short cable might mean you have to balance both notebook and drive on your lap at the same time.

PC cards & slots

PC card is a more recent name for PCMCIA cards (short for Personal Computer Memory Card International Association). Notebook computers have PC card slots into which these credit-card sized devices can be fitted when you need to use them. A PC card device might be a hard drive, CD-ROM drive, modem, or extra memory – almost anything you can buy for your desktop computer can be bought in PC card form. The main difference (if you ignore the high cost of these cards) is that only one or two of them can be plugged in at any time, although cards are just beginning to appear that combine several accessories into one device.

PC card slots come in two different sizes: the Type II slot which takes smaller cards such as RAM and modems, and the Type III slot for larger accessories including additional hard disks. The usual notebook specification now includes two Type II slots mounted one above the other, allowing two small cards or one large one to be inserted.

When a PC card is connected to your notebook it's still drawing battery power whether you're using it or not. Make sure you remove any cards after use.

The size and weight of these cards make them easy to carry around in a pocket or briefcase, but the prices are considerably higher than those for comparable full-sized devices. For notebook users on a budget, one option is to buy the smallest full-size device you can get your hands on and connect it to the notebook's serial or parallel port when you need it, but of course you'll need access to a mains supply and you're now carrying a larger piece of kit plus two cables instead of one small card.

Cards on the desktop

PC cards aren't limited to notebook PCs – you can buy a PCMCIA interface card for your desktop machine and use PC cards with that too. Clearly this isn't the kind of expansion option that the typical desktop user will regard as a must-have: why pay twice the going rate for a modem that keeps getting lost among your other office clutter? For the confirmed notebook user, on the other hand, it might be a worthwhile investment. If most of your work is done on the notebook and you keep a desktop machine for occasional use, a PCMCIA interface will let you use the accessories you've already bought rather than having to equip the desktop with similar full-size devices.

The better battery

The 'external device' you can't live without if you have a notebook PC is the battery, or perhaps *batteries* if you'll be relying heavily on your machine. Notebook batteries are all removable and rechargeable, and come in two delicious flavours: nickel metal hydride (NiMH), or lithium.

The NiMH battery is the cheaper and more common of the two, but the more expensive lithium battery can power your notebook for longer. Using PC card peripherals will discharge your battery a lot faster, so it's worth looking for a notebook that uses the lithium battery if you expect to be using these cards for much of your computing time.

> **TIP**
>
> When buying a notebook, always find out how long it takes to recharge the battery (some batteries will recharge fully in as little as two hours) and how many hours you can get from a fully charged battery in normal use. Another good question to ask is whether you can continue to use the PC while the battery is recharging.

Printing on the move

The first thing to point out on this subject is that mobile printing is to be avoided if possible. Although portable printers are cheaper than their full-size counterparts, they lag behind on quality and speed. In addition, of course, you're giving yourself another couple of kilos to lug around, so you might prefer to print your documents when you get back to your desktop computer (if you have one), or buy a full-size printer and leave it at home.

If a portable printer is a necessity, you'll be looking for a colour inkjet printer such as Canon's BJC-70 or BJ-30, or Hewlett-Packard's DeskJet 340. There's a catch with some models to watch out for though: to be truly portable, a printer should be able to run on batteries rather than mains, but some manufacturers insist on regarding the battery pack as an optional extra and charging for it separately!

At home with the notebook

In the past, many notebook users had a desktop PC at home or in the office that they regarded as their 'main' computer, and the notebook acted as a useful accessory that they'd use when they had to. The notebook is easy to use like this: it can run the same Windows operating system and all the applications you use on your desktop PC. Windows' Direct Cable Connection accessory makes it easy to connect the two computers together and transfer files back and forth, and the Briefcase accessory can track different versions of the documents you work on to make sure that you've got the most recent version on both machines.

A couple of years ago, the reason for having both a notebook and desktop PC was that the notebook simply wasn't much fun to use: the small drab screen, poky keys, fiddly mouse control, and the speed and capabilities of a notebook couldn't come close to matching the power of the desktop. But things have come a long way since then. Although notebook technology still lags slightly behind that of the desktop, these machines are much more usable, and at last make a credible alternative to the desktop.

This leads us to two extra add-ons worth considering that add a little extra flexibility to the notebook as a desktop replacement:

Port replicator – This is a reasonably cheap device into which you can slot your notebook; it gives you an easy way to connect typical desktop peripherals such as a full-sized monitor, keyboard and printer.

Docking station – A more advanced (and expensive) device that adds the other useful abilities of the desktop system unit: drive bays for access to extra disk drives and backup drives, and expansion slots to give you access to the cheaper desktop expansion cards.

In effect, either of the above devices will give you the best of both worlds. You have easy access to the desktop features you need without the full expense of buying and maintaining a desktop PC.

Chapter 8

Buying a New PC

In This Chapter...

Pick the best desktop or notebook system for your needs

You'll get a warranty, free software, and an operating system

Tips for trouble-free buying

Where and how to set up your desktop computer

Buying a New PC

Over the last few chapters we've examined the major widgets and gadgets and bodily functions of the PC and by now you should have a pretty good idea of what's available. The time now comes to put it all together in a single unit that can do everything you want it to do – in other words, it's decision time!

Of course, a set of specifications that's ideal for one user may be overkill for another, and hideously under-powered for a third. In theory, you should choose a PC according to the software you want to use – after all, it's the software that makes the PC a useful tool. For example, if you just need to run an integrated package like Microsoft Works or one large application at a time like Lotus WordPro, you could get by with a Pentium 166MHz with 16Mb RAM. But while it's obviously sensible to make sure you choose a PC that can cope with your choice of software, it's hard to be sure that that's all you'll want to use the PC for in a year's time. So the single most important piece of advice to keep in mind as you decide what to buy is: *think ahead*!

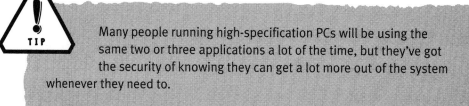

TIP
Many people running high-specification PCs will be using the same two or three applications a lot of the time, but they've got the security of knowing they can get a lot more out of the system whenever they need to.

● *If you're unsure about what software you need, turn to Part 3 for a close look at some of the popular types and titles.*

Buying a desktop PC

The desktop machine is by far the cheapest route to take both in terms of initial cost and in the price of add-on hardware. All the same, a high-specification PC is still a major purchase so you don't want to get it wrong. The table below shows the specifications of four example computers, ranging from a minimum specification to a high-spec machine, with a few explanatory notes beneath. These specifications are included for guidance only – to save on initial costs, you can add extra RAM, a CD-ROM drive, soundcard and so on later if you need to. Pay particular attention to processor, monitor and hard-disk capacity, the elements that are expensive or (sometimes) complicated to either upgrade or replace later. The example specifications assume that you want to run Windows 98 and a typical range of the latest home/office software.

	Minimum	Low	Recommended	High
Processor type	Pentium	Pentium MMX	Pentium II	Pentium II or Xeon
Processor speed	120	200 or 233	333	450+
Cache memory	256K	256K	512K	512K
RAM	16Mb	32Mb	64Mb SDRAM	128Mb SDRAM
Hard disk	1.6Mb	2.5Gb	5.4Gb	9Gb
Floppy-disk drive	1	1	1	SuperDisk drive
Backup/archive drive	–	–	1	1
Monitor size	14-inch	15-inch	17-inch	19 or 21-inch
Graphics card	1Mb RAM	2Mb RAM	4Mb RAM, AGP	8Mb RAM, AGP
CD-ROM drive	4 speed	16 speed	32 speed	DVD-ROM drive
Soundcard	–	16-bit	32-bit wavetable	32-bit wavetable
Stereo speakers	–	Yes	Yes	Yes
Modem	–	–	56Kbps	56Kbps
MPEG Card	–	–	–	Yes

Minimum – If you hunt around, you might find a new PC with a lower specification, but this is the minimum worth buying. Like each of the four machines listed, this will run Windows 95/98, but that 16Mb RAM will have Windows trotting rather than sprinting. Despite the CD-ROM drive, this isn't a multimedia system: the drive itself is too slow for gameplay and smooth video playback, and there's no soundcard for playing audio CDs or game soundtracks. The graphics card will display a respectable 800×600dpi desktop, but at only 256 colours which isn't sufficient for working with colour graphics and photographs. In summary: a no-frills machine suitable for occasional small office/home use with a package such as Microsoft Works, or for someone wishing to 'test the water' before committing to a more expensive system.

Low – A far more practical base for running Windows with a reasonable turn of speed. From solid office software such as Microsoft Office to games and multimedia, this machine will deliver. This is the lowest possible end of the multimedia spectrum, however, and would benefit from a faster CD-ROM drive and a 32-bit wavetable soundcard. Although a machine of this specification is unlikely to come bundled with a modem, there's no reason not to add one yourself: this system is more than adequate for full Internet use. In summary: a good machine for the kids, a more suitable machine for small office/home use than the Minimum specification, but lacking in punch for heavy-duty use. This system will quickly start to groan under the demands of next year's software.

Recommended – If you're looking for a machine that handles everything well, this is it. The combination of large monitor and 4Mb of video RAM makes this a pleasant system to work with for long periods, with good support for graphics and image processing. The fast PII processor, larger cache and 64Mb RAM make the system responsive, and heavyweight software titles like Microsoft Office will perform well. Multimedia and game support is good, but as it stands this is an enjoyable business machine; to push it more into the 'great multimedia' bracket, consider adding an MPEG card for quality video playback, or perhaps swapping it for the backup drive. For desktop publishing or frequent work with large spreadsheets, you might still want to increase the size of the monitor. The capacity of the hard disk is suitable for the greedy Windows 98 and Microsoft Office, leaving plenty of room for your own files and other programs you need to use.

High – You want the best, and you don't care what it costs! Actually, by the time you read this, that processor should be in the shops at over 500MHz and a 12Gb hard disk should be standard in a machine like this. The graphics card should ideally be a 3D video card to make the latest games come alive, and you might want to swap that DVD-ROM drive for a rewritable CD-ROM drive (CD-RW). Here you've got the biggest and fastest of everything, and the best 'future-proofing' possible, with the Recommended specification unlikely to reach this point for over a year. In summary: if this is *your* system, *we're* envious!

Buying a notebook PC

Although the purchase of *any* PC should never be taken lightly, buying a notebook takes even more care than buying a desktop since its components are either much more expensive or totally impossible to replace. PC cards give you the ability to add extra RAM or a second hard-disk, but they fill a slot you could be using for something else if the PC itself were better-equipped.

The four specifications in the following table assume that you need to use your notebook for exactly the same tasks that you'd use a desktop PC for – in other words, as your sole computer. It's worth noting that notebook specifications are always following several steps behind the desktop.

	Minimum	Low	Recommended	High
Processor type	Pentium	Pentium MMX	Pentium MMX	Pentium II
Processor speed	133	166	233	300
RAM	16Mb	16Mb	32Mb	64Mb EDO-RAM
Cache memory	256K	256K	256K	512K
Hard-disk	1.6Mb	2.6Gb	4.1Gb	5.1Gb
Floppy-disk drive	1	1	1	1
Screen	11.3-inch Dual-scan	11.3-inch Dual-scan	12.1-inch TFT	13.3-inch TFT
Max. screen resolution	640 × 480	640 × 480	800 × 600	1024 × 768
Slots	2 × Type II	2 × Type II, 1 × Type III	2 × Type II, 1 × Type III	3 × Type II or 1 × Type II + 1 × Type III
CD-ROM drive	Swappable with floppy drive	Swappable with floppy drive	Yes	DVD-ROM
Soundcard	–	–	Yes	Yes
Stereo speakers	–	–	Yes	Yes

Have I wasted my money?

Regardless of what you buy now, in six months' time you'll see systems with the same specifications advertised at prices perhaps 20 percent lower. The instinctive feeling is that you should have waited, or that you've somehow been conned, but don't torture yourself! In the computer world technology moves very fast, and there's an endless array of bigger and better products arriving on the market that push down the prices of existing products. If you'd waited six months before buying, you'd see exactly the same effect six months after that.

The fact that there's no escaping this cycle serves to underline an important point in computer buying: *buy what you need*. You can interpret that in two ways:

- If you know exactly what tasks this computer will have to perform and what software you'll use, a computer that can handle these now will still handle them in ten years' time. Provided you don't hanker after the latest software version and hardware add-ons every year, you're future-proof.

- If you *do* want to keep up with the latest software, multimedia add-ons and PC capabilities, buy with an eye to expansion. A large hard disk and fast processor, along with vacant drive bays and expansion slots, will take everything you can throw at it for two or three years, and perhaps longer. Eventually you'll reach a point at which some element of your PC can't cope with the device or application you want to use, but a good base machine can be kept alive longer with a few economic upgrades.

Warranties

All new computers should come with at least a one-year warranty as standard. Many packages (as well as one-off peripheral purchases) give you the chance to extend the warranty to three or more years in return for cash. Don't be tempted! There are two reasons why the standard one-year warranty is enough: first and foremost, if a component is going to curl up and die, it's usually going to do it long before the first year is up; second, if it fails after the first year, prices will have fallen still further and you'll probably be able to replace the part yourself for a lot less than the price of the extra cover!

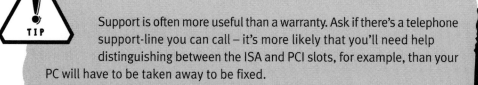

TIP Support is often more useful than a warranty. Ask if there's a telephone support-line you can call – it's more likely that you'll need help distinguishing between the ISA and PCI slots, for example, than your PC will have to be taken away to be fixed.

Bear in mind that your basic one-year warranty will be of the 'back to base' type: if something goes wrong, you'll have to pack up your machine and send it away for repair. You might want to consider paying extra for an on-site warranty if you rely on your PC for daily use.

You get free software!

Most computer packages include a range of software, most of which has already been installed when you take delivery (with the exception of games and multimedia titles intended to be run from CD-ROM). This bundle of software will include an operating system (see below), together with a range of office applications such as a word-processor and spreadsheet, perhaps a few games, and so on. The software bundle will look very tempting (it's supposed to) and, being free, amazingly good value.

The first point to remember is: *nothing is free*! This software is included in the price you pay and the best you could say is that it's cheap. Being cheap isn't a crime of course, and one of the most popular integrated office applications, Microsoft Works, costs very little even if you buy it at full price. If this is included in the bundle, it's probably worth considering – you're sure to need these types of application at least occasionally, whatever the primary use of your PC will be. A full office suite like Microsoft Office or Lotus SmartSuite can seem a very attractive proposition, but they're large and powerful applications with many more features than the average user is ever likely to need and might just find unwieldy for day-to-day working.

This highlights the second point: do you really need this software? Hopefully you'll have a pretty good idea of what you'll be using your PC to do; if this software isn't what you had in mind, you may be able to find a similar computer with no bundled software at a cheaper price, and use the saving to buy the software you want.

Finally, make sure you'll be provided with the manuals for all this software, and the installation disk(s) in case you ever need to re-install the software yourself, preferably on CD-ROM if you have a CD-ROM drive.

- *Turn to Chapter 24 for details of the office suites and integrated applications mentioned above.*

The all-important operating system

Whether your new PC comes with a bundle of software titles or not, it should definitely include an operating system. The operating system should be installed on the hard-disk already so that you can just switch on and start using the computer. Although installing an operating system is rarely more troublesome than installing any other type of software, you don't want that to be your first computing experience. As with the software bundle, make sure you're provided with the original installation CD-ROM.

Almost without exception, the operating system installed on a new PC will be Microsoft's Windows 98. Almost 90 percent of the world's computers run a Windows system, and this is the most recent version for which vast numbers of software titles are available.

There are other PC operating systems, of course, but to explain the use of each would be well beyond the scope of this book. Here's a quick description of some that you might see mentioned:

Windows 3.1 – This version of Windows was available in several forms (such as Windows 3.11), sometimes collectively referred to as Windows 3.x. This was the forerunner to Windows 95, and was just as easy to use although it looked very different. A huge amount of software was (and still is) available. Windows 3.x was less power-hungry than 95 or 98, running happily on slow pre-Pentium systems with 4Mb RAM, but it required MS-DOS to be installed on the PC too. Rather than an operating system in its own right, this version of Windows was a 'friendly face' for MS-DOS.

MS-DOS – The original PC operating system, which few people use by choice nowadays. Instead of Windows' colourful attractive features, clickable icons, and simple menus, DOS offered a plain screen on which cryptic text commands had to be typed to make anything happen. (If you choose to, you can get a flavour of DOS by clicking the MS-DOS Prompt icon in Windows.)

Windows NT – Microsoft's full-strength operating system, aimed at the demanding corporate network environment. Versions 4.0 and 5.0 closely match the look of Windows 95 and 98 respectively, but this system demands a more powerful computer. Certain software designed for the Windows 3/95/98 series won't run on NT, and the current version of Windows NT has very poor support for some of the fancy devices you may want to add, such as scanners or rewritable CD-ROM drives.

OS/2 Warp – This IBM operating system is a sometime challenger to Windows that takes a similar approach to Windows 95. Unfortunately, it failed to capture the PC-user's imagination in the same way that Windows did, with the result that there's a comparatively tiny amount of software available and some areas of computing have no OS/2 software at all. Add-ons to the basic OS/2 system do enable it to run some Windows 3.x-compatible software.

Quickfire buying tips

Apart from choosing the PC itself and any other peripherals and software you want, a few other points need attention when buying. Here's a list of the more important ones that apply equally to whole computer systems and to single add-on devices:

- For extra security, try to pay by credit card.

- Always check what the final price will be, including extra peripherals or software you asked to be added, tax and delivery, and get it in writing.

- When you place an order, tell the vendor what you want to use the computer for. This will give you extra leverage if the PC doesn't prove fit for the task.

- Find out what your options are for refund or replacement if you're unhappy with your purchase. Make sure you get written confirmation of these terms.

- If you order by telephone, keep records of who you spoke to and when, and make notes on what was offered and at what price. Follow up with a fax or letter detailing the order, agreed terms and price. If a delivery date was given, and is vital, include the words 'Time is of the essence'. This is a legal term that gives you the right to cancel the order if delivery isn't made by the quoted date.

- When you sign for the delivery, add the words 'Goods not inspected' before your signature.

- When you receive the goods, set everything up and check it carefully. Make sure you inform the vendor immediately if something is missing or not working – if you leave it too long, you may find it more difficult to justify a refund or replacement.

- Keep all the cartons and packaging in case you need to return the system or send it for repair sometime in the future.

- Keep *all* the paperwork that came with the computer in one place.

- Don't fill in any warranty or registration cards for hardware or software until you know it's complete and it works.

Setting up your PC

Where you site your desktop PC takes some careful thought. You'll need to be within easy reach of power-sockets (and a phone socket if you have a modem), and to have enough desk-space for external devices such as keyboard, mouse and printer to be accessible. Remember that monitors take up a lot of space – if necessary, pull your desk out from the wall a little way so that you can move the monitor further back. Also, make sure the monitor is situated and angled in such a way that it can't reflect sunlight or a lightbulb into your eyes.

The system unit is the other bulky device that needs to be found a home. You'll need to leave at least six inches of fresh air behind it, partly because of the cables that have to be plugged in, but primarily to ensure that its internal components don't overheat. Desktop cases are intended to be placed behind your keyboard with the monitor placed on top of them, though you may prefer to place it elsewhere. Small tower-cases are usually placed on the desk beside your monitor; larger tower-cases are intended to be placed on the floor under your desk. Remember you'll need to reach the floppy-disk and CD-ROM drives, and avoid putting the case anywhere it can be jolted or kicked: if this happens while the hard-drive is working, it can cause serious damage to both disk and read/write head which might mean loss of data and a replacement drive if you're unlucky.

If you have a desktop case with a CD-ROM drive (rather than a tower case), never stand it on its side: CD-ROM drives must be mounted horizontally.

Make sure none of the connected cables is stretched taut between devices, and keep all the spaghetti at the back as tangle-free as you can. Take special care to secure all this cabling in some way so that no-one can drag it off the desk by getting their feet caught up in it! Lastly, choose somewhere comfortable: your monitor should be in front of you, and at eye-level without the need to stretch or slump; you'll need room to rest your hands in front of the keyboard; you'll need space on your desk for a mouse-mat, and some elbow-room to move the mouse.

The various ports and sockets on a PC are detailed in Chapter 3, and plugging everything in should be a simple job. However, never *ever* plug or unplug devices on the system unit while the computer is switched on! If you brought additional devices to install yourself (particularly internal devices such as expansion cards), don't install them until you're sure the rest of the system is working perfectly.

When you're not using your PC, unplug the whole system from the mains after turning everything off. To guard against electrical spikes and storms, you might also choose to add a surge protector.

Turning on, turning off

The most important rule to remember in turning your PC on and off is: *Try not to do it!* In general, try to turn your computer off only when you won't be using it again for several hours. The surge of power into the unit each time you start up, and the change in temperature of the internal components, can shorten their life-span if it happens unnecessarily often. Turning the PC off and immediately back on again should only be done in desperate circumstances and you should pause for a few seconds in between. Whenever a restart is necessary, use the Reset switch on the system unit to do it.

Whenever you switch on your system, there's a routine that should be followed to ensure that everything is powered-up in the correct order and avoid damage to components and devices. Your PC's manual should give precise details, but the usual routine is to switch on the system unit, then the monitor, then any peripherals. When you've finished for the day, follow the same steps in reverse.

What about the Year 2000 bug?

You've almost certainly heard mention of the 'millennium bug', so you're probably wondering whether your new PC and software will suffer from it. Let's start with a quick explanation of what the millennium bug actually is.

In years gone by, many software writers took shortcuts when telling their programs how to handle dates, telling them to take the '19' for granted when given a year number like 98. Rather short-sightedly, it didn't occur to them that their software might still be in use at the turn of the new millennium. Therefore, when the year 2000 comes around, these programs will see that the date is '00' and assume that to mean 1900. Clearly this could cause mayhem if the software in question determines bank interest, flight departures, or anything else that relies on the system knowing the correct date.

In fact, although the media has jumped on this issue and hyped it relentlessly, the so called millennium bug matters little to ordinary computer users like you and me. Our computers and software are almost certainly programmed to use four-figure year numbers, and have been for quite a while. The Year 2000 issue is important only to companies relying on software that was written years ago and has never been updated, or software that they commissioned specifically to handle a particular task. These companies should be actively testing for year 2000 compliance, and many are. A more valid fear for the rest of us concerns the companies that are not testing their systems, and how their computers affect our lives.

Meanwhile, one result of the hype is that companies have started trying to sell us software that will check our system to see if it can handle the new millennium. Of course, in almost all cases, the software will look at your system for an expensive few minutes, reply that everything looks okay, and never be used again. If you have a recent PC and you're not using any old or custom-written software, spend your money on something more useful – almost anything qualifies.

Part Two

Getting to Grips with Windows

In This Part...

Starting & Exploring your PC

Finding your Way Around

Working with Programs & Files

Getting more out of Windows

Customizing Windows for Speed & Style

Keep your System Running Smoothly

Install & Set Up New Hardware

Chapter 9

Starting & Exploring your PC

In This Chapter...

How to start and shut down your computer

Make friends with the mouse for easy computing

The Windows desktop: icons, Taskbar and Start button

Drives, files, and folders in My Computer and Windows Explorer

Starting & Exploring your PC

So you're the proud owner of a shiny new PC. You've diligently attached everything that needed to be attached, and you're sitting comfortably and waiting expectantly. Over the next few chapters you'll learn how to find your way around Windows, work with programs and documents, and customize things so that they look and work the way you want them to.

As you read on, remember this one simple fact about computers: they exist to help you do what you need to quickly and easily. Essentially, that means creating, opening, saving, and printing files. They can do other things too, such as playing audio CDs, but you didn't buy a PC because you wanted a really expensive CD player!

Getting started

Task number one needs little introduction: to use the PC for anything remotely useful you'll need to switch it on! Plug the PC into the mains, along with any other devices you want to use, such as your printer or external modem. Press the power switch on the PC's system unit, then switch on the monitor followed by the other devices.

To begin with, you'll see a plain black screen with some technical-looking text. Within a few seconds this dull screen will be replaced by something more colourful. Within about 30 seconds, the hard disk will finish its churning and grinding, and the colourful picture will vanish to reveal the Windows desktop.

Instead of the colourful picture, you might see a line that says **Invalid system disk. Replace the disk and press any key**. This means that there's a floppy disk in the floppy drive that doesn't contain the type of information your PC needs to start Windows. Just remove the disk and then press any key on your keyboard, and Windows will start to load.

Don't worry if there's a CD in your CD-ROM drive when you start the computer. When the system starts it only looks at your floppy drive and your hard disk.

Shutting down Windows

When you've finished work for the day and you're ready to switch off your computer, don't press the power button yet. Just as Windows has some work to do before it can start, it has to do a few things before it stops. Instead, follow this routine:

1. Save any documents you're working on (if you want to keep them), then close any applications still running and any open windows.

2. Click the **Start** button at the bottom left of the screen to open the Start menu.

3. Click on **Shut Down** at the bottom of the Start menu.

4. A small window called a dialog will appear, like the one shown in the next screenshot, giving you several options. The dot beside the words **Shut down** means that this option is selected. This is the option you want, so click the **OK** button.

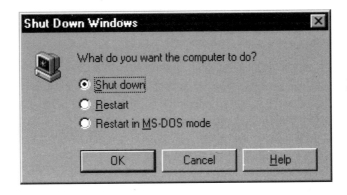

The Shut down dialog: choose what you want to do, then click OK to make it happen.

5. A large picture will fill the screen asking you to wait while Windows shuts down. After some hard disk churning, you'll see a message telling you it's safe to switch off your computer.

6. Switch off peripheral devices such as your printer, followed by the monitor, and finally the computer itself. Then unplug everything from the mains.

Arriving at the Windows desktop

When Windows has finished loading you'll see the desktop, shown in the next screenshot. At the moment it looks empty and uncluttered, with several small labelled pictures called icons, and a grey strip along the bottom called the Taskbar. In the centre of the screen you'll see the pointer, which you control by moving the mouse. Here's a brief explanation of what these features do:

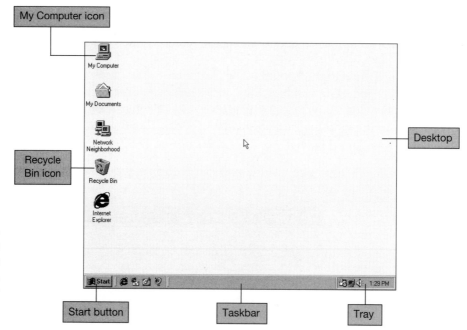

The Windows desktop and its main features.

Taskbar – Almost everything that happens in Windows happens in a window; that's how the operating system got its name. A window is a box that opens on the desktop to show you the program you're using, the file you're editing, and many other things. As soon as a window opens, a button will appear on the Taskbar with the same name as the window. During normal everyday work, you might have several windows open at once, putting several buttons on this bar. As well as telling you at a glance what's currently open, these buttons can be clicked to let you see a window that might be hiding behind all the others. We'll take a closer look at the Taskbar in Chapter 10.

Start button – This is your key to getting things done in Windows. When you click this button, a menu will appear that holds entries for all your programs along with some other useful options. Starting a program or selecting an option is as simple as moving the mouse pointer on to it and clicking the left button. The Start button and its menu are covered in more detail in Chapter 10.

Tray – This is a sunken area at the right of the Taskbar containing a digital clock and a few small icons. You might have only one icon here (which looks like a small loudspeaker), or you might have several, depending upon what programs are installed on your PC. These icons usually give quick access to settings or options; for example, if you click the loudspeaker with the left mouse-button, a slider will appear to let you change the volume of your soundcard. (To make it go away again, click the mouse somewhere else.) You can also find extra information by resting the pointer over these icons: if you move over the clock, a little message will appear to tell you the date.

Icons – You'll find icons scattered all the way through Windows, and you'll soon start to recognize and distinguish between the different 'pictures'. Every application you use has its own distinctive icon, and any documents you create with it will be given the same icon along with any name you choose. That way, you can tell at a glance which program you used to create a particular document. You'll have several icons on your desktop at the moment, although you can add more later if you want to, to give quick access to favourite programs or documents. Later in this chapter we'll look at the most important of those icons – My Computer.

What's on your desk?

The layout of Windows follows a 'desktop' metaphor that's intended to make the organization of your disks and files intuitive. The idea is that just as your desk might be covered in objects that you pick up and use, so the objects in your computer (applications, documents, printer, modem, and so on) should be presented as pictures on the screen that you can 'pick up' (click with the mouse) and use in a similar way.

On your desk you have a computer, hence that icon labelled My Computer. Although technically *under* your desk, there's a bin for all your trash called the Recycle Bin, and the Taskbar corresponds to the jumble of papers on your desk from which you might pick something up to work with for a while (by clicking its Taskbar button) before putting it down and looking at something else (clicking a different Taskbar button).

Handling the mouse

Although Windows can be used entirely from the keyboard, it wasn't designed for easy keyboard-only use. A little time spent getting used to controlling the mouse pays huge rewards in speed and simplicity. So before we start looking at Windows itself, now is a good time to make friends with your rodent.

First, make sure the mouse is the right way round: when you place your palm on the body of the mouse, your second and third fingers should rest lightly on the buttons and the cable should be running towards the back of your desk. Moving the pointer on the screen is simple: move your hand to the left, and the pointer moves left, and so on.

If you're left-handed the mouse buttons will probably seem uncomfortable to use. Turn to Chapter 13 and use the Control Panel's Mouse applet to switch the buttons about.

Now let's try a little exercise in clicking. There are three terms you'll come across: click, right-click, and double-click:

Click means to press the left mouse-button once. You can test this by moving the pointer on to the Start button: click once to make the Start menu appear; click again to make it vanish.

Right-click means to click once using the right mouse-button. If you move the pointer to an empty space on the desktop and right-click, a menu containing options such as Arrange Icons and Line Up Icons will appear. Click on a different area of the desktop to make it disappear.

Double-click takes a bit more mastering. Like 'click', this tacitly refers to the left mouse-button, but you need to click twice in quick succession. To try this out, move the pointer on to the Recycle Bin icon, and double-click. If you're successful, a window will open on your desktop like the one in the next screenshot. You can close this window by clicking the Close button (marked with an '**x**') in the top right corner. It's worth trying this routine a few times to get the hang of it.

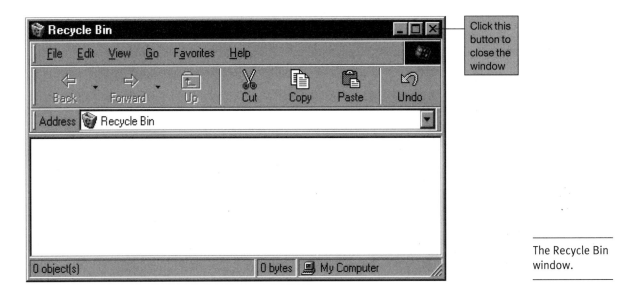

Click this button to close the window

The Recycle Bin window.

Drive names – learn your ABC

Whenever you want to use a particular file, you have to tell the computer what it's called. Even though the data is stored on the disk itself, you tell the computer which *drive* to look at to find the file rather than which *disk*.

Because the normal computer had one floppy drive, it came to be called Drive A. If a second floppy drive was added, it would be called Drive B. When the hard drive arrived on the scene, it was automatically assigned the name Drive C. So on a standard PC with its one floppy drive and one hard drive, these are called Drive A and Drive C respectively. Recently, more and more PCs have extra drives, such as CD-ROM and backup drives, and the computer simply assigns these the next

available letter name: your CD-ROM drive will usually be Drive D, and your
backup drive Drive E.

Drives & folders in My Computer

So far, you've taken it on trust that there are files on your hard disk. After all,
Windows started, so there must be *something* there! The quickest way to take a look
at what files are on a particular disk is to open **My Computer** by double-clicking
its icon. When you do this, a window like the one shown in the next screenshot will
open to display My Computer's contents.

You can view
your drives and
their contents in
My Computer.

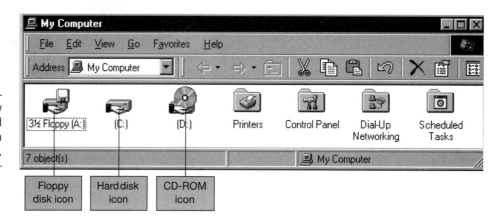

You'll probably have the same three icons shown here for floppy-disk, hard disk
and CD-ROM drives, and you might even have one or two more. To look at the
contents of one of these disks, just double-click its icon. The important thing to
remember is that only your hard disk is permanently attached to your PC; if you
double-click the icons for your floppy or CD-ROM drive without first inserting a
floppy disk or a CD, a message will appear to tell you that the drive is unavailable.

If you're finding the double-click action tricky, you can cheat: click
once on an icon, which will highlight it to show it's selected, then
press the Enter key on your keyboard to open it.

Start by double-clicking the icon for your hard disk, labelled **C:**, and another window will open to display its contents as a collection of icons. Although the contents of your hard disk will be different from mine, this window will look a lot like the one in the following screenshot, showing a mixture of folders and files.

The hard disk is best thought of as a filing cabinet. In a well organized office, every time you start work on a new project, you'd grab a new folder, scribble a memorable name on the front of it, and put all the documents relating to that project inside it to make them easy to find. Then you'd store that folder alphabetically inside the cabinet with all the other folders. The hard disk works in a similar way: when Windows was installed, it created a folder called Windows and another called Program Files, and it placed files inside both. Most other programs you install will create their own folders in the same way, and you can create new folders yourself to organize your own files, as you'll learn in Chapter 12.

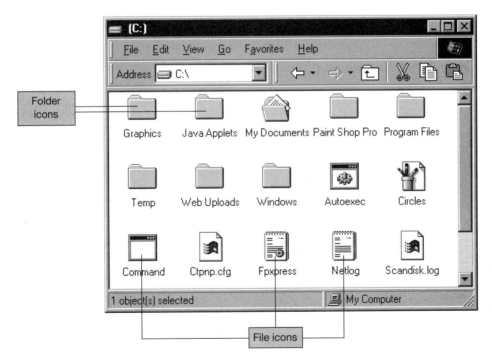

Folders and files on Drive C.

As you can see from the window you've just opened, Drive C contains several folders and a small bunch of files. The folders are easy to spot – they all use the same yellow icon. Files can have many different icons according to what type of file they are, but the most important thing for now is to recognize a folder.

Folders don't necessarily contain just files, though. If you double-click the **Windows** folder to open it, you'll see more folder icons including **Command**, **Fonts** and **System**, along with yet more files. And, indeed, if you open the **System** folder, you'll see more folders inside that. When one folder is inside another, it's referred to as a *subfolder* (so the System folder is a subfolder of the Windows folder). Conversely, the Windows folder is said to be the *parent* of the System folder.

Working with My Computer

There are two ways to look at the files and folders on your system: one way is to use My Computer, and the other is to use Windows Explorer (more on that in a moment). You can use whichever method you like, whenever you like, but most users seem to favour one method over another. Here's a few tips to help you navigate your system using My Computer:

- If you lose track of which folder's contents are being displayed, look at the extreme top left of the window. Beside a small folder icon you'll see the name of the current folder.

- If you open a subfolder and want to move back to its parent folder, either press the Backspace key, or click the button on the toolbar showing a tiny folder with an upward-pointing arrow. (If you can't see the toolbar, click the word **View** on the menu bar, move the mouse onto the word **Toolbars** and click **Standard Buttons** on the menu that appears beside it.)

- Remember you can close any window by clicking the **Close** button (marked with an 'x' symbol) in the top right corner.

- You can choose between four different ways of displaying icons and information in a window. Open the **View** menu by clicking the word **View** on the menu bar, and choose from Large Icons, Small Icons, List and Details. If you're using Windows 98, you can also switch on Web view by clicking **as Web Page** on the same menu: every time you click on a file or folder in the window, information will appear in the coloured area describing the item you clicked. With some types of file, a small preview will also be shown. (If you decide you're not keen on Web view, go back to the View menu again and click the same option a second time to switch it off.)

The view from Windows Explorer

Windows Explorer offers another way to view the drives, folders and files on your system. One of the great benefits of Explorer is that icons for all your folders and drives remain visible while you look at the contents of one particular folder. This can make it easier to tell at a glance where you are and what you're looking at, with the added bonus that copying and moving items from one place to another is simple (as you'll learn in Chapter 12).

There are two ways to open Windows Explorer:

- If your keyboard has the extra Windows keys, press and hold the **Win** key (marked with a 'flying window' icon) and press **E**.

- Click the **Start** button, then point to **Programs**, as shown in the next screenshot. The Programs menu will open and you can click the **Windows Explorer** entry.

Opening Windows Explorer from the Start menu.

Explorer shows a neat split-window view of your system. In the left pane of the window you'll see icons for your desktop, My Computer, Recycle Bin, and your drives. In the right pane you'll see the contents of whatever you selected in the left. When Explorer first opens, the right pane displays the same items you see in My

Computer. In fact, if you choose to, you can use Explorer in exactly the same way as you use My Computer: just ignore the left pane, and double-click drives and folders in the right pane to open them.

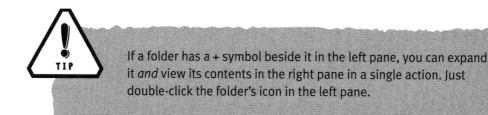

If a folder has a + symbol beside it in the left pane, you can expand it *and* view its contents in the right pane in a single action. Just double-click the folder's icon in the left pane.

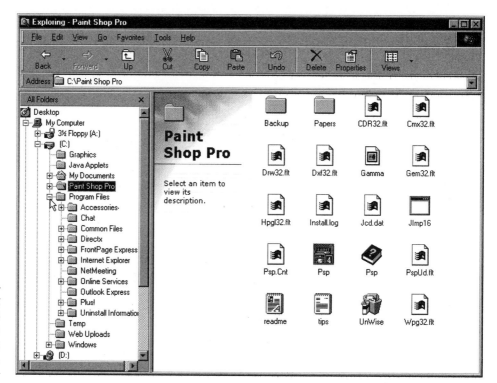

Browsing through drives and folders in Windows Explorer.

The neatest way to use Explorer, though, is with the left pane (and you don't need to double-click!). Every drive has a tiny + symbol beside it, indicating that it contains folders. If you click the + symbol beside the icon for your C drive, the list

(or 'tree') will expand to show its folders, and the + symbol will turn into a –
symbol. To collapse that part of the tree again, click the – symbol.

If a folder contains subfolders, you'll see the same + symbol beside it, and you can
expand and collapse it in the same way, as shown in the screenshot above. Click on
any drive or folder in the left pane to view its contents in the right.

TIP

You can choose how wide the two panes of the window should be.
Move your pointer on to the bar that splits them, and you'll see it
turn into a vertical bar intersected by an arrow. Press the left mouse-
button and, without releasing it, drag the bar to where you want it.

Chapter 10

Finding your Way Around

In This Chapter...

Navigate the Start menu to run programs

Switch from one window to another with the Taskbar

Open, close, move, and resize windows

Learn how to work with dialog boxes and file names

Finding your Way Around

Whatever you're planning to use your computer for, there are three fundamental elements you need to be familiar with: the window, the Taskbar, and the Start menu. The significance of the window shouldn't come as much of a surprise, given the name of the operating system. The Taskbar and Start button remain visible whatever you're working on, and these are your essential tools for working with different programs. In this chapter, you'll learn how to use these elements, and pick up the basic information you need to start working with programs and files.

The mighty Start button

It may not look like much, but the Start button on the left of the Taskbar is your key to being productive in Windows. Along with a few other options we'll be looking at in Chapter 12, this is where you find quick access to all the programs on your computer. Click the Start button and the Start menu will open. Move your pointer up to the **Programs** entry and pause there for a second, and another menu (called a *submenu*) will pop out. On this, you'll see program groups such as Accessories, Internet Tools, and StartUp.

Entries for program groups all have a black arrowhead beside them and identical folder-like icons: when your pointer pauses over a group, a new submenu will open to show its collection of icons (which may contain still more groups). Entries on these menus that don't have the arrowhead and folder icon will run a program when you click on them.

If your computer came with a bundle of software, such as Lotus SmartSuite or Microsoft Works, you'll probably see extra program groups for those programs. Most software you install on your PC adds its own little set of icons on a separate submenu.

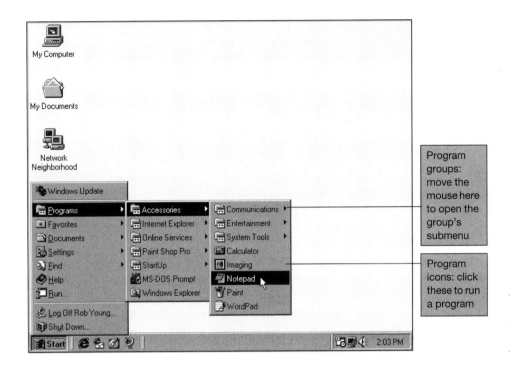

Program groups: move the mouse here to open the group's submenu

Program icons: click these to run a program

Program groups and icons on the Start menu.

Using Windows' own accessories

Even if your new PC didn't come with a bundle of extra software, you'll still find a range of accessories supplied by Windows itself in the Accessories and Internet Explorer program groups. Although most of these add-ons lack the advanced features you'd expect to find in a fully fledged (and more expensive) piece of software, they're all still perfectly usable and useful. (If you can't see all of these programs on your Start menu, they may not be installed. Turn to Chapter 13 to find out how to add them.)

 Notepad – A handy 'jotter-style' text editor for creating simple text files that can be opened in any word processor.

 WordPad – A more advanced word processor than Notepad, for creating longer documents using different text styles, colours and sizes, and paragraph formatting.

 Paint – A simple graphics program for drawing and editing pictures.

Calculator – An onscreen calculator with Standard and Scientific layouts, which you can select from its View menu.

CD Player – For playing your audio CDs, and creating playlists that can skip the tracks you don't like.

Media Player – The multimedia 'everything' player: movie files, audio CDs, animations and sound files.

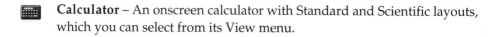

Internet Explorer – If you have a modem and a connection to the Internet, this is your number one Net-surfing tool, as you'll learn in Part Four.

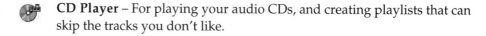

Outlook Express – If you're using Windows 95 you may have two separate icons instead, labelled Internet Mail and Internet News. These programs let you send and receive email messages and read newsgroup messages, provided you have an Internet connection.

Along with the accessories listed above, you'll find a Games group containing a few simple computer games, and a System Tools group containing utilities to keep your PC running smoothly. You'll learn about these system utilities in Chapter 14.

Anatomy of a window

The window is the fundamental element of Windows operating systems. A window is a box on the desktop which displays a document or application, or groups of icons representing the files on your hard disk. You might have several windows open at the same time and switch between them when you need to. For example, in one window you might have your word processor running to type a sales report; another window could contain your spreadsheet application so that you can refer to your sales figures; and a third window might display icons for all the spreadsheet documents you've created this year, so that you can select which month's figures you need to look at.

In this example, the word-processor window would usually be in the foreground so that all your keyboard input would be entered into the report you're typing. The other two windows would be, quite literally, in the background: the word-processor window is covering them up like the top sheet on a stack of papers, perhaps leaving just a corner or an edge visible. When you switch to the spreadsheet window, this will move to the foreground (the top of the stack) instead, and the word-processor window will disappear behind it. The fact that you can no longer see this window doesn't mean it's not there, or that the report you were typing into it has been lost – you can switch it back to the foreground whenever you want to, or you can place the windows side by side on the screen so that you can refer to one as you type into the other.

Almost every window you work with will have the same features as those shown in the screenshot below. Some of these features let you change the way the window looks, such as its size and position, and others let you work with the information displayed in the window.

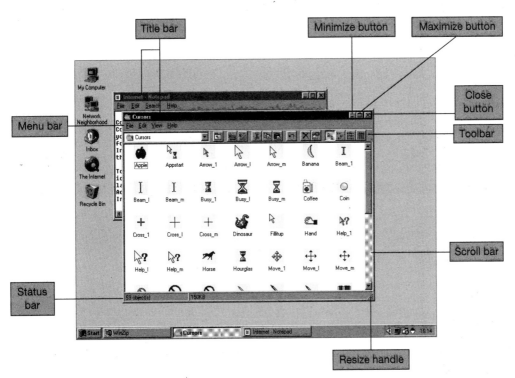

The major body parts of a window.

Title bar – The title bar displays the name of the folder you're looking at, or the name of the application in that window. It has an extra useful function: you can use it to move the window wherever you want it. Just click on the bar, and drag the window without releasing the mouse button. The colour of the title bar tells you which of your open windows is active. Inactive windows will have a dull grey title bar, but the active window's title bar will be blue (unless you've changed your colour scheme – see Chapter 12). The active window is the one that will react to your keyboard input; only one window can be active at a time.

Resize handle – Move your pointer on to this area at the corner of a window, and the pointer will change into a double-headed arrow. Click the left mouse-button and drag the corner of the window in any direction to change its size. (With slightly more skilled mouse-positioning, you can do the same thing at any edge of the window too.)

Close button – We've seen the Close button before, and it does what you'd expect: click it, and the window will close. (If the window contains a document you've been working on and haven't saved, a dialog will appear to ask if you want to save it first.)

If you prefer to work from the keyboard, holding Alt and pressing F4 will close a window in exactly the same way as clicking the Close button.

Maximize button – Clicking this button increases the window's size to make it cover the entire desktop. Any other open windows will be covered too, but you can switch to them at any time by clicking the appropriate buttons on the Taskbar. When the window is maximized, the Maximize button changes into a Restore button: if you click this, the window will return to its original size and position.

Minimize button – This makes the window vanish from your desktop, making the screen less cluttered and easier to work with. It doesn't close the program and document you were working on in that window, however – its button remains on the Taskbar and can be clicked to make the window reappear. You could think of the Minimize button as a 'make temporarily invisible' button.

Status bar – This is a simple information bar. If a window is displaying the contents of a folder, it might tell you the number of items in that folder, or the size of an item you've clicked. In a word processor, the status bar might tell you the total number of pages in your document.

Scroll bar – If a window contains more information than it can display, a scroll bar will appear to let you wind the window contents up and down (rather like winding a long piece of paper through a typewriter). The scroll bar contains a long box called a scroll box, and scroll arrows at either end. To move quickly through the window contents, you can drag the scroll box up and down; for more controlled scrolling, click and hold one of the scroll arrows to move through the window a line at a time.

Toolbar – Not all windows have a toolbar, and for those that do you can usually choose whether to hide or display it. The toolbar contains a collection of buttons that give one-click access to some of the often-used options in a program. The same options can usually be selected from menus on the menu bar, but the toolbar buttons will help you work more quickly.

If you're not sure what a toolbar button does, place the pointer over it for a couple of seconds; in many programs, a small 'tooltip' message will appear with a brief explanation.

Menu bar – The menu bar is a feature of most (though not all) windows. It's a narrow horizontal strip below the title bar containing a row of words such as **File**, **Edit**, **View** and **Help**. Each of these words is the name of a menu: clicking on the word **File**, for example, will cause a drop-down menu to open that contains options such as **New** (to start creating a new document), **Open** (to open an existing document), and **Save** (to save the document you're working on to disk), as shown in the next screenshot.

If you prefer to use the keyboard rather than the mouse, menus are just as easy to deal with. Every menu on the bar has an underlined letter. To open that menu, hold the **Alt** key and type that letter on your keyboard. To select an option from the open menu, press the option's underlined letter. For example, to select the **Save** option shown in the screenshot on the next page, press **Alt+F** to open the File menu, then press **S**.

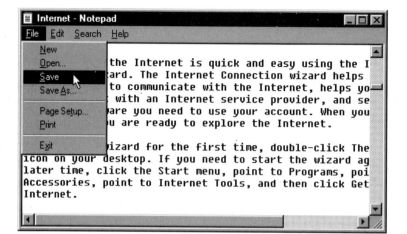

Click File to
open the File
menu, then click
the option you
want.

Many of the options you see on these menus end with an ellipsis – **Open...**, for example. The ellipsis indicates that selecting this option won't carry out a command straight away, but will open a dialog box to let you provide more information. In this example, 'Open' by itself is clearly meaningless until you tell the program what document you want to open.

Switching between open windows

One of the things that made Windows so popular was the ability to have multiple windows open and to switch between them (known as 'multitasking'). The introduction of the Taskbar in Windows 95 made this not just possible, but easy. Every window you open immediately places a matching button on the Taskbar which remains there until the window is closed. Because the Taskbar stays visible, even when one or more of your windows is maximized, you can tell at a glance which windows are open, and switch to any window by clicking its Taskbar button

In the screenshot on the next page, you can see two open windows and three buttons on the Taskbar. The Cursors window is active, and its Taskbar button is depressed as an indication. Behind this window you can see part of an inactive window with the words Internet – Notepad on its title bar, and its Taskbar button. If you wanted to work with this window, you'd click its Taskbar button to bring it to the front and make it active. You could also bring it to the front just by clicking any part of it that's visible.

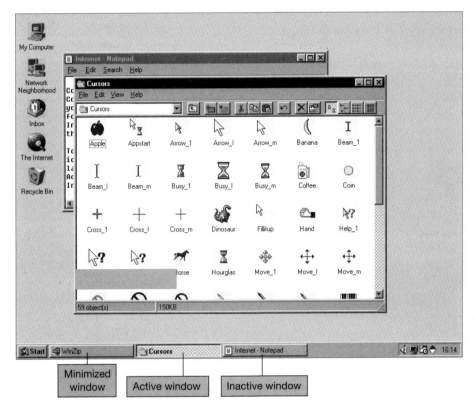

A quick glance at the Taskbar tells you what's open.

The third button on the Taskbar indicates that there's a window open running a program called WinZip, but where is it? It might be a tiny window hiding behind the other two, or it might have been minimized, effectively making it invisible. In fact, it doesn't matter: to work with the WinZip window, just click its button to make it appear at the top of the stack looking just as it did the last time you saw it.

Remember that you won't lose your work by minimizing its window or hiding it behind another window – it's no more risky than closing your eyes! The window and the document it contains will still be there waiting for you.

If you're a keyboard fan, or you're working with the keyboard and don't want to break off and reach for the mouse, here's another couple of window-switching options:

Alt+Tab – Press and hold the **Alt** key and then press **Tab** repeatedly until the icon for the window you want to switch to is highlighted on the pop-up panel, then release both keys. (Alt+Tab cycles only through program-windows' icons – dialog windows don't feature in the list.)

Alt+Esc – Press and hold **Alt** and press **Esc** repeatedly. This cycles through the actual windows themselves (rather than icons for them) bringing each to the foreground in turn. Release both keys when the window you want comes to the surface. (Alt+Esc *does* include dialog windows in its cycle, but it doesn't include minimized windows.)

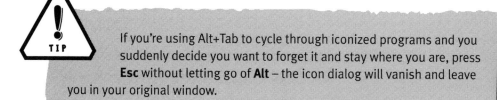

If you're using Alt+Tab to cycle through iconized programs and you suddenly decide you want to forget it and stay where you are, press **Esc** without letting go of **Alt** – the icon dialog will vanish and leave you in your original window.

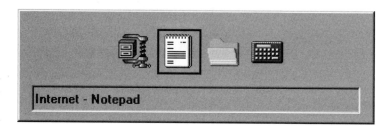

The Alt+Tab panel.

Tricks with the Taskbar

As one of the main navigation tools for getting your work done in Windows, the Taskbar offers some useful customization options, along with some handy features for rearranging your open windows.

- By clicking on an empty area of the Taskbar, and dragging it without releasing the mouse button, you can place the bar at any edge of your screen.

- As you open more windows, the buttons on the Taskbar get progressively smaller, making their labels difficult to read. One option is to hold your pointer over a button for a couple of seconds: a tooltip message will appear containing the button's label. Alternatively, move the pointer to the edge of the bar until it turns into a double-headed arrow, then drag upwards: the Taskbar can be stretched to fill half your screen!

● Right-click on the **Taskbar** and choose **Tile Windows Vertically** or **Tile Windows Horizontally** to have all your open windows arranged neatly side by side. You can also select **Minimize All Windows** to get back to your desktop quickly. After choosing any of these actions, you can right-click the Taskbar again and choose **Undo Tile** or **Undo Minimize** options to return to your previous layout.

● By right-clicking the **Taskbar** and selecting **Properties**, a dialog will appear containing some useful options such as **Auto Hide** (the Taskbar will only appear when you move the pointer to the bottom of your screen), and **Show small icons in Start menu**.

Dealing with dialogs

A dialog box is a window that gives you information about a task that Windows is carrying out, provides you with a warning or prompt when you do something you might regret later, or asks you for information.

Prompts & informative dialogs

As dialogs go, the prompt and the progress dialog shown in the next screenshot are pretty straightforward. The prompt dialog warns you of the consequences of an action you tried to carry out – if you're happy to carry on and do it you click the **OK** button; if you'd rather not, click on **Cancel**. This dialog won't go away until you choose one or the other. A slightly different type of prompt may ask you a question, and give you three buttons for **Yes**, **No** and **Cancel**.

The progress dialog indicates how far the system has got in copying a file from one place to another. When the copy process has finished this dialog will disappear automatically, but until it does you can cancel the operation by clicking its single button.

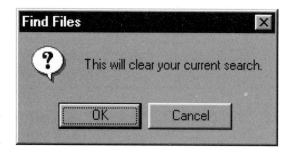

A prompt dialog.

A progress
dialog.

All dialog boxes have a default button, indicated by a dark outline (like the OK
button in the prompt dialog). If you want to select the option indicated by the
default button, you can just press the **Enter** key on your keyboard instead of
moving the pointer to the button and clicking.

Selection dialogs

The more complex type of dialog box is the one that asks you for information. In
some cases, the information required might just be the name of a file that you type
into a space and then click an OK button, or, as in the next screenshot, there may be
a range of options that you can choose from, or several pieces of information that
you need to enter, with another small group of graphic objects.

Scrolling list box – A small box that looks like a miniature window. It contains a
list of options that may be longer than the box can display, so the scroll bar to its
right is used to bring the remaining options into view. You select an option by
clicking its name – the option will be highlighted to confirm your choice. Only one
option can be chosen from the list.

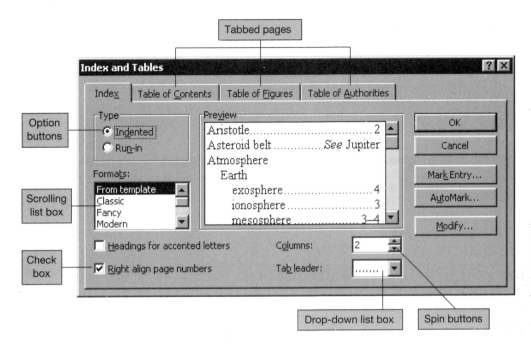

Common
methods of
making choices
in dialog boxes.

Drop-down list box – This works like the scrolling variety, but in its normal state only one option can be seen. If you click the arrow-button beside it, the box will drop downwards, displaying a list of options. When you click on an option, the list will vanish, and the option you chose will be displayed in the box.

Option buttons – These occur in groups of two or more, and let you choose a single option. The selected option has a black dot on its button; if you click on a different option the dot will move to that button instead.

Check box – These are straightforward selection boxes, and you can choose as many of these as you need to. To select an option, click on the box and a check-mark will appear; if you want to de-select the option, click it again to remove the check-mark.

Spin buttons – A pair of Up/Down arrow buttons that increase or decrease the value in the box by 1 each time you click one, or you can hold a button down to spin rapidly through the values. These are not the most user-friendly of buttons, and it's often easier to click once inside the box, use the Delete or Backspace key to erase the value, and just type in a new one.

Tabbed Pages – In modern powerful applications, there are often lots of functions that you can customize to suit your methods of working. All these options together could easily fill the entire screen and wouldn't be pleasant to work with, so instead they're organized into groups, with each group on a separate 'page', and each page having its own tab. Clicking on one of these named tabs will bring the corresponding page to the front. (From the keyboard, hold **Ctrl** and press **Tab** repeatedly to move from page to page.)

In addition to these objects, and the ubiquitous OK and Cancel buttons, there are several other buttons on the page whose labels end with an ellipsis (...). An ellipsis beside an option means that by selecting it you won't be committing yourself to anything just yet, but you'll be presented with another selection dialog.

Understanding file names

Before you start creating and saving files, it helps to know a bit about the way file names work. Any time you create a new file, you choose a name for it and select which folder you want to save it in, but a folder can't contain more than one file of a particular name. For example, if a folder already contains a file called Letter.doc and you try to save a newly created file into the same folder using the same name, you'll be asked if you want to replace the original Letter.doc with this new one, or cancel the operation. You could get around this by choosing a different name, such as Letter2.doc, or, if you're really determined to use this name, you could save the new file into a different folder.

You *can* have multiple files in the same folder with the same file name provided the extension for each is different. For example, a folder could quite happily contain Letter.doc, Letter.txt and Letter.pdf.

As you can see from the file names in the previous paragraph, files are named in a particular way: a few characters, a dot, and several more characters. The characters to the left of the dot are known as the **file name**, and the characters to its right are the **extension**.

Choosing a name for your file

Unlike MS-DOS and older versions of Windows, Windows 95 and 98 use a system of long file names that makes it easy to choose names for your files. A name can be up to 255 characters long, and can include mixed upper- and lower-case characters and a few extra symbols. The symbols you can't use are \ / : * ? " < > |, but you can use one or more dots in the name itself. Handy though these long filenames are, if you actually tried to give a file a 255-zcharacter name, you'd hardly ever be able to see this whole name because Windows just hasn't got room to display it! A more sensible length is about 25 characters, which still gives you plenty of scope to choose a descriptive and easily recognizable name, such as Letter to Sandy or Sales Report Q1 1998.

File extensions & icons

You won't have to bother about file extensions very often. Whenever you create or save a file, the program you're using will add the default extension on the end automatically, and Windows hides the extensions from view to prevent you from worrying about them.

> If you'd like to be able to see the file extensions, open **My Computer** or **Windows Explorer**, open the **View** menu and click **Folder Options**. Click on the tab labelled **View** and then click on '**Hide file extensions for known file types**' to remove the check-mark, and click **OK**. To hide the extensions again, follow the same routine to replace the check-mark.

The function of the extension is to identify what type of file it is: different types of file have different icons so that you can tell them apart, and Windows chooses the correct icon to use by looking at the file's extension. The result is that, although you can look at the extensions yourself, you get the same information in a much friendlier way from the icon. As you learnt in Chapter 9, every application has its own individual icon, and the files you create with that application will be given the same icon. That way, as you look through your folders in Explorer or My Computer, you'll be able to tell at a glance which program is used to open and edit a particular file.

Chapter 11

Working with Programs & Files

In This Chapter...

Open existing files and create new ones

Learn how to save and print your files

Work with several files at once in MDI applications

How to edit different types of information in your files

Working with Programs & Files

Unless you're a huge games or multimedia fan, the main reason you bought a computer was for storing and retrieving information – in other words, creating, opening, saving, and editing files. Part of the power of Windows lies in the fact that there are several ways to do almost everything, and you can choose the one that seems simplest according to what you're currently doing. Don't feel that you have to remember all the available methods though: until you become familiar with Windows, what matters most is that you get the result you want, even if you haven't found the quickest way of doing it!

Opening a file

Although you can see the icons and names of your files in My Computer and Explorer, you can't see the information they contain. To be able to view the contents of a file you have to open it in a program. This can be treated as two separate operations: first, you have to start (or *run*) the program that can work with the type of data in your file; second, you have to load (or *open*) the file itself into that program, which will display the file's contents in its window in a form that you can work with. The program and the file must be compatible with each other; for example, a paint program can't open a database file, and a database program can't open a picture file.

One of the quickest ways to open a file is to look for its icon in My Computer or Explorer, and then simply double-click it. Windows knows which program it needs to run for this type of file, so it handles everything automatically: the program will start and your file will be displayed in its window.

Of course, the program you want to use might be running already: perhaps you've just finished working on a report in your word processor and you want to type a letter. Open the program's File menu and select the **Open...** option (or click the toolbar button containing an open yellow folder if you can see one) and you'll see the dialog shown in the next screenshot.

If you've worked with a particular file recently, and you want to open it again, open the **Start** menu and move the pointer up to the **Documents** entry. On this submenu you'll see the names of the 15 documents you've opened most recently. To reopen one, just click its entry.

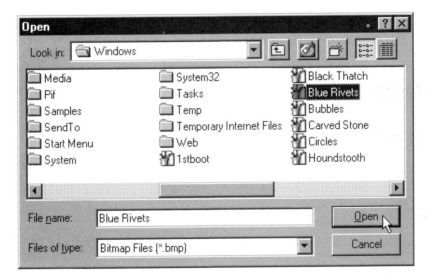

Click the name of the file you want to open, then click on Open.

The main window of this dialog looks like a mini version of My Computer, and it works in just the same way. You can double-click folders to open them, click the arrow-button on the toolbar to move up to the parent folder, or open the drop-down list box beside 'Look in:' to switch to a different drive.

Most programs can work with several different types of file, but specialize in one type. This will be displayed in the 'Files of type:' box, indicating that only files that match this type are being displayed in the main window of the dialog. If the file you want to open belongs to a different type, you can choose it from this box.

When you find the file you want to open, either double-click it, or click it once and then click the **Open** button. The dialog will vanish and your file will open to let you view or edit it.

Some programs offer a much faster way to open a document. They keep track of the names and locations of the last few documents you opened, and place them on the File menu. To reopen one of these documents, just open the File menu and click the name of the document.

Saving an edited file

When you open a file, it isn't removed from the disk it was on. So if you use one of the options above to open a file, take a look at it, and then close the application you were using, the file will still be on the disk unchanged next time you want to open it.

However, if you make some changes to a file you've opened, you must save the file if you want to keep this updated version. (In fact, if you change a file and then try to close the application without saving it, a dialog will appear to ask whether you want to save it.) If you choose not to save an edited file, the changes you made will be permanently lost and the file on your disk will remain as it was before you opened it. When you save a file you've edited, you can choose whether you want to replace the original version with this newer one, or keep both:

- To replace the original file with this edited version, open the File menu and choose **Save** (or, in most programs, just press **Ctrl+S**).

- If you want to keep the old file as well, you'll have to save this new one with a slightly different name or save it into a different folder. Open the File menu and click **Save As...** (which tells the program you want to save the file as something different). The dialog that appears looks exactly like the 'Open' dialog shown above, except that the Open button is replaced by a Save button. Choose the folder into which you want to save the file (if you want to save it to a different folder from the original). If you want to save the file with a different name, type it into the **File name** box. Click the **Save** button to complete the task.

When you save a file, the program and file remain open and you can continue to work on the file. In fact, it's advisable to save a file every few minutes so that if something goes wrong you won't lose all the changes you made to it. If you used Save As to save a file to a different location or under a different name, the program will remember these details in future, so subsequent saves can be made by selecting **File**, **Save** or pressing **Ctrl+S**.

> **TIP**
>
> Some programs offer the option of creating an automatic backup of a file when you save – in other words, keeping a copy of the previous version and replacing its original extension with .bak. This is an option well worth taking: if you mess up your document and then save it, you can open the backup and use that to replace it.

Creating a new file

To be able to create a new file, you have to run the application that works with the type of information you want to use in the document, so the first decision to be made is what sort of document you want: for a text-based report or letter you need to run your word-processing software; for a drawing or picture you'll need your paint program; to enter and manipulate sets of numbers you'll run your spreadsheet application. In almost all cases, that's all there is to it! When the window opens containing the application you selected, it will start with a 'clean sheet of paper' so to speak – a large white space into which you can begin typing your letter or drawing your picture, or a grid of boxes in which to begin entering your numbers.

Of course, the application you need to use may already be running. In this case, you just open the application's File menu and click on the word **New**. If you already have a document open in the window, the new blank document will replace it (although, as usual, if you've made changes to it and not yet saved it, a dialog will first appear to ask if you want to do so).

Saving a new file

When you create a new file, as above, it doesn't exist on disk until you save it. When you try to close the application, the usual prompt to save will appear: if you select No, this newly created file will be gone forever!

As usual, you should save this file every few minutes as you work on it. The first time you do so, the application doesn't know what you want to call it or where you want to store it. From the File menu you can choose either the **Save** or the **Save As...** option – both will result in the *Save* dialog appearing. Choose a folder in which to save the file, and type a name for it in the **File name** box, then click the **Save** button or press **Enter**. As you continue working on the file, you can simply select **File**, **Save** (or press **Ctrl+S**) to overwrite the stored file with the updated version.

Printing a file

Along with opening, saving, and creating files, printing them is something you'll be doing pretty frequently (as long as you've got a printer, of course). Print options and commands are listed on the File menu and are fairly standard from one application to another, so we'll take a look at each of the entries you're likely to come across.

The **Print...** option is often followed by an ellipsis indicating that it leads to a dialog rather than printing immediately. To print a single copy of the document on the default (or only) printer, click on **OK** or press **Enter** when this dialog appears. Provided your printer is switched on and has paper, the document will print.

The Print dialog itself can vary from one application to another, but you'll find many of the same options there somewhere. The default printer will be shown together with the port it's connected to (usually LPT1) – if you have more than one printer you can select which you want to use from a drop-down list box. A box with spin-buttons will show the number of copies to print, defaulting to one, and there will usually be some method of specifying a range of pages to print if you don't want to print the whole document.

In many applications, you'll find another pair of print-related options on the File menu:

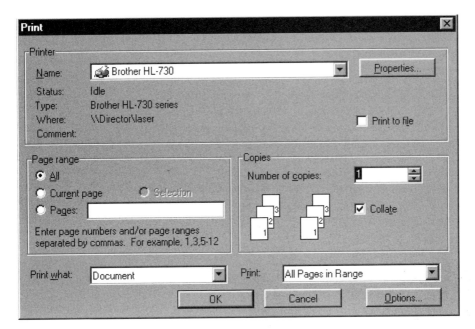

A typical Windows print dialog.

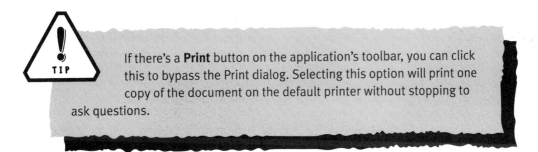

TIP

If there's a **Print** button on the application's toolbar, you can click this to bypass the Print dialog. Selecting this option will print one copy of the document on the default printer without stopping to ask questions.

Page Setup... – Like the Print option, this will lead to a dialog from which you can set options such as paper size and orientation, and the sizes of margins. The settings you choose will usually be reflected in the layout of the document on screen – for example, if you increase the sizes of the margins in a word-processor document, the margin-size will be increased by similar amounts on screen to give you an impression of how the document will appear when printed.

Print Preview – Selecting this option displays the whole of the page you're working on by shrinking it to fit on the screen to let you check the overall appearance and layout of the page before printing. In some applications, you may have an option to view two or more pages side by side, which involves shrinking them still further. Clicking somewhere on the page will often allow you to zoom in and out on a particular area of the page, and you can usually cycle through a multi-page document using the PageUp/PageDown keys.

Working with multiple document interfaces

A handy feature found in some applications is the multiple document interface (MDI), which allows several documents to be open in the same application at once. Each document is given its own window inside the application's own window, and you can arrange these document-windows to be side by side, one above the other, or in a 'stack', so that only the top window is visible. Just as only one application at a time can be active, in an MDI only one document at a time can be active, indicated by the colour of its title bar.

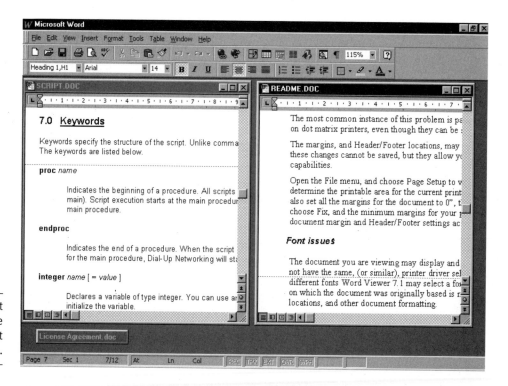

Microsoft Word's multiple document interface.

In the screenshot above, the document-window on the right is active, so any keys you type on the keyboard, and any options you select from the toolbar or menus, will be applied to this document. Like any other window, document-windows have Maximize, Minimize, and Close buttons: the Close button will close the document (prompting you to save it if necessary); the Maximize button will make the document-window expand to fill the whole application-window; the Minimize button will reduce the document to a rectangular icon at the bottom of the application-window.

To switch from one open document to another you can click the mouse in the window you want to work with to make it active (if you can see it), or hold **Ctrl** and press **F6**, or click on the **Window** menu and choose from the list of open documents. And just as you can close an application-window from the keyboard by using the keystroke **Alt+F4**, you can close the active document-window in an MDI by pressing **Ctfl+F4**. You can also close a document by clicking its window's **Close** button, or by choosing **Close** from the File menu.

Editing a file

One of the main reasons for opening a file is to add to it or change it in some way – in other words, to edit it. Since any application that allows you to create and save a document will also allow you to edit it, the Edit menu is as much a fixture on the menu bar as the File menu. In fact, most of the other menus you'll find are also geared towards making the editing easier, but their names, and the entries they contain, will vary widely from one application to another depending upon the type of information you're working with (for example, a database application has no need of a menu called 'Sound Effects'!). The Edit menu has its own variations too, of course, but there are a few entries here that turn up in almost every application.

Cut, Copy & Paste

These three commands form a group of the most useful editing tools you'll come across, enabling you to move or copy large chunks of a document around instead of needing to repeat work you've done once already.

These commands work with the **clipboard**, a temporary storage place provided by Windows that any application can access whenever it needs to. The clipboard can hold any kind of data you select – a picture, a block of text, a snippet of sound or video, or even a whole document. (The various ways of selecting the data to be edited are explained in 'Selection Methods' below.)

- The **Cut** command works rather like the Delete key on the keyboard: the item you selected will vanish from the screen in the same way, but it will be placed on the clipboard rather than disappearing forever.

- The **Copy** command 'photographs' the item you selected and stores a copy of it on the clipboard. The original text, picture or document isn't affected.

- The **Paste** command places the item currently on the clipboard into your document. In a word processor, spreadsheet, or other text-based application the pasted item will be placed at the position indicated by the flashing cursor (the *insertion point*); in a graphics-based application the pasted item will usually appear surrounded by a dotted-box attached to the pointer – just move the pointer until the item is where you want it to be, and click.

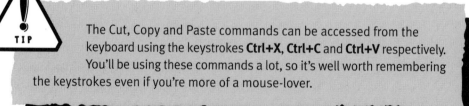

TIP The Cut, Copy and Paste commands can be accessed from the keyboard using the keystrokes **Ctrl+X**, **Ctrl+C** and **Ctrl+V** respectively. You'll be using these commands a lot, so it's well worth remembering the keystrokes even if you're more of a mouse-lover.

The clipboard can hold only one item at a time, so if you cut a section of text, and then cut another one it will replace the first. Also, since there's only one clipboard, if you copy something with one application, then switch to another application and copy something else, the first copy will be replaced on the clipboard. However, once something has been placed on the clipboard (using either Cut or Copy) it can be pasted as many times, and to as many different places, as you want it.

Undo

As the name suggests, this is the command you head for when you do something you didn't mean to. It could be something as minor as typing a wrong letter in a word-processor document (although the Backspace key would take care of this more easily!), or something as major as accidentally deleting a paragraph or part of a picture – selecting Undo will make it like it never happened.

Some applications have several levels of undo; for example, Windows' Paint program will let you undo your last three actions by selecting Undo three times. (An 'action' refers to the period of time between clicking a mouse-button in the drawing area and releasing it again; in this time you might have made just a single dot or you might have drawn a large and intricate freehand shape.)

In most applications, you can undo your last action by pressing **Ctrl+Z** instead of sending your mouse off to the menu bar.

Find and Replace

These are options found in text-based applications such as word processors, spreadsheets, databases, and so on. Find and Replace are actually two separate dialogs, but they work in a similar way. **Find** allows you to search a document for all instances of a particular word or phrase that you type into its box; when an instance is found you can stop and make a change to it, or search for the next. A **Match Case** check-box lets you narrow down your search to instances using the same combination of upper- and lower-case characters that you have specified. Checking a second box marked **Find Whole Words Only** ensures that the search ignores longer words containing the letters you entered – for example, if you wanted to search for instances of the word 'rant', checking this box would prevent the search from finding the word 'currant'.

In the **Replace** dialog, you type a word or phrase (or just a single character) to be searched for, and a second entry to replace it. Clicking the **Replace All** button will automate the process, and a final dialog will tell you how many instances were replaced in the document. If you prefer, you can step through the document from one instance to the next, clicking the **Replace** button to replace the text that was found, or the **Find Next** button to ignore it and move to the next instance.

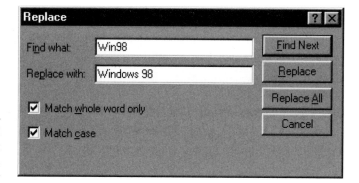

Select All

This is another option found more often in text-based, rather than graphics-based, applications. Choosing this option (or pressing **Ctrl+A**) will highlight the contents of the entire document in preparation for a global editing action. There are a few occasions when this might be useful: one is so that you can 'Copy' the document to the clipboard ready to 'Paste' into a different document or application; another is so that you can apply a formatting command to the whole document, such as changing the font or text-size.

Selection methods

Whenever you want to carry out an editing action on a part of a document you first have to select that part, otherwise the action might have no effect at all or, worse still, it might affect the whole document! There are various selection methods, and which one to use will depend on the type of document you're working on and how much of it you need to select.

In graphics applications, such as Windows' Paint, a 'selection tool' called Scissors or Pick is used to mark the area you want to select. After choosing this tool, click the mouse button at one corner of the required area and drag diagonally – a dotted box will expand as you do so, as shown in the next screenshot. When the required area is outlined by this box, release the mouse button and choose the editing action you want.

A similar method is used to select multiple cells in a spreadsheet or table: click in one cell and drag the mouse vertically, horizontally, or diagonally to highlight the

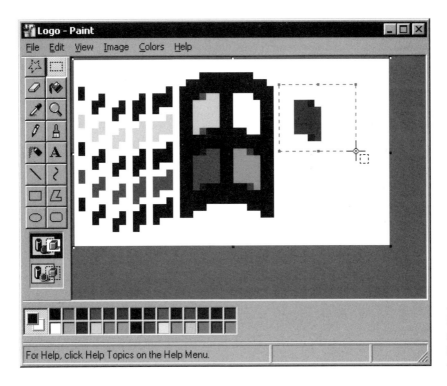

Using the selection tool in Paint.

cells you want to work with. Another method (which is also used to select multiple files in My Computer or Windows Explorer) is to press and hold **Ctrl** and click in each of the required cells. In this way, you can select cells scattered throughout the document rather than having to select a block of adjoining cells.

When working with text there are several possible methods you can use, one of which is dragging. Move the pointer to the left of the first word you want to select, and simply click and drag along the line or diagonally down the page until you've highlighted all you want. Here's a quickfire list of other methods (some of which are limited to Microsoft applications):

● To select characters one by one using the keyboard, hold **Shift** and use the left or right arrow-keys to highlight consecutive characters.

● To select a single word, double-click it with the mouse.

● To select words one by one using the keyboard, hold **Ctrl+Shift** and use the left or right arrows-keys to highlight consecutive words.

UK ▾	NZ/Au ▾	Total ▾
34	22	56
6	10	16
21	14	35
18	6	24
30	8	38
13	2	15
4	2	6
6	4	10
19	2	21
32	30	62
21	7	2p
44	7	5†
6	3	9
8	3	11
26	2	28

Drag the mouse over adjoining cells in a spreadsheet to select them.

- To select a whole line from the keyboard, move the cursor (insertion point) to the beginning of the line and press **Shift+End**.

- To select a whole line (as an alternative method for some Microsoft word processors) move the text-pointer to the extreme left of the line: when it turns into a right-slanted arrow, click once.

- To select a whole paragraph, triple-click it with the mouse. This is a Microsoft trick requiring the mouse-button finger to be much more nimble!

- To select a whole paragraph (another alternative Microsoft method), move the text-pointer to the extreme left of the paragraph: when it turns into a right-slanted arrow, double-click.

- To select all text between the insertion point and the end of the document press **Ctrl+Shift+End**.

- To select all text between the insertion point and the beginning of the document press **Ctrl+Shift+Home**.

- To select the whole document (a Microsoft alternative to the Select All menu-option), move the text-pointer to the extreme left margin once again: when it turns into a right-slanted arrow, triple-click.

Chapter 12

Getting More out of Windows

In This Chapter...

Access to online help wherever you are

Working with floppy disks and CDs in Windows

Learn how to create, rename, copy, and move files and folders

Retrieve accidentally deleted files from the Recycle Bin

Work faster with the power and flexibility of shortcuts

Getting More out of Windows

The fundamental role of the computer is to help you create, by allowing you to open, edit, and save files, which you learnt how to do in Chapter 11. The next step is to organize the way you work and find ways to make the whole creation process faster and easier, and in this chapter we'll explore some of the countless methods offered by Windows to help you do just that.

Getting help when you need it

Whatever you're doing, and whatever knotty problem you're trying to solve, Help is at hand to give you a few clues. Windows itself, and its accessories and the applications you install yourself, all come with their own help files, and they're always within easy reach:

- The general Windows help files can be opened by clicking **Help** on the Start menu, or by opening the Help menu in My Computer or Windows Explorer and selecting **Help Topics**. If your keyboard has the extra Windows keys, you can also press **Win+F1**.

- Get help on a specific Windows accessory by opening its Help menu and choosing the same Help Topics entry.

- Applications have a Help menu too. It might contain the same Help Topics, or it might have a **Contents** entry (leading to its main Contents page) and a **Search for help on...** entry leading to the index page, both of which are explained below.

- Remember the magic key: wherever you are, press **F1** and 'context sensitive' help will appear to explain what you're looking at and how it works.

Double-click a 'book' to reveal or hide its contents

Double-click a Help topic to read it

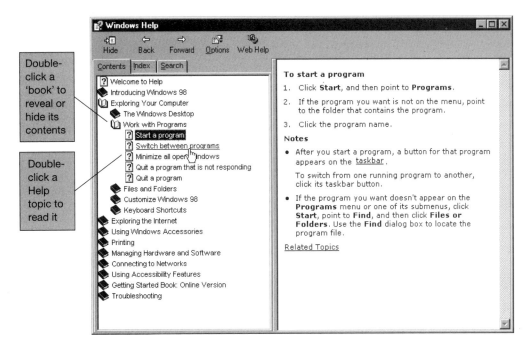

To start a program

1. Click **Start**, and then point to **Programs**.

2. If the program you want is not on the menu, point to the folder that contains the program.

3. Click the program name.

Notes

*   After you start a program, a button for that program appears on the taskbar.

    To switch from one running program to another, click its taskbar button.

*   If the program you want doesn't appear on the **Programs** menu or one of its submenus, click **Start**, point to **Find**, and then click **Files or Folders**. Use the **Find** dialog box to locate the program file.

Related Topics

Every Windows program includes a Help file like this.

The Contents page is usually a good place to start when you want to learn how to use a new program or carry out a particular operation such as printing a file. The different topics covered by the help file are grouped into sections indicated by a book icon, and the topics themselves have a page icon. Click a book icon to reveal its contents, then click the topic that sounds most promising.

If you can't see a topic that seems to cover what you're looking for on the Contents page, click the **Index** tab and type a keyword into its topmost box: as you type, the list of possible topics below will adjust to display those that match. Pick a topic that looks relevant and double-click it. If you still haven't found the answer, click the **Find** tab. The very first time you do this, Windows will need to create a list of words in the Help file, which will take a few seconds. You can then type in a descriptive keyword, and the list below will show all the Help topics that contain that word.

Windows 95 uses a slightly different type of help system, and you'll probably come across programs that still use this older type even if you're using Windows 98. Although the layout is similar, the book and page icons must be double-clicked to open them. And, disconcertingly, as soon as you double-click the topic you want to read, the main window vanishes and a new window opens to display the topic. To return to the main window again, click the button marked **Help Topics** in the topic window.

Sometimes you'll find yourself wishing you could just point at something on the screen and say 'What's that?'. Well, sometimes you can. Almost all of the dialogs and tabbed pages in Windows offer this type of context-sensitive help which appears in tooltip messages.

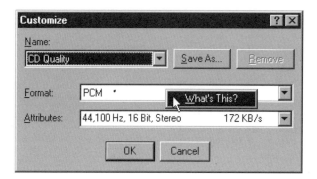

The question-mark button and 'What's This?' menu.

There are three different ways of opening these tooltips. If a window's title bar contains a button with a question-mark icon, click the button and then click the item you want to be explained. If there's no button (or if there is, but you prefer this method), right-click on the item and a tiny context menu will appear with the words **What's This?** on it – just click the context menu. The third option is to click the item once to select it and then press **F1**. There are times when this third method is no use; for example, if the item in question is a button, by the time you've clicked it, it'll be too late to press F1 – for better or worse, you'll have just found out what the button does!

Working with floppy disks

Modern floppy disks are enclosed in $3\frac{1}{2}$-inch slim plastic cases, making them much more resistant to dirt and dust than the older cardboard $5\frac{1}{4}$-inch variety. All the same, they're still fragile devices so always keep them in a box when they're not in use, and store them away from magnetic fields such as speakers and mobile phones. In one corner of the disk there's a little plastic tab called the Write-Protect Tab: when this is moved upwards (so that you can see through the hole it was covering) the read/write head will be unable to write any new data on to the disk and, more importantly, will be unable to delete its existing data.

Insert floppy disks into the drive with the sliding metal cover going in first and the label side up (or pointing away from the eject button if your drive is mounted vertically). The disk is held steady in the drive with a spring mechanism so press it firmly until it clicks into position. To eject a floppy disk, make sure its drive light is out, then press the eject button.

The $3\frac{1}{2}$-inch disk comes in two flavours, double-density (DSDD) and high-density (DSHD), referring to the capacities of the disk. The double-density disk has a total capacity of 720K, the high-density a capacity of 1.44Mb. You can identify a high-density disk by a small engraved 'HD' symbol beside the metal shutter. The standard $3\frac{1}{2}$-inch floppy drive included as standard in all PCs can work happily with both disk capacities.

You can save a file to a floppy disk in just the same way that you save it to your hard disk. Choose **Save As...** from your application's File menu, then open the drop-down list box marked **Look in** and click your floppy drive's icon. Click the Save button to save the file.

Preparing a floppy disk for use

Before you can use a new floppy disk it has to be formatted. In its 'out-of-the-box' state, the $3\frac{1}{2}$-inch blank floppy disk is a standard disk type that can be used by many different types of computer, and other electronic devices with disk drives. Different computers create their own format on a blank disk so that they can use it, and the PC can only use disks with a 'DOS format'.

You can reach the Format command by right-clicking on your floppy drive's icon in My Computer or either pane of Windows Explorer and selecting **Format...** from the context menu. Choose whether you want to perform a Quick or a Full format by checking the appropriate box – a new disk will need a full format, a previously used disk can be quick-formatted to save time – and click on **Start**. When formatting has finished you can click **Close**, or insert another disk and click **Start** again. (If you've got a bunch of disks to format, you can save some time by removing the check-mark beside **Display summary when finished**.)

It's possible to buy boxes of floppy disks ready-formatted for a PC to save you the trouble of doing it yourself. They cost a little more, but they're worth considering if you buy and use in bulk.

You can format a disk that you've already used and which still contains data if you want to, but be warned: formatting a disk erases it completely and (usually) irrevocably! Always make sure you've put the correct disk in the drive before you choose the Format command.

Copy the floppy

Windows makes it easy to make an exact copy of a floppy disk, even if you have only one floppy drive (as most PCs do). Put the disk containing the data you want to copy in your drive, then right-click your floppy disk icon in My Computer and choose **Copy Disk...** from the context menu. A dialog will appear containing two small windows labelled **Copy from** and **Copy to**. The icon for your floppy drive will be highlighted in both if you have only one floppy drive; if you have two floppy drives or a backup drive, place a blank disk in the second drive and make sure its icon is selected in the **Copy to** window.

Click the **Start** button on this dialog to begin copying. If you're copying from one drive to another, you can just wait until Windows tells you the process has finished. If you have a single floppy drive, Windows will read the data from the first disk, and then ask you to remove this disk and insert a blank one in the same drive so that the data can be written to it.

Using audio CDs & CD-ROMs

The number one thing to remember about CDs is: don't believe the nonsense you hear about them being indestructible. They're certainly resilient, and they might survive a drop from a tall building, but a misplaced fingerprint on the silver data-surface might make some of the data unreadable. Always handle CDs by their edges, and keep them in their case when you're not using them.

CD drives in computers are just like those in home stereos: in most cases, you'll press an Eject button to slide out the disk tray, place the disk in the tray, and then press the button again to close it. If your CD drive uses a multi-disk cartridge, place the disk in the cartridge, then slot the cartridge into the drive. Bear in mind that different drives expect the disk to be inserted label-up or label-down: make sure you check the instructions for your drive!

Windows can tell the difference between an audio CD and a data CD-ROM. When you insert an audio CD, the CD Player accessory will start automatically and begin to play the disk. If you insert a CD-ROM, Windows searches the disk for a program called Autorun, which it again runs automatically. The Autorun program may be a multimedia presentation that introduces the contents of the disk in a friendlier format than just a plain list of files, or it may start your CD-based game automatically.

If the CD-ROM doesn't have an Autorun program on it, nothing will happen at all. To look at the contents of the disk, open My Computer or Windows Explorer and double-click on the CD drive's icon.

If you don't want your CD or CD-ROM to run automatically when you insert it, hold the Shift key when you close the drive tray, and until the drive light goes out.

- If you need to clean a CD, wipe it gently with a soft cloth. Always wipe in straight strokes from the centre to the edge of the disk – wiping in circles could damage the surface.

- If a CD gets stuck in the drive and the tray won't eject, find a paper clip and straighten it out, insert it into the tiny hole in the front of the drive unit and push. The tray will slowly slide out. If the tray won't close by pushing the button after you've removed the offending CD, push it gently back into the unit and restart your PC as soon as you can to let the drive reset itself.

Organizing your files & folders

An important key to productivity in Windows is organizing your files and folders so that you know where to find everything without frantic clicking. One popular way to stay organized is to create a single folder on your hard disk that will contain all the documents you create. You might call this folder Documents. Inside the Documents folder you could create subfolders – Pictures, Letters, Accounts, and so on. Whenever you create or save a new file, either pick the appropriate subfolder for the file, or create a new one.

If you use Windows 98, a folder called **My Documents** has already been created, and you can open it by clicking the 'My Documents' icon on the desktop. When you first save a newly-created file, Windows will usually suggest this folder as a place to store it. You can store your own files in this folder, or create subfolders inside it for better organization. Or, if you choose to, ignore Windows' suggestion and choose a different location to save the file.

Over the next few pages, we'll look at the various options for creating, moving, copying and renaming files and folders. The important thing to remember when you do this is: never move, rename, or delete a file or folder that you didn't create yourself!

Creating new folders

As an illustration, let's take the example mentioned above and create a folder called Documents on your C drive.

1. Open **My Computer** and double-click the icon for your **C** drive.

2. Right-click on any blank space in the window (not on an icon) to bring up the context menu, and move the pointer down to the **New** entry. When the submenu opens, click on the word **Folder**, as shown in the next screenshot.

3. A new folder icon will appear in the window named **New Folder**. Type the word **Documents**, and as you begin typing, this new name will replace the highlighted one. Then press **Enter**.

You can create subfolders in just the same way. For example, to create a subfolder called Letters inside your Documents folder, double-click the Documents folder to open it, then follow steps 2 and 3 above, typing **Letters** as the new name for the folder you create.

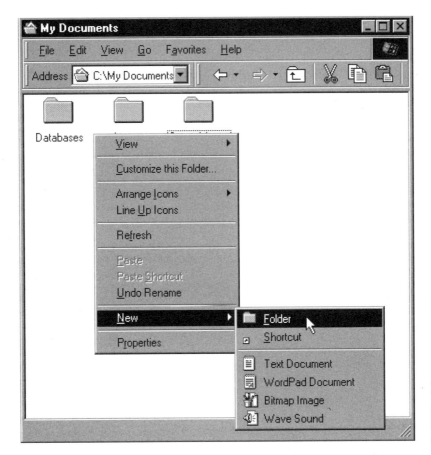

Two clicks, and you've got a new folder.

Renaming files & folders

There are three different ways to change the name of a file or folder, and you can choose whichever seems easiest at the time. A name can use up to 255 characters, with upper- and lower-case letters and spaces, but the characters \ / : * ? " < > | won't be allowed – if you try to use them, Windows will tell you to try again.

● Right-click on a file or folder icon and choose **Rename** from the context menu. A box will appear around the current name. Type the name you want to use instead and it will replace the current name. Press **Enter** when you've finished.

● Click once on the file or folder, then press **F2** and type the new name.

- Click the file or folder icon, then click on the label below the icon. (Make sure these are two separate clicks, not a double-click.) The same box will appear for you to type a replacement name.

Copying or moving files & folders

There are many different ways to copy and move folders and files in Windows. One way to copy a file, for example, is to open it in an application, and then save it to a different location. If you then delete the original file, you've effectively moved it!

One of the neatest ways to copy either a file or a folder is to use the Copy and Paste options. In either My Computer or Windows Explorer, right-click on the icon and choose **Copy** from the context menu. You can then casually click your way to the folder or drive in which you want to create the copy, right-click on a blank space in the window, and choose **Paste**. (If you want to create a shortcut to the item instead of copying it, choose **Paste Shortcut**. See 'Fast access with shortcuts' later in this chapter for more details.)

If you want to move the item rather than copy it, follow the same routine, but select the Cut option after right-clicking the icon. You'll see the icon fade slightly, but it won't actually be moved until you choose the **Paste** option.

> **TIP**
>
> If you'd rather use the keyboard than the context menu, click the icon to select it and press **Ctrl+C** to copy, or **Ctrl+X** to cut. Open the target folder and press **Ctrl+V** to paste.

 Yet another option is to use the buttons on the toolbar in My Computer or Explorer, shown on the left, after clicking the required icon once to select it. The three buttons, from left to right, correspond with Cut, Copy and Paste.

A final method is to use drag and drop, which is easiest in Windows Explorer. In the right pane, make sure you can see the file or folder icon to be copied or moved. Then adjust the left pane so that you can see the target folder or drive.

Finally, right-click the file or folder icon and drag it into the left pane until it's over
the target icon, then drop it by releasing the mouse-button. As soon as you let go of
the file, a context menu will appear like the one in the next screenshot, asking
whether you want to Copy or Move the item, create a shortcut to it (see 'Fast access
with shortcuts' later in this chapter), or cancel the operation: click an option to make
your choice.

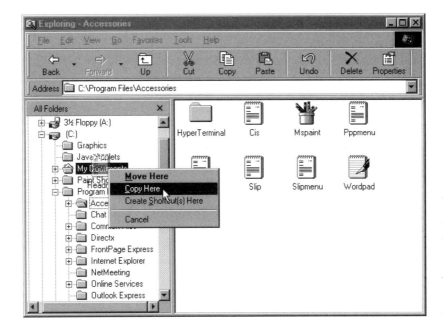

Drag an icon to
the target with
the right mouse-
button, then
choose the
result you want
from the menu.

If you want to copy or move several files to the same place in one operation, you
need to select each item first. To select a continuous row or column of files, click the
first file you want, then hold **Shift** and click the last – all the icons in between will
also be selected. To select several files from different parts of the window, press
Ctrl as you click each icon you want. In either case, if you find you've selected an
icon by accident, hold **Ctrl** and click it again to de-select it.

If you copy, move, rename, or delete a file or folder and then wish
you hadn't, you might be able to undo it. Provided it was the last
thing you did, click the **Undo** button on the toolbar, or press **Ctrl+Z**.

Recycle Bin – deleting & retrieving files

Files and folders are easy to delete: one of the simplest ways is to click an icon once to select it, then press the delete key on your keyboard. You can also click the button marked with an 'X' on the toolbar in My Computer and Explorer, or right-click the icon and select Delete. Finally, if you can see the Recycle Bin icon on your desktop or in Explorer, you can drag and drop an item into it using the left mouse-button.

The Recycle Bin exists because files are so easy to delete, and because people make mistakes. When you 'delete' a file using one of the methods above, the file isn't actually erased from your hard disk. Instead, it's moved into a hidden folder. By double-clicking the Recycle Bin icon, you can see the rubbish you've thrown away and, more importantly, rescue any of it you threw away by accident.

Be careful not to take the Recycle Bin for granted. Files deleted from a floppy disk won't be placed in the Bin but will actually be deleted.

To undelete a file from the Recycle Bin, right-click its icon and choose **Restore**. The file will be replaced in the folder from which it was deleted. (If you deleted the folder that contained the file, it will be recreated automatically.) You can find out where a file will be restored to by double-clicking it: on the properties page that appears, look at the entry beside **Origin**. If you'd prefer to restore a file to a different location, you can use any of the methods covered in 'Copying or moving files & folders' earlier in this chapter.

If you use Windows 98 and you delete a folder, the folder and its entire contents will be moved to the Recycle Bin. Restoring the folder will automatically restore everything that was in it. Unfortunately, if you're not sure what was in it, the only way to find out is to restore it and then open it to have a look.

Here are three useful tips for using the Recycle Bin:

● The Bin can expand to cover 10 per cent of your hard disk if you keep deleting files without emptying it. To reclaim this space, periodically examine its contents to make sure there's nothing there you want to keep, and then select **Empty Recycle Bin** from the File menu. When you do this, those files are gone for good.

● If you're quite sure you want to delete something without the option of retrieving it later, you can bypass the Bin. Highlight the file you want to delete, then hold **Shift** as you press the **Delete** key. The file will be instantly deleted. (Note that you can't use Undo to bring back a file deleted in this way.)

● If you're tired of being asked whether you're sure when you try to delete something, right-click the Bin's icon, choose **Properties**, and remove the check-mark beside **Display delete confirmation dialog box**.

Finding files & folders on your disks

However well you've organized your folders and files, there are bound to be times when you need to find something in a hurry and can't remember where it is. At times like this, the Find option leaps into action. Open the Start menu, move the pointer up to **Find** and choose **Files or Folders...** from the submenu to open the dialog shown below.

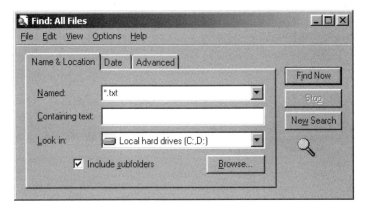

Type the name of the file or folder you're looking for, choose a drive or folder to search, and click Find Now.

The first tabbed page, marked **Name & Location**, is the important one, letting you find files or folders with a particular name and/or containing specified text anywhere on your system. Just type the name (or part of it) into the **Named** box, and either choose a drive or folder to search from the drop-down **Look In** box or click the **Browse** button and double-click the folder you want to start from. If you want to find files that contain a particular word or phrase, type it into the **Containing text** box (Windows 95 users will find this box hidden away on the **Advanced** tab). Click on **Find Now** and the window will expand downwards to display the list of matching items found.

Looking at the results in the Find dialog is exactly like looking at files in My Computer or Explorer: you can double-click a file to open it, right-click it for the usual Cut, Copy and Rename options, move or copy it to a different location, and even delete it. The Find dialog is a powerful tool, so here are a few tips to help you make the most of it:

- You can use the * (asterisk) symbol to replace a group of letters in the file name if you're not sure what they should be; for example, a search for **fin*.doc** would find files on your system such as **Fines.doc, Final.doc** or **Finsbury Park.doc**. Similarly, searching for ***.txt** would find any file with a **.txt** extension, and ***.*** finds every file on your system (up to a limit of 10,000).

- Switch off the Case Sensitive setting on the Options menu (by clicking it to remove the check-mark) if you want Windows to display all matches regardless of upper- and lower-case characters. If you enter something into the **Containing text** box, remember that the search will take longer: Windows has to search *inside* every file rather than just looking at files' names.

- You can choose how you want the results sorted in the lower window: click one of the bars labelled **Name, In Folder, Size, Type** or **Modified**. Clicking **Name**, for example, will sort the results alphabetically. Clicking the same bar again will sort them counter-alphabetically.

- When browsing through My Computer or Explorer, press **F3** to open the Find dialog with the current folder selected in the Look In box. If your keyboard has the extra Windows keys, you can press **Win+F** to open the dialog wherever you are.

Using context menus

Before the arrival of Windows 95, the right button was just an unnecessary extra weight that the mouse had to drag around with it – it couldn't be used to accomplish anything useful. Windows 95 changed all that by introducing the context menu (sometimes called the shortcut menu).

When you click almost any object in Windows with the right mouse-button, a menu will appear containing a variety of options that apply to that object. The options you'll see on the menu vary according to the type of object you clicked. For example, you can click a file or folder icon to cut, copy, rename, or delete it; click inside a folder window to create a new folder or change the folder view; click on selected text in your word processor to format it, and much more.

Although most of the same options can be found elsewhere, the context menu is very often the quickest way to get at them.

Fast access with shortcuts

Over the last two chapters we've talked about organizing and finding the folders and files on your system using My Computer and Windows Explorer, and you've learnt how to run programs from the Start menu. These are vital things to know, but there's still a problem: you won't find every file you're likely to need listed on the Start menu, and trawling through My Computer or Explorer to find a frequently used file soon starts to get on your nerves.

This is where shortcuts come in handy. A shortcut is a tiny 'pointer' file that tells Windows the location of the 'real' file or folder. In fact, shortcuts aren't restricted to pointing at files or folders – you can create a shortcut to a drive, a printer, a networked computer, and many more objects. Not only that, you can create as many shortcuts to a single item as you want to!

In effect, having shortcuts to a file is like having lots of copies of the file in different places, but while the file itself might be several megabytes in size (and you wouldn't want unnecessary copies of a file that size hanging around your hard disk!) a shortcut is roughly 360 bytes.

The place you'll usually want to create shortcuts is on the desktop, where they're always within easy reach, and the simplest way to create a shortcut is to use drag and drop. Open the folder containing the file, folder or program for which you want a shortcut, and in one action, click its icon with the right mouse-button, drag it to the desktop and release the mouse button. From the context menu that appears, click on **Create Shortcut(s) Here** (shown in the screenshot above) and hey presto, you have a shortcut.

Drag an item
from one place
to another with
the right mouse-
button, choose
Create
Shortcut(s)
Here, and
you've got a
shortcut.

TIP

If you're not a big fan of drag and drop, right-click on the icon and choose **Copy**, then right-click on your desktop and choose **Paste Shortcut**.

When you create a shortcut, it has two distinctive features that enable you to distinguish it from a 'real' file: the icon's label will be prefixed with the words **Shortcut to**, and its icon will gain a small black-and-white arrow. The arrow symbol can't be removed (it's there to help you distinguish between a shortcut and a 'real' file, so that you don't delete the wrong one accidentally), but you can rename the shortcut anything you like – turn back to 'Renaming files & folders' earlier in this chapter for details.

Double-clicking the shortcut to an object will give exactly the same result as if you had double-clicked the object itself. The important thing to remember is that you can move, rename, and delete shortcuts and this will have no effect on the original object. (If you delete a shortcut accidentally you can either retrieve it from the Recycle Bin, or just create another one to replace it.)

Customizing shortcuts

Shortcuts probably sound pretty useful so far, but they have a few extra features tucked away. More than any other type of file on your system, a shortcut can be customized to suit the way you want to work with it. These options are hidden away on the shortcut's Properties sheet. You can open the Properties sheet for a shortcut (or any other file) in several ways, and one of the simplest is to right-click its icon and choose **Properties**; alternatively, click the icon once, and press **Alt+Enter**.

A shortcut's Properties sheet consists of two tabbed pages headed General and Shortcut. Most of the excitement happens on the second of these: the first applies to the shortcut file itself, showing its size, location, and other pretty dull information. Move to the second tab (shown in the following screenshot) and it's a whole new ball game.

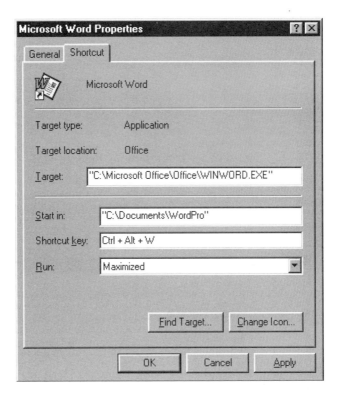

The feature-packed second tab on a shortcut's Properties sheet

- You can choose a hotkey combination in the **Shortcut Key** box. Click once in this box and type **W**, for example, and you'll be able to open this program or window simply by typing **Ctrl+Alt+W** on your keyboard, regardless of what application you're currently using. (Windows inserts the Ctrl+Alt automatically; if you'd prefer to use **Shift+Alt** or **Ctrl+Shift** instead, press those keys along with the W.)

- The drop-down list beside Run gives you the choice of Normal Window, Maximized or Minimized. Most of the time you'll want a normal window. Maximized will open the program or window full-screen; Minimized will open it as a button on the Taskbar that you can click when you're ready to use it.

- The Start In box is useful in shortcuts to applications. As an example, if you keep all your word-processor documents in a folder called C:\Word-Pro, create a shortcut to your word processor and type the path **C\Word-Pro** in this box. Whenever you want to open a file or save a newly created one, the word processor will offer you this folder in its Open and Save As... dialogs, saving you a lot of clicking or key-pressing to navigate to the right folder!

Path

A path is a list of the folders that Windows has to search to find a particular subfolder or file, similar to the way you have to click through My Computer's folders to find the file you want. The path C:\Documents\Word-Pro\Letter.doc tells Windows to start at Drive C, look inside the Documents folder, then the Word-Pro subfolder, and open the file called Letter.doc that it finds there. The drive-letter is always followed by a colon, and each drive, folder, or file must be separated by a backslash.

Shortcut suggestions

So what are shortcuts good for? Here are a few ideas for shortcuts you might find useful:

- Open My Computer and drag each of your drive icons out to the desktop. A dialog will appear that says you can't move or copy them here, offering to create shortcuts – click **Yes**. You can now open your drives quickly without first opening My Computer.

- Open My Computer and your Printers folder, and drag your printer-icon to the desktop in the same way. To print a file fast, just drag it on to this icon.

- If you have files that you use regularly, such as an appointments file or a list of regular contacts, create a shortcut to the file on the desktop.

- Create shortcuts to the folders you use most often, to save yourself piling through Explorer or My Computer to find them.

- If you find yourself using Control Panel a lot (see Chapter 13), drag its folder out of My Computer in the same way as the drive icons. Or, if you use just a couple of Control Panel applets regularly, drag out the icons you want.

Send it to where you want it:

Windows has one more powerful feature that makes use of shortcuts, and its full potential is often overlooked by beginners. If you right-click on any file or folder you'll see a *Send To* entry on the context menu, the submenu of which contains an icon for your floppy-disk drive and perhaps two or three more entries.

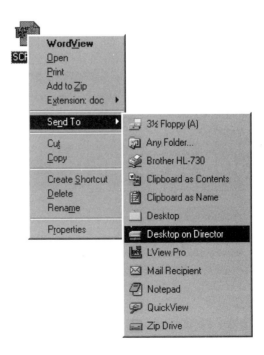

The Send To option and its submenu of shortcuts.

- The Send To option works like an automated 'drag and drop', sending the item you clicked to the drive, folder, or program you chose from the submenu. For example, if you click on **3½ Floppy (A)** the file or folder you selected will be copied to the disk in your floppy drive. One aspect that is often overlooked is that you can customize the options that appear on the Send To submenu. Open your Windows folder, and then open its Send To subfolder, and you'll see that all the entries on the menu are actually ordinary shortcuts! To outline the uses of the Send To option, here are a few suggestions for shortcuts you might want to add to this folder

- Add a shortcut to Notepad (**C:\Windows\Notepad.exe**). Any time you come across a text-based file with an unusual extension you can open it in Notepad by right-clicking it and choosing **Send To/Notepad**. This is also handy if you don't know whether it's a text-based file or not – you'll soon find out!

- Add a shortcut to your printer by dragging it from My Computer/Printers. You can print a file by 'sending' it. This is useful if you have more than one printer and need to choose which one to use for a particular file.

- If you have certain folders that you seem to keep moving things into, put shortcuts to these folders in Send To. If the folder is on the same drive as the item you 'send', the item will be moved; if the folder is on a different drive, the item will be copied. If you want to take control over whether an item is copied or moved, you can use the Ctrl or Shift keys to force a copy or a move respectively. For example, to force something to be moved to a floppy disk rather than copied, hold the Shift key as you click on $3\frac{1}{2}$ **Floppy (A)**.

If you use Windows 98, you have a useful option to send items to the desktop as shortcuts. You can use this to create shortcuts to folders and programs you use most often, or just create shortcuts to the files you want to work with during this Windows session and then delete the shortcuts again when you've finished work on each.

Chapter 13

Customizing Windows for Speed & Style

In This Chapter...

Turbo-charge your Start menu for quicker access

Create your own colour, sound and mouse-pointer schemes

Choose the best settings for your mouse and keyboard

Set up screensavers and power-saving features

Learn hotkey combinations for fast access to menu options

Customizing Windows for Speed & Style

One thing that all computer users want to do is to stamp their own style on Windows. With PCs acquiring new talents every few months, more and more of us are using them for many hours a week, so it's only natural that we want to coax as much speed and enjoyment out of the system as we can. The more you use Windows, the more tricks and shortcuts you'll find, but in this chapter you'll learn some of the most useful customization options to get you started.

Rearranging your Start menu

One of the wonders of the Start menu is that everything you need is close at hand, whatever you happen to be doing. Almost every new program you install will create its own submenu and add a new collection of icons. Unfortunately, many software writers seem to have no control over their egos: along with the vital entry that starts the program itself, you'll often find entries for text files that you'll probably read only once, help files that are available from the program's own Help menu, links to the company's Internet site, and other paraphernalia. So let's streamline that Start menu to make the important stuff easy to find.

The Start menu is actually a subfolder of your Windows folder, and the Programs menu is a subfolder of that. The easiest way to view and edit the contents of these folders is to right-click on the **Start** button and choose **Explore** from the context menu, then double-click the **Programs** folder in the left pane to open and expand it in one go (as shown in the next screenshot). If you look at the contents of the Programs folder, you'll see that all the submenus you see on the Start menu are actually subfolders containing ordinary shortcuts to programs and documents. The folders have more colourful icons than all your other folders, but apart from that they're no different.

In the same way that you organize files and folders elsewhere on your disk, you can move or delete shortcuts and folders on the submenu to make it easier to work

The Start menu folders and its subfolder.

with. (Remember that if you delete a shortcut accidentally, you can restore it to the same location from the Recycle Bin.) Just one caveat – don't rename or delete the folder called StartUp; the shortcuts inside this folder run automatically as soon as Windows starts, and Windows expects to find this folder inside the Programs folder. However, you can place more shortcuts inside it if there are particular programs you want to use every time you run Windows.

Here are a few suggestions for ways to streamline your Start menu:

- Work your way through folders added by software you've installed and remove shortcuts to Help and text files. If you ever need to read these files, you'll be able to find them in the folder into which the program was installed.

- Create a new folder called **Control Panel** inside the Programs folder, then open the real Control Panel folder and use the right mouse-button to drag all the icons into the new folder to create shortcuts. This gives much faster access to any Control Panel applet when you need it.

- Create a new folder called **Folders**, and create shortcuts to the folders you need to open most often by dragging them into it with the right mouse-button. You could also create a shortcut to My Computer here in the same way.

- As with any shortcut, you can assign these hotkey combinations to reduce the time you spend navigating this menu to find the entries you use most often.

- For much faster access to everything in your Programs folder, select every item in the folder (apart from the StartUp folder) by holding **Ctrl** and clicking each icon in turn. In one action, click any selected icon with the left button, then drag and drop on to the Start Menu folder in the left pane. The result: your submenus will now appear on the Start menu itself, as shown in the next screenshot, saving the need to scrabble around inside the Programs menu. (If you have so many icons that the Start menu can't display them all, right-click on the Taskbar, select **Properties**, and choose **Show small icons in Start menu**.).

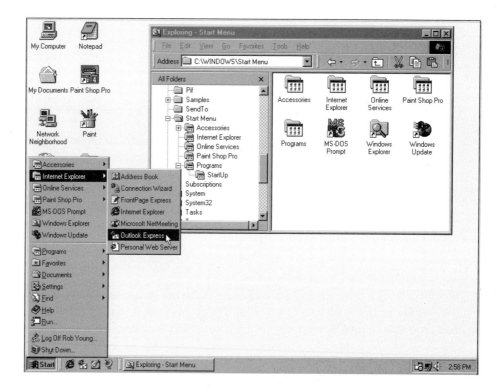

Move the folders inside Programs to the Start menu folder to place them on the Start menu itself.

In Windows 98, you can drag items around on the Start Menu itself to arrange them into a different order. In one action, click an item with the left mouse-button, drag to wherever you want it, and let go. If you want to move it from one folder into another, drag it to the target folder and wait for a moment; the target folder's menu will open so that you can drop the item onto it. If you right-click an item on the menu, a context menu will appear that lets you cut, copy, delete or open items, and you can use the right mouse-button to drag Start Menu items to your desktop to copy or move them there.

Adding & removing Windows components

If your PC came with Windows pre-installed, or you chose the 'Typical' installation option, you may be missing out on a few useful accessories. To see what else is available, to add extra components, or to remove any you don't need, open the **Control Panel**, double-click **Add/Remove Programs** and click the **Windows Setup** tab.

All the components are collected into groups under headings such as Accessories, Multimedia and Communications. Click one of these group-names and click on the **Details** button to see which components the group contains. You can add a component from this group by checking the box beside the component's name, or you can remove it from your system by clearing the check-box. When you've made all the selections you want from one group, click **OK**, then choose another group from the list to look at.

When you've worked your way through each group in this way, click **OK** on the main Windows Setup page and Windows will carry out all the additions and removals you've chosen. Depending what you selected, you may be prompted to restart Windows when all this is finished; if so, click the **OK** button and be patient – it might take a little longer than usual to restart while Windows updates the system.

Working with the Control Panel

The Control Panel consists of a collection of separate small programs (known as applets) that automatically appear in one window, and allow you to view or change various features of Windows such as colour and sound schemes, mouse and keyboard settings, and vital system behaviour. To open the Control Panel, click on **Start/Settings/Control Panel**, or click its icon near the bottom of the tree-view in Explorer, or double-click it in My Computer. Run an applet by double-clicking its icon. Each Control Panel applet functions as a separate entity, so you can have as many as you want open at the same time.

Because Windows gives you so much scope to customize, tabbed pages are much in evidence in the Control Panel and most applets have a daunting array of options, check-boxes and buttons. You can find out what each applet does by clicking it once and looking at the Control Panel's status bar for a brief description, but when you come to navigating these pages and changing settings, use the context-sensitive Help to find out what each element on a page is for (see 'Getting Help when you need it' in Chapter 12). Over the next few pages, we'll look at some of the features of the Control Panel you're likely to need most.

In most of the Control Panel applets you'll see a button marked Apply. This puts into action the changes you've made without closing the applet's window – if you don't like the result, you can change the settings immediately.

Setting the clock

The Date-Time applet lets you change the time and date shown by your clock, and alter your time zone (particularly useful for globetrotting notebook PC-users). To change the date, select the required year and month from the drop-down lists, and click a date in the area below. To change the time, click inside the box below the large analog clock, then use a combination of the delete, backspace and number keys to replace the displayed time with your new time. If it all goes wrong click Cancel and start again.

To change the time zone, click the **Time Zones** tab. Here you can either choose the new time zone from the drop-down list, or click on areas of the map below. When you've made all the settings you need in this applet, you must click **Apply** before clicking **OK**, or your changes will be ignored.

A quicker way to reach the Date-Time applet is just to double-click the digital clock on the extreme right of the Taskbar.

Personalizing your mouse

The Mouse applet is a multi-paged epic with plenty of options to give your rodent a makeover. The first tab, labelled Buttons, is the practical one: from here you can switch mouse-buttons for left-handed use and set the double-click speed. The Motion tab lets you adjust the speed at which your mouse moves across the screen, and gives you the option to show pointer-trails (ghost-pointers that follow your mouse around to help you see where you are) and to adjust their length.

The **Pointers** tab is one of Windows 95's many 'scheme' pages: from this tab you can choose which types of pointer you want to assign for different actions, and save this as a scheme that can be recalled any time. You can choose which scheme to use from the drop-down list at the top of the page, or create your own by clicking one of the pointer-types in the window and using the **Browse** button to find and select one of the pointer or animated-cursor files on your hard disk. When you've chosen all the pointers you want, click **Save As...** and type your own choice of name for the scheme, which will be added to the list in the **Schemes** box, and click **OK**.

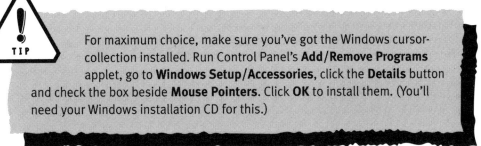

TIP

For maximum choice, make sure you've got the Windows cursor-collection installed. Run Control Panel's **Add/Remove Programs** applet, go to **Windows Setup/Accessories**, click the **Details** button and check the box beside **Mouse Pointers**. Click **OK** to install them. (You'll need your Windows installation CD for this.)

To use animated cursors you must have at least a 256-colour, 800 x 600 display. You can make these settings on the Settings tab of Control Panel's Display applet, but make sure your monitor and display adapter support them first.

Getting audio accompaniment while you work

Sounds is a single-page applet that works in a similar way to the Pointers tab in the Mouse applet; it allows you to assign sound effects to system events and dialogs, such

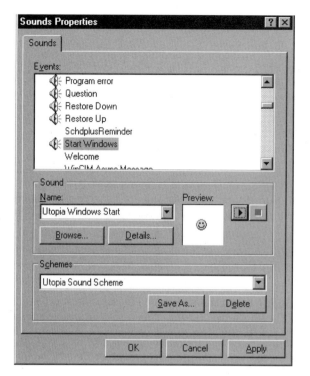

Choose a sound scheme from the drop-down list, or create a new scheme by assigning sounds one at a time from the Browse button.

as maximizing or minimizing a window, starting or quitting Windows, or selecting a menu option. The sounds are all digitally recorded files that have a .wav extension. This is another 'scheme' applet that allows you to choose the collection of sounds you want to assign, and save them as a list of your own sound schemes. To use one of Windows' preset schemes (or one you made earlier), choose it from the **Schemes** box at the bottom of the page and click **OK**. Or follow these steps to create your own scheme:

TIP

Using the Sound Recorder accessory, you can create your own sound effects by recording from a CD or with a microphone. Double-click the loudspeaker icon in the Tray to open the mixing desk and set recording levels before you start.

1. In the **Events** window, click an event for which you want to assign a sound (you don't have to assign a sound for all of them unless you want to).

2. Click the arrow beside the drop-down list box labelled Name to display the .wav files in C:\Windows\Media. Click on one of these entries and click the **Play** button (with the arrow icon) beside the Preview window to hear it.

3. If none of the sounds from the Media folder are suitable, click **Browse** and search your hard disk for other .wav files – you can preview these in the same way using the same button at the bottom of the Browse dialog. Click **OK** when you find the one you want to use.

4. Repeat steps 1–3 to assign sounds to other events. If you choose a sound file from a different folder, the contents of this folder will be listed in the Name box so you can choose the next one.

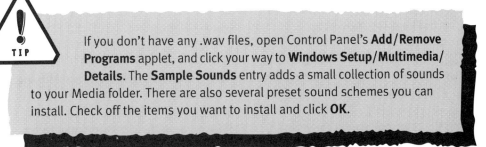

If you don't have any .wav files, open Control Panel's **Add/Remove Programs** applet, and click your way to **Windows Setup/Multimedia/ Details**. The **Sample Sounds** entry adds a small collection of sounds to your Media folder. There are also several preset sound schemes you can install. Check off the items you want to install and click **OK**.

5. When you've selected sounds for all the actions you want, click **Save As...**, type a name for the scheme and click **OK**.

6. Click **Apply** and/or **OK** to put the new scheme into effect.

Adjusting keyboard response

There isn't much that can be changed about the humble keyboard, but what there is you'll find on the Speed tab of the Keyboard applet. The slider for Repeat delay lets you choose how long Windows should wait before repeating a character when you hold down a key. The Repeat rate slider adjusts the speed of those character-repeats. A text-box lets you test your settings before applying them. There's also a slider for Cursor Blink Rate which determines how fast the insertion-point cursor should flash in text-based applications.

A second tab, labelled Language, adds the option to switch languages and keyboard layouts quickly. Click the **Add...** button and add the languages you want to use, then highlight them one at a time and click **Properties** to change the keyboard layout for each. You can specify a hotkey combination to switch between languages, or check the box marked **Enable indicator on taskbar**. The indicator is a two-letter abbreviation of the currently selected language – click once to display a menu of your chosen languages and select one to switch to, or right-click the icon and choose **Properties** to get back to this Language tab quickly.

Changing your windows wallpaper

At the moment, your desktop is probably the greenish colour that Windows sets automatically when it's installed. Whether you're a big fan of green or not, sooner or later you'll probably want a change, and Windows offers many ways to customize how things look. One of those is to cover the desktop with a wallpaper image or a pattern.

Open the **Display** applet (or right-click a blank area on the desktop and choose **Properties**) and make sure the **Background** tab is selected. From the left-hand list you can choose a pattern which adds an overlay to the desktop while keeping its current colour; pick one of these and you'll see the results displayed in the preview window above.

The list on the right lets you choose a bitmap image file (with the .bmp extension). Choosing **Center** places the image in the middle of your screen; **Tile** uses multiple copies of the image to cover the entire desktop. If you have Windows 98, you'll also find a **Stretch** option that expands the image to cover your entire desktop. By default, the list shows bitmap files from your Windows folder, but you can use a .bmp image from any folder by using the **Browse** button to locate and select it.

Getting creative with colour schemes

If you prefer not to use a wallpaper image, that greenish colour on the desktop is just one of many colours you can change by clicking the **Display** applet's **Appearance** tab. As in the Mouse and Sound applets, you can choose an existing scheme from a drop-down list (the default scheme is Windows Standard) and click **Apply** to see how it looks, or create your own custom theme and save it.

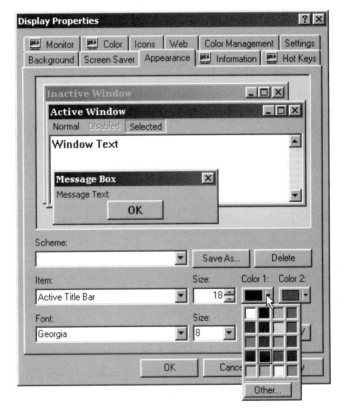

Pick an existing colour scheme, or create your own by selecting items and changing their colours and fonts.

To create your own theme, start by clicking on items in the interactive preview window to select them, and then choosing colours, fonts and sizes for them from the controls at the bottom. If an option is 'greyed out', it can't be changed for the item you've selected. Some of the items that you can edit, such as the colour of tooltip messages, don't appear on the preview, but you can select them from the **Item** list.

> Always audition colour schemes you create yourself by clicking the **Apply** button and looking at a few windows and menus before closing the applet. If you choose colours unwisely, it's possible to make some items 'invisible', which could make it difficult to find your way back to the Display applet to put things right.

Keeping track of your print jobs

You can open the Printers folder from within Control Panel or from My Computer. Inside this folder you'll find icons for any printers connected to your system, along with 'software' printers such as Microsoft Fax. Double-clicking a printer icon will open a small window to display the print queue – the list of documents waiting to be printed. By right-clicking a document you can pause, resume or cancel printing. To change the order in which documents are printed, drag entries up or down in the queue. From the Printer menu, you can choose Purge Print Jobs to stop printing and remove all print jobs from the queue.

Like most objects in Windows, each printer has its own properties sheet which can be opened by right-clicking and selecting **Properties**, or clicking once and pressing **Alt+Enter**. The tabbed pages you'll find here will vary according to the make and model of your printer, but you should find options that let you choose the default paper size and orientation, print quality, and other (sometimes quite exotic) settings.

Installing & removing fonts

Fonts are sets of instructions that tell Windows how to display text on the screen and how to print it, and each font is a separate file on your hard disk. Some fonts are used by Windows itself to display the text on menus and tabbed pages; others are fonts that you can choose from drop-down lists in your applications for use in your own documents. Windows supplies a small set of fonts, including Arial, Times New Roman, and WingDings, but it's easy to add your own fonts to the collection. (Some people find fonts irresistible, and have several hundred of them!)

To see which fonts are installed already, open Control Panel's **Fonts** folder. The fonts look like any other file on your system and come in two types. The type you'll probably choose to use yourself are the TrueType fonts, which have blue 'T' icons; those with the red 'A' icon are required by Windows, but don't have the flexibility of TrueType fonts for your own uses. Double-click any of these font files to see examples of the typeface.

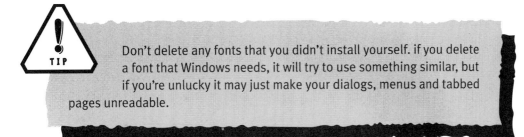

TIP Don't delete any fonts that you didn't install yourself. if you delete a font that Windows needs, it will try to use something similar, but if you're unlucky it may just make your dialogs, menus and tabbed pages unreadable.

Deleting fonts is easy. In fact, some would say it's *too* easy! Click the font file you want to get rid of, and press the **Delete** key. A prompt will ask if you're sure, and the deleted font file will be sent to the Recycle Bin from where you can rescue it if

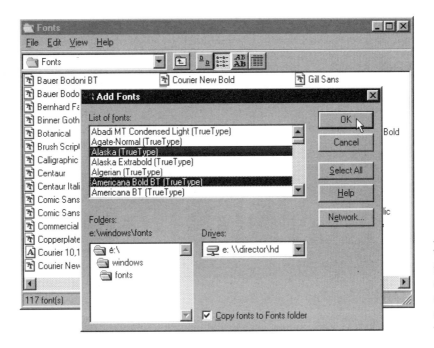

You can install fonts from any drive or folder on your system or network.

you need to, but only its icon will be recognizable – the Fonts folder is a special folder that displays font files with a friendly name, but as soon as a file is moved elsewhere it reverts to its own unusual-looking file name.

To install new fonts, you must have some font files to install, of course, and there are many cheap CD-ROM packages of TrueType fonts available from computer stores or by mail-order. Choose **Install New Font...** from the File menu and you'll see the dialog in the screenshot above. Use the Drives and Folders lists to navigate to the location of your new fonts (or click the **Network** button if you want to install fonts from another PC on your network). When you arrive at a folder containing font files, Windows will list the fonts it found in the upper portion of the window. To install them all, click **Select All** followed by **OK**. If you want to install just some of them, click the names of the required fonts while holding the **Ctrl** button, then click **OK**.

All In One – Desktop Themes

Desktop Themes are complete sets of wallpapers, icons, sounds, mouse-pointers and screensavers with names like Dangerous Creatures, Mystery, Science and

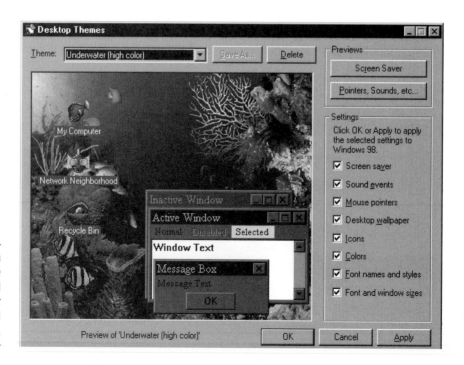

Choose a Desktop Theme from the list and transform your desktop and windows.

Underwater. Windows 95 users had to buy an add-on pack called Microsoft Plus to get their hands on Desktop Themes. For Windows 98 users things are different: a set of 17 Themes is included on the Windows 98 CD-ROM, although they may not be installed on your system. If you like them, you can buy a similar add-on pack called Microsoft Plus 98 to add another 18 to the list.

You can use the Windows Setup tab of the Add/Remove Programs applet in Control Panel to install new themes or remove any you don't like: select the **Desktop Themes** entry and click **Details** to choose from the list. Bear in mind that each theme takes a hefty slab of disk space, so you probably won't want to install all of them. When you have one or more themes installed, you'll find a new **Desktop Themes** icon in Control Panel. Double-click this icon and pick one of your installed themes from the **Theme** box to preview it, choose whether to use all the theme's elements such as icons and colours by checking or un-checking the boxes on the right, and click on **Apply** or **OK** to put the theme into action.

Accessibility help for the disabled

If you have difficulty seeing the screen clearly, hearing sounds, or working with the mouse or keyboard, Windows 95 and 98 both have a range of options that can help. In fact, some of these can be useful for any Windows user. To install the accessibility features, go to the Windows Setup tab of the Add/Remove Programs applet in Control Panel, select **Accessibility** and click on **Details**, then check the box beside **Accessibility Options**. Windows 98 users also have an Accessibility Tools option here with new features that are well worth installing. Click **OK** to install them, and double-click the **Accessibility Options** icon in Control Panel to choose the options you want to use from the tabbed pages.

● **StickyKeys** – lets you type keystrokes like Ctrl+S by pressing one key at a time.

● **ToggleKeys** – plays a sound whenever you press the Caps Lock or Num Lock key (something we all do by accident when typing).

● **SoundSentry** – displays a message for the hard-of-hearing whenever Windows plays a sound.

● **High Contrast** – changes the Windows screen to use more easily-visible fonts and colours.

- **MouseKeys** – lets you move the pointer using keys on the numeric keypad instead of the mouse.

Windows 98's Accessibility Tools include Microsoft Magnifier, which displays an enlarged view of the portion of the screen containing the pointer (also a useful tool for anyone working on high-definition graphics), and an Accessibility Wizard that lets you tailor individual items to your precise needs, such as the size of text, icons and window elements. The Wizard also includes the options contained in the Control Panel's Accessibility Options applet and presents them all in a much more user-friendly (and *accessible*) form. You'll find Magnifier and the Accessibility Wizard in the Accessories group on the Start menu.

Setting up a screensaver

Screensavers are fun, but they serve a useful purpose: when you leave your computer and monitor on for long periods without using them, the image can literally 'burn' into the coating on the inside of the screen. This, needless to say, is bad news, because it leaves permanent ghost-images on your monitor. One answer is to turn off your monitor when you wander away for a while, but on some PCs that's not possible. A more enjoyable answer is the screensaver which kicks in after a predetermined time and continually changes the screen image. When you're ready to start work again, just move the mouse or press a key on the keyboard, and the saver will vanish leaving everything as it was before you left.

Windows comes with its own set of screensavers, but you can pick up many more on disks given free on magazine covers, on the Internet, or as complete stand-alone software packages such as Berkeley Systems' superb After Dark series, or Microsoft Scenes.

You can switch between different screensavers and adjust their options by selecting the **Screen Saver** tab on Control Panel's **Display** applet, shown in the next screenshot. If you choose to, you can also set a password for the screensaver by checking the box. After the screensaver has started, it can only be stopped by entering the correct password, thus preventing anyone prying into your system while you're away from your desk.

An increasing number of monitors now include power-saving features, and you can opt to use these instead of (or as well as) a screensaver. Click the **Settings** button at the bottom-right of the dialog to open the Power Management page.

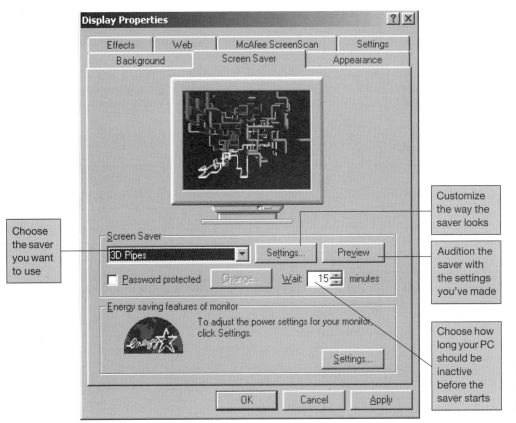

Choose the saver you want to use

Customize the way the saver looks

Audition the saver with the settings you've made

Choose how long your PC should be inactive before the saver starts

Setting up a Windows screensaver.

In the boxes at the bottom you can choose to put your monitor and hard disk to sleep after specified periods of inactivity. As with a screensaver, just moving the mouse or pressing a key will wake them up again. Most users will be happy to settle for a single power-saving setting, but you can use the upper section of the dialog to save and recall different 'power schemes' if you want to. (You can also reach this page by double-clicking the Power Management icon in Control Panel.)

> **TIP**
> Remember that your data, windows and unsaved documents aren't affected when the screensaver kicks in, or when your monitor is switched off – you could compare it to the effect you have on BBC1 when you turn off your television.

Get there faster with hotkeys

Even if you're a big fan of the mouse, there are times when tapping a couple of keys on the keyboard to get something done is much quicker. For those times, here's a short list of hotkey combinations for use in Windows itself or in applications you run.

Open the Start menu	Ctrl+Esc
Close any open menu or dialog	Esc
Open selected item's context menu	Shift+F10
Open or run the selected item	Enter
Rename the selected item	F2
Delete the selected item	Delete
Delete, bypassing the Recycle Bin	Shift+Delete
Open the properties sheet for the selected item	Alt+Enter
Open the Find dialog in a folder	F3
Iconic list of open windows and applications	Alt+Tab
Cycle through open windows, applications and dialogs	Alt+Esc
Open a menu	Alt+underlined letter
Select a menu to open	Underlined letter
Cycle through tabbed pages	Ctrl+Tab
Switch between controls in dialogs and tabbed pages	Tab
Close a window or quit an application	Alt+F4
Open a file	Ctrl+O

Print the current file	Ctrl+P
Save the current file	Ctrl+S
Cut selected item	Ctrl+X
Copy selected item	Ctrl+C
Paste selected item	Ctrl+V

Here are a few extra hotkeys you can use if your keyboard has the additional Windows keys:

Open the Start menu	Win
Open Windows Explorer	Win+E
Open the Find command	Win+F
Open the Run command	Win+R
Minimize all windows	Win+M
Restore all windows after minimize	Win+Shift+M
Open the Control Panel	Win+C
Open the System applet	Win+Break
Open the Mouse applet	Win+I
Open the Keyboard applet	Win+K
Open the Printers folder	Win+P
Open the Windows help file	Win+F1

Quick Windows tips

Windows has an almost inexhaustible supply of customization possibilities, options and shortcut methods that can make the operating system and its accessories easier, faster or more enjoyable to use. Here's a few of them:

- When you select the **Shutdown** command from the Start menu, you have the option to Restart the computer. If you only want to restart Windows itself (which is much faster), select **Restart the computer**, then hold **Shift** as you click on **OK**.

- If you don't like using the right mouse-button when you drag and drop files and folders, try using these in conjunction with left-button dragging: hold **Ctrl** to force a copy; hold **Shift** to force a move; or hold **Crtl+Shift** to create a shortcut.

- If your Send To menu is getting too full you can turn it into a mini-Start menu! Just go to C:\Windows\SendTo and create new folders inside it, then start dragging items into it from the Send To folder to organize them into groups. This is useful if you've created Send To shortcuts to lots of different folders on your system – create a folder called Folders and drag all these shortcuts into it to keep them separate from the other items.

- When viewing any list of files in Windows – whether in Explorer, My Computer, Find, or anywhere else – type the first three letters of the entry you want (in quick succession) to move straight to it.

- If you want your screensaver to start immediately when you leave your desk, create a shortcut on your desktop to one of the .scr files found in C:\Windows. You can just double-click it to start it running or assign it a hotkey combination.

- Experiment with your Tray icons – many have different options on their menus depending whether you click with the left or right mouse-button. The option shown in bold type is the action that occurs if you just double-click the icon.

Chapter 14

Keep your System Running Smoothly

In This Chapter...

Make a startup disk for emergencies

How to keep backups of your system and vital documents

Use Windows' utilities to keep your system purring sweetly

What to do when a program hangs or Windows won't respond

Computer viruses: don't panic, but do get some protection

Keep your System Running Smoothly

Windows is able to look after itself pretty successfully to keep everything working but once in a while things may go wrong. In this chapter we'll take a look at the ways you can get everything back to normal again when a program (or Windows itself) starts misbehaving. But prevention is better than cure – if you prepare for disasters now, you should never experience anything worse than an inconvenience in future!

Create a startup disk

When you installed Windows you were given the option of creating a startup floppy disk to start the system in the event of a serious crash. If you didn't (or if your computer arrived with Windows pre-installed, thus denying you the prompt), grab a high-density floppy disk and your Windows installation disk(s) and do it now:

1. Start the **Add/Remove Programs** applet in the Control Panel.

2. Click the **Startup Disk** tab and then click on **Create Disk**.

Once the disk has been created, you need to make sure it actually works! Shutdown the computer from the Start menu's Shut Down command, and then restart the computer using your PC's Reset button with this emergency disk in the drive. You should arrive at the DOS command-prompt (A:\>).

If you do, your startup disk is working properly. Remove the disk from the drive and restart the computer again. Write-protect this emergency disk (see 'Working with floppy disks' in Chapter 12), label it Windows Startup Disk and keep it somewhere safe.

Backup your system configuration

Although few computer books tell you to do this, it's something I absolutely swear by. Admittedly, I fiddle around with my system more than the average user, but these backups have saved my bacon on more than one occasion!

The settings for your entire system are stored in something called the Registry: this covers your hardware settings, details of all the software you've installed, and much more. Unfortunately, the files that make up the Registry are too large to fit on to floppy disks. The good news is that Windows supplies a simple program you can use to keep backups on your hard disk. Grab your Windows CD and follow these steps to install the program and make a backup:

1. Using Windows Explorer, open the **other** folder on your Windows CD, then open its **misc** subfolder, and finally the **cfgback** subfolder. You should see two files both named **cfgback** – an application and a help file.

2. Copy both files to your Windows folder, either by dragging them into the left pane or by using copy and paste.

3. Create a shortcut to **cfgback.exe** and place it somewhere handy, such as your Start menu's System Tools folder, and rename the shortcut **Configuration Backup**.

4. Run this program. Instructions will appear, so click the **Continue** button several times to skip past the instructions and start the program itself.

5. In the upper box, type a name for your backup to help you remember it later, and click the **Backup** button. Click **Yes** when prompted to continue, then sit back and wait a few minutes.

This program will let you create up to nine backups in this way, and will list them all in order of date (although you should note that the date is in the US month/ day/year format). Ideally, you should aim to run this program every month or two so that you always have a recent backup, but only do it when you know your system is working perfectly – there's no point in creating a backup of a system with problems. As time goes on, you can delete your earliest backups by selecting them from the list and clicking **Delete**.

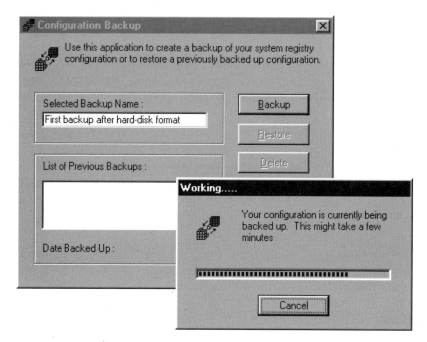

Type a name, click **Backup**, and a few minutes later you have a safety copy of your system settings.

The point of these backups is that you can restore the system if you get into problems that you can't fix (preferably after seeking some expert help too). Re-run this program, select the most recent backup that you know to be okay from the list, and click the **Restore** button. After a few minutes, you'll see a prompt to restart your computer. If that backup really was okay, the problem should have disappeared. However, if you've installed any software or hardware since making that backup, you might need to reinstall the application or re-run the setup program for the device so that the system knows about it.

Check your hard disk for lost data

Although the hard-disk is a reliable device, occasionally small errors can appear on its surface that could mean you occasionally lose small chunks of files, or that Windows can't use areas of the disk. To keep your hard disk squeaky clean, run ScanDisk regularly every week or so to automatically identify and fix any errors that appear.

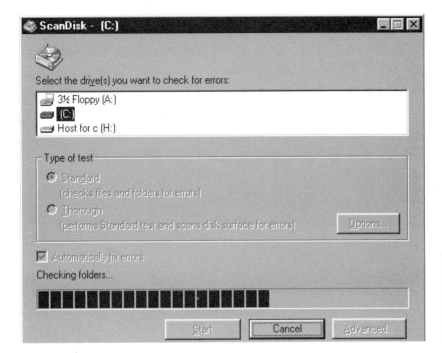

Run ScanDisk
regularly to
keep your hard
disk in tip-top
shape.

1. Click the shortcut to **ScanDisk**, which you'll find in the System Tools subfolder
   on your Start menu.

2. By default, your hard-disk will be selected, and the option button beside the
   Standard test will be checked. If you want ScanDisk to fix any errors it finds
   without asking you first, check the box beside **Automatically fix errors**. Click
   Start to begin checking.

3. When ScanDisk has finished (usually after only a few minutes), it will display a
   summary of the results: what you're most interested in is the first line, which
   will usually tell you that no errors were found.

4. Every month or so, you should run ScanDisk and check the option button for a
   Thorough test, which checks the surface of the disk as well as the files and
   folders on it. This might take an hour or more, so you'll need to pick a time when
   you won't need to use the PC. You should also override your screensaver by
   selecting **(None)** from Control Panel's **Display/Screen Saver** tab.

If ScanDisk finds any lost pieces of files, it will save them to your hard disk with the names File0000.chk, File0001.chk, and so on. Take a look at these files in Notepad or WordPad before deleting them. If you recognize something from one of your own documents, check to make sure that document is still intact, and use this .chk file to replace it if necessary. If the contents of the .chk file look like meaningless drivel, it might be part of an application: run the applications you installed most recently to test them, if an application won't run, you'll need to reinstall it.

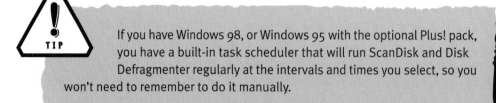

If you have Windows 98, or Windows 95 with the optional Plus! pack, you have a built-in task scheduler that will run ScanDisk and Disk Defragmenter regularly at the intervals and times you select, so you won't need to remember to do it manually.

Get optimum speed from your hard disk

Although Windows presents your files in a friendly way in Explorer, in reality they look nothing like that on the hard disk. Disks store files in small chunks called clusters, and a sort of address-book on the disk tells Windows where to find all the pieces that make up a particular file. For fastest response, all the clusters for a file should be grouped together in a chain; that way, Windows doesn't have to scoot around the disk gathering together pieces of file from far and wide when you want to use one. In practice, that doesn't happen: for example if you edit a file and make it larger, it won't fit into the same number of clusters it occupied before, so some will have to be placed elsewhere. After you've worked with files for a few weeks, your hard disk will start to look a bit of a mess! Fortunately, Windows includes a nifty program called Disk Defragmenter that can group all these pieces of file back together again, speeding up your access to the hard disk. (In Windows 98, the system also keeps track of the programs and files you use most often, and this program moves those files to the fastest area of the disk so that they start more quickly.) Once again, this is something you should aim to run every week or two, and you should override your screensaver while it's running.

You'll find Disk Defragmenter in the System Tools folder along with ScanDisk. When you run it, it will automatically select your hard disk (although you can

TIP

Before running Disk Degragmenter, empty the Recycle Bin – if you empty it afterwards, you'll undo all the good defragmentation work!

defragment a different disk if you need to), so click **OK**. You can wander away and leave it to do the job, but it's fun to click **Show Details** and watch a graphic portrayal of all these chunks of file flying about!

● *If you use Windows 98, you can use the Maintenance Wizard to run ScanDisk and the Disk Defragmenter for you automatically at regular times – see page 170.*

Clear out unnecessary files

Even if your hard-disk is particularly large, one thing you don't want is to fill it with unnecessary space-wasting files. However much you pride yourself on being organized in this area, Windows and some of your applications may conspire against you by creating temporary files on your hard disk and not deleting them and these could easily amount to many megabytes of wasted space.

Fortunately, Windows 98 includes a utility called **Disk Cleanup**, which you'll find in the Accessories\System Tools group on the Start Menu. Click **OK** when the dialog appears with your hard drive selected, and you'll see the main Disk Cleanup window showing several types of file that can be safely removed and telling you how much space you can regain by doing so. Check the boxes beside the types of file you want to delete and click the **OK** button.

If you use Windows 95, you don't have the Disk Cleanup utility, but you can still manually delete any unnecessary files. When you do this, always do it immediately after starting Windows and before you run any applications, and leave the files in the Recycle Bin for a day or two just in case you accidentally deleted something you shouldn't have!

Here are some ways you can reclaim space on your hard-disk:

● Open **C:\Windows\Temp** and delete any files you find inside it; these are temporary files that should have been deleted when the program that created them was closed, but this doesn't always happen.

● Look around your system for any files or folders whose names begin with a ~ sign: these are also temporary and can be deleted.

● Look in the root folder of your hard disk (C:\) for files called File0000.chk, File0001.chk, and so on; these are orphaned pieces of file found by ScanDisk (see above).

● Make sure you empty your Recycle Bin regularly: if you let it get full you're wasting tens (if not hundreds!) of megabytes.

If you have an archive drive, you might want to move little-used files such as help files, screensavers (.scr files) and large multimedia files to it. Always try to keep *at least* 100Mb of free space on your hard disk.

If you're using Windows 98, you have a couple of additional utilities that can automate the process of keeping your system in shape. The first of these is the **Maintenance Wizard**, found in the System Tools group on the Start Menu. Choose the **Express** option, and choose a period when you're least likely to be working on your PC from the Wizard's second page. In future, Windows will run ScanDisk, Disk Defragmenter and Disk Cleanup automatically once a week during the chosen period.

The second utility is **Task Scheduler** which you can open from the System Tools group as usual or by double-clicking its icon in the tray. The Task Scheduler window displays a list of the utilities that Windows runs automatically, along with their schedule times. You can add new programs and tasks to be added by double-clicking the **Add Scheduled Task** icon, or double-click on any task to alter its settings or change its scheduled running time.

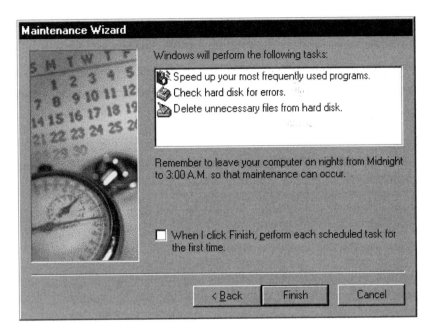

Run the
Maintenance
Wizard once,
and then leave
your system to
look after itself!

Backup your important documents

If the worst happens and your hard disk stops working, the thing that's going to hit
you hardest is the loss of your files – not your applications which can easily be
reinstalled from the original disks, but the documents you create yourself. To guard
against loss of irreplaceable documents, you should get into the habit of regularly
making backups of your files to a tape drive or a set of floppy disks, and Windows
includes a utility called Backup to help you do this. If you don't have Backup
installed, open the Control Panel's **Add/Remove Programs** applet and click the
Windows Setup tab. Double-click on System Tools, check the box beside **Backup**,
and click **OK** twice to install. (Windows 95 users have a different, and not quite as
easy-to-use, version of Backup. You'll find this in the **Disk Tools** section of the
Windows Setup tab if you want to install it, but you may prefer to use the utility
that came with your backup drive or buy a copy of Seagate Backup, the utility that
Windows 98 users have.)

When Backup starts, you're given the option of creating a new backup job (a list of
files that you want to backup), opening a list you created previously, or restoring a
set of backed-up files from your archive drive to your hard disk. Choose the option
to create a new backup job, and follow these steps:

1. In the left-hand window, use the familiar Explorer layout to expand drive and folders by clicking the + signs. Click the box beside a drive or folder to add it to the list of items to be backed up. All the files and subfolders in the selected drive or folder will be added to the list. (To remove a tick from one of these boxes, just click it again.) If you want to select only individual files from a folder, click the folder itself and its contents will appear in the right-hand pane with similar check-boxes beside them.

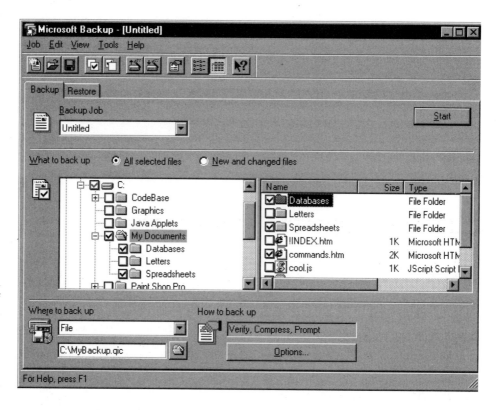

Create a list of files and folders to be backed up by checking the boxes beside them.

2. Choose whether to backup every selected file or just the files that have been added or changed since you last backed them up, by clicking the appropriate option beside **What to back up**.

3. In the **Where to back up** section, choose your backup drive (if you have one and want to use it), or select **File** and enter a name and location for the single compressed backup file to be stored.

4. Click the **Options** button, select the **Advanced** Tab, and check the box beside **Back up Windows Registry** (on the basis that you can never have too many backups of these vital files!) and click **OK**.

5. Click the Save button on the toolbar (or press Ctrl+S) if you want to save this list for reuse.

6. Click **Start** to begin the backup process. Depending on the number of files to be backed up and the speed of your backup device, the process might take quite a while to complete.

You can edit the backup job file you created at any time in the future to add more files to the list or remove them. And if the worst happens and you lose one or more files from your hard disk, click Backup's **Restore** tab, pick the file(s) you want to restore, and click **Start** to copy them from to their original locations on your hard disk. Make sure you backup your files regularly so that you won't be faced with restoring a very out-of-date copy of a lost file.

Surviving a program crash

Very occasionally, you might do something as innocuous as clicking a toolbar button in an application, and the program will 'hang' – in other words, it will stop reacting to any mouse or keyboard input. (This is why you should get in the habit of saving the document you're working on every few minutes!) It doesn't happen often, and when it does it shouldn't stop Windows working, but your only option is to shut down that program.

To do this, press **Ctrl+Alt+Del** and you'll see the Close Program dialog, containing a list of the programs currently running. Your misbehaving program should be at the top of the list, and it might have the words 'Not responding' beside it. Make sure the correct program is selected in the list, and click the **End Task** button to close it. Be patient at this point: Windows sometimes has to grapple with the program for a while before it can present you with a confirmation dialog.

After closing the offending program, you could probably continue working in Windows, but it's best to restart the computer as soon as you can to banish any lingering after-effects. Select **Shut Down** from the Start menu, and click **Restart the computer** followed by **OK**.

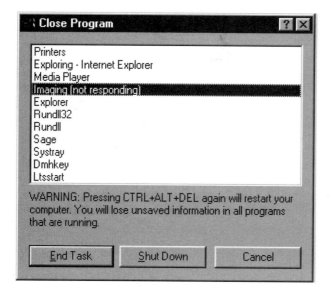

The Close
Program dialog
– handle with
care!

There are two important points to remember about the Close Program dialog: first, it isn't an alternative to the usual ways of closing a program when you've finished work and second, pressing Ctrl+Alt+Del again while this dialog is on the screen will restart your PC without prompting you to save open documents, and without updating Windows' own system settings, so only do this in times of extreme desperation (see below).

How to deal with a Windows crash

In more severe situations than that mentioned above, Windows itself may hang. If it does, your aim is to shut down or restart the computer. Begin by trying to open the Start menu and select **Shut Down**, either by using the mouse or by pressing **Ctrl+Esc** followed by **U**. If that doesn't work, press **Ctrl+Alt+Del** to call up the Close Programs dialog mentioned above. If a program has the words 'Not responding' beside it, click its entry in the list, and click the **End Task** button: once that program has been closed, the system may recover enough for you to shut down properly.

Failing that, the next thing to try is clicking the **Shut Down** button on this dialog. In many cases, this will do the trick but sometimes this dialog will then hang as well and nothing more will happen: if so, press **Ctrl+Alt+Del** twice to try to restart the computer.

If this doesn't work, the only remaining option is to press your PC's **Reset** button to restart the computer from scratch. In Windows 98 and later versions of Windows 95, a version of ScanDisk will run before Windows restarts to check your disk for errors – this is normal behaviour that occurs whenever Windows detects that it was shut down improperly.

Solve problems in safe mode

In normal everyday use of Windows, you simply switch on your computer, wait 30 seconds or so, and the Windows desktop appears. Most of the time this is exactly what you want, but there are times when it's the last thing you want! For example, if you changed your display settings and the whole screen went blank, you don't want the computer to just return you to Windows when you restart because you'll still have a blank screen!

At times like this you can start the computer in a special mode called Safe Mode, in which Windows loads only generic driver files for display and mouse, and disables any non-essentials to display a low-resolution 16-colour screen. Although the layout is unattractive and basic, it does give you the chance to put the problem right and then restart the computer normally.

To start Windows in Safe Mode, follow the steps below. We'll do it the hard way, assuming you've arrived in Windows to find the screen completely blank; if you've got a different problem and you can still see the desktop, the routine will be even easier.

1. Wait until the hard disk stops working and you know Windows has finished loading, press **Ctrl+Esc** to open the Start menu (although you won't see that happening if your screen is blank!), press **U** and then **R**, and then press **Enter** twice to shut down.

2. If you're using Windows 98, press and keep holding the Ctrl key when the computer begins its restart process. If you use Windows 95, watch the screen carefully with your finger poised and press F8 as soon as you see the message **Starting Windows 95**... appear.

3. A short list of numbered options called the Windows Startup Menu will appear on the screen, and one of its entries will be Safe Mode. Type the number beside the Safe Mode option, and Windows will start to load in this special mode (which will take somewhat longer than usual).

Once you've put the problem right you can choose the Shut Down option again, click on **Restart the computer**, and Windows will restart in the normal way.

Other startup options

Another thing you might need to do in times of trouble is to start the computer running MS-DOS. This and several other options can be selected from the Windows Startup Menu. As your computer starts or restarts, follow step 2 above to interrupt it and display the menu. You can then run any of its options by typing the number beside them or selecting them with the up/down arrow keys and pressing Enter. Here's what each of those options does:

Command-prompt only – Boots in the normal way but stops at the MS-DOS prompt instead of loading Windows.

Step-by-step confirmation – Asks you for confirmation before processing each command in the system files Autoexec.bat, Config.sys and Io.sys to let you bypass any commands you think may be causing problems.

Safe Mode Command-prompt only – The same as the Command-prompt only option, but doesn't process Autoexec.bat or Config.sys.

Logged – Starts Windows in the normal way, and creates a file called Bootlog.txt in your root folder listing the startup sequence.

Normal – Starts Windows in the usual way.

Safe Mode – As described above.

Safe Mode with network support – Starts the computer in Safe Mode but loads network drivers. You may want this option if you need to use files from your network to correct a configuration problem.

Keep your computer virus-free

You've probably heard of computer viruses. Viruses are tiny programs maliciously inserted into a program which start to run as soon as you begin using that program. The way viruses work and the effects they have on your system can vary: some are of the 'jokey' variety that make your PC go beep once a year; others might turn your files into meaningless gobbledegook or fill your hard disk with trash to make it unusable.

The first thing to get straight about viruses is that the threat is almost always hysterically overstated: viruses are simply not as common as some folk would have you believe. On the other hand, they certainly do exist, and they're commonly transferred from one computer to another in two ways: one is to run programs given to you on a floppy disk (or some other type of removable disk), and the other is to run files from a network or downloaded from the Internet. What these two situations have in common is that you don't necessarily know where the program came from, or whether the computer that provided you with the program was infected.

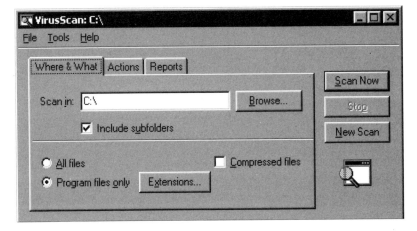

Anti-virus utilities such as McAfee VirusScan check programs as you start them to prevent a virus taking hold.

However, viruses are easily avoidable. There are specialist utilities available such as Dr Solomon's Anti-Virus Toolkit or McAfee VirusScan (shown in the screenshot above) that can identify and stamp out viruses before they can cause a problem. These utilities check the vital system files every time you turn on your PC, and then monitor every program you run to prevent a virus from working. You can also select particular files or disks to scan before you start to use them.

If you use Windows 98, you can buy an add-on pack called Microsoft Plus 98. Along with additional Desktop Themes (see page 156), several games and system utilities and a very stylish CD player, you also get a copy of McAfee VirusScan.

To work effectively, virus scanners need to know what to look for, and new viruses are appearing all the time. For maximum safety, make sure you update your anti-virus software regularly according to the details in the manuals.

Chapter 15

Install & Set Up New Hardware

In This Chapter...

Fitting new internal and external devices

Doing it the easy way with Plug & Play hardware

Installing and updating device drivers

Understanding and assigning hardware resources

Buying and installing extra memory

Install & Set Up
New Hardware

Adding new hardware to your computer has traditionally been viewed as something you shouldn't do on a full stomach. Its not the physical installation of the device that causes the problems – it usually just slips into an expansion slot, or plugs into a port – it's the configuration of the thing once it's there. Windows' support for Plug & Play has made the configuration of new devices much easier, but with so many manufacturers selling so many products, instant success isn't guaranteed.

In this chapter we'll begin by looking at the automated methods of installing and configuring hardware and lead on to some of the manual changes you might have to make in order to get everything working as it should. But first, a more pressing question...

What is installation?

The installation of new hardware is actually two things tied up neatly in one word. The first and most obvious of these is that you have to physically attach the new device to the computer: with some devices this is the easy bit; with others it's more or less the only bit! How to attach the hardware will depend upon whether it's an **internal** or an **external** device. Once the device has been connected, the next step is to set it up properly to tell the computer what it is, where it is, and how to communicate with it.

Never install a new device with the computer switched on – you might damage the PC, the device, yourself, or all three. Remember too that expansion cards and memory chips are susceptible to static electricity: handle one of these boards only by its edges, and leave it in its packing until the last possible moment.

Fitting an internal device

Internal card devices are plugged into the ISA or PCI expansion slots described in Chapter 3. You'll be able to see which type of slot is which by comparing the size of your card to the size of the available slots, but your PC's manual should provide a diagram of the system unit's layout. These cards and their slots contain all the connections necessary to power the devices and pass data to and from them.

If you're installing a new internal drive, remove the plastic cover from a drive slot, slide the drive in carefully, and then bolt it to the restraining brackets to hold it firmly in place. Drives will also need at least two cables to be connected: first, they need to be connected to the computer's power-supply, and there are usually several spare power-connectors in the system unit for this purpose, second, they have to be connected to the main bus in order to send or receive data. You'll see a 2-inch-wide grey ribbon inside the case (the interface cable) with several plastic connectors on it: one of these connectors needs to be attached to the new device. (If the new device is a CD-ROM drive you'll also have to connect its Audio Out cable to your soundcard's Audio In if you want to use it to play audio CDs.)

TIP

Don't install more than one piece of hardware at a time! If you install several and your PC doesn't work properly next time you start up, it might be difficult to tell which device is causing the problem.

Hooking up an external device

External devices are very simple to connect: they usually have just one cable that has to be connected to a port (or socket) at the rear of the system unit to enable data transfer. Along with a mains cable, that's all there is to it!

Well, that's almost all there is to it. You have to make sure you plug it into the correct socket, some of which are known as ports. Ports are similar to the sockets you'd find on just about anything, in the sense that you plug something into them, and they're usually labelled. The main difference is that the PC's sockets are configured in different ways to enable them to deal with different types of data doing different things at different speeds. There are three common types of port:

Serial ports – Your PC will have at least two serial ports, called COM1 and COM2 (short for 'Communications port'). The mouse should be connected to COM1, and the modem (if you have one) to COM2. Serial ports are still not standardized and you see both 9-pin and 25-pin connectors (you can tell which type you've got by counting the pins in the socket or the tiny holes in the plug). If your device and your computer use different types you can buy a very cheap adapter to get around the problem. Serial ports transmit and receive data in a one-bit series, the format needed to send data over a telephone line.

Parallel ports – You'll usually have only one of these called LPT1 (for Line Printer port), although some computers offer two or three. To the LPT port(s), unsurprisingly, you attach your printer(s). The connectors for parallel ports are standardized, but few devices other than printers and scanners are ever connected to parallel ports. The parallel port sends data in 8-bit chunks, and is able to check that the printer is ready to receive more data.

USB ports – This is a new type of port found on recent PCs, designed to make installation and use of new devices quick and simple. Unlike other devices and ports, you can plug a device into a USB port with the computer switched on and Windows running; Windows should spot the device immediately and you can start to use it straight away. The device must be specifically designed for plugging into a USB port, and up to 127 devices can be connected to a single port by chaining them together with cables. If your PC has a USB port and you can find a USB version of the hardware you want, buy it! If you do, you should never need to look at the rest of this chapter!

Drivers – making everything talk

When you add almost any new device you'll also have to install a device driver to go with it. A device driver is a program that helps the PC to talk the same language as the new device, and it will usually be provided on a floppy disk or CD bundled with the hardware itself.

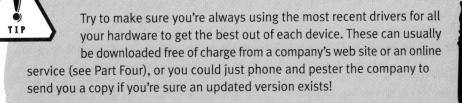

Try to make sure you're always using the most recent drivers for all your hardware to get the best out of each device. These can usually be downloaded free of charge from a company's web site or an online service (see Part Four), or you could just phone and pester the company to send you a copy if you're sure an updated version exists!

How you install the driver will vary from one device to another, and indeed from one manufacturer to another, but in general there are two methods. The neatest of these is that the manufacturer supplies a small program on disk that will copy the driver to your hard disk and make sure the computer knows where to find it when it needs it. The second method is less automated, but not particularly difficult: the Add New Hardware applet in the Control Panel gives step-by-step help with installing a driver, as we'll see later in this chapter.

Understanding resources

Many types of hardware that you add to your system (and particularly expansion cards) raise the question of resource settings. Resources are one of the most complicated areas of PCs you're likely to come up against, but you shouldn't have to deal with them too often unless you plan on buying new hardware every few weeks. (And if you do, they'll soon seem pretty easy anyway!) Let's try looking at this in simpler terms first.

A car has resources – it has petrol, oil, and water. Some of its components need petrol, some need oil, others need water. So car manufacturers assign these resources where they're needed: for example, if a particular component needs petrol, for example, they make sure there's a hose connecting it to the petrol-tank.

There are also three typical resources that different components of a PC might have – I/O Port Address, IRQ and DMA – and these should be clearly listed in the device's manual. Here's a quick description of each:

I/O Port address – Identifies a particular area of the memory that a single specific device can use.

IRQ – Whenever a device is called upon to do something (for example, your soundcard needs to play a sound), it has to interrupt whatever the processor is doing at that time. So it sends a request for processor time (an interrupt request) down a line to the processor, and these lines are numbered – the lower the number assigned to a particular device, the higher its priority in the queue when the processor is busy.

DMA – These are numbered channels rather like IRQs. A DMA channel is a direct line to the computer's memory, bypassing the processor. This gives an improvement in response times from the device, coupled with the fact that the processor is left alone to get on with other things in the meantime.

The most important aspect of these resources (which, sadly, doesn't remotely fit our car metaphor) is that these settings must be unique to each device: for example, if two devices are assigned IRQ2, one or both of them will be unable to work, causing a situation known as a hardware conflict.

In a similar way to device drivers (mentioned above) there are two methods of allocating resources to a newly installed device. If you're lucky (or you bought carefully), the device will come with a help disk. The program will examine your entire system to see which resources are available (those that aren't already assigned to another device) and tell you which ones you should choose. Most of the time this will be as simple as agreeing to the program's suggestions and letting it update the system for you, but once in a while you might need to change settings on the hardware itself, and the device's manual will explain how to do that.

If you're unlucky, you might have to configure these resource settings yourself. This will involve looking at the resources already allocated to all the other devices attached to your computer and making notes of any available ones. You'll then need to check the manual for the new device to see which settings are suitable. For example, despite the fact that there are 15 IRQ lines, some devices (typically the cheaper ones) might be able to work with only two or three of them. If these two or three lines are already being used, you've got the added thrill of checking the manuals of other devices to see if you can swap the IRQs around and free-up one of the lines you need.

Installing with Plug & Play

The idea of Plug & Play is that the first time you start your computer after connecting the new hardware, Windows will notice this new device, determine what it is, and add the necessary drivers for it automatically. If all goes smoothly, you should see just a brief onscreen message as your desktop appears, announcing that a new device has been detected and is being configured. As well as installing driver files, the Plug & Play system covers the allocation of resources for the device, such as assigning correct and non-conflicting DMA channels and IRQs if necessary.

Microsoft supplies its own drivers for a huge range of hardware: you might be prompted to insert your Windows installation CD so that the required files can be copied to your hard disk. If Windows detects a Plug & Play device but can't provide a driver for it, you'll be prompted to insert the disk containing the driver-files that was packaged with the hardware.

Full Plug & Play support relies on having a Plug & Play BIOS as well as Plug & Play hardware. Nevertheless, if one or both of these items are non-Plug & Play compatible, Windows will still have a brave stab at identifying the new device. If neither are Plug & Play compatible, however, you'll probably find you need to get your hands dirty in Device Manager to assign non-conflicting resources. This will always depend upon the type of hardware you're installing, and what's installed already (see 'Making Resource Settings' below).

Changing hardware drivers

Despite its name, the Add New Hardware wizard in Control Panel lets you change hardware drivers as well as install new hardware. If Windows didn't manage to detect your device, or you want to install an updated driver, go to Control Panel and run the wizard, then follow these steps:

1. Click **Next** in the first dialog to begin the process. In the second dialog click the **No** button to prevent Windows searching for the device.

2. On the next page, shown in the screenshot below, double-click the type of hardware for which you want to change or install drivers.

3. If Windows failed to detect your hardware after you started your PC, look at the Manufacturers and Models lists to see if the device is listed. If it is, select it and click **Next** to install it. If you want to install an updated driver, or the driver that came with the software, click **Have Disk...** and direct Windows to the location of the files.

4. Installing new drivers will always require that you restart the computer for the change to take effect.

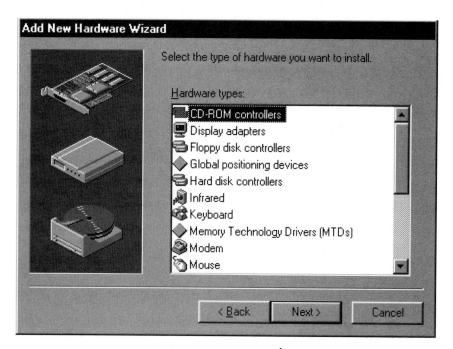

Choose the type of device you want to install and configure.

Installing an unrecognized device

Sometimes Windows just hasn't got a clue what your device is: it can't detect it, and it doesn't list a driver for it. If the manufacturer didn't package a driver with the hardware, all is not lost! Many drivers will work with different devices, so use the Add New Hardware wizard to try a few. It's a trial-and-error process, so it could involve a lot of starting and restarting of your computer, but you'll usually find something that will give you at least basic control of the device.

If there are devices of the same type as yours listed by the same manufacturer, start by trying those, following steps 3 and 4 above. If none of those work (or your manufacturer isn't listed at all), try the range of generic drivers supplied for most device types: after clicking the **No** radio-button as in step 1 above, double-click **Other Devices** in the **Hardware types** list. You'll see a list of bracketed entries in the left pane such as **(Standard display types)** and **(Standard mouse types)**.

Click the correct type and choose what you think is the closest match in the right pane, then click **Next** to continue the installation.

Finding system settings in Device Manager

Almost all the nitty-gritty of your system that affects (or is controlled by) Windows can be found in Control Panel's **System** applet. You can either double-click this icon or, for quicker access, right click on **My Computer**, and choose **Properties**.

Following the basic information on the **General** page, the first tab you come to is **Device Manager**. This follows the familiar 'tree-structure' used in Explorer's left pane. From this page, you can:

- view all the devices connected to your computer;

- add/remove or disable/enable devices;

- see which drivers are used for particular devices and change them;

- check and change settings, addresses and IRQs;

- check and alter port settings (mouse, modem, printer, etc.); and

- make sure that each device is working properly.

It's well worth taking a browse through Device Manager even as an inexperienced user: expand trees, select devices and choose the Properties button for each. Provided you don't actually change anything, this is risk-free. For the nervous, the simple way to avoid changing anything is: never click **OK** – always use **Cancel** to close a dialog.

By selecting the **Computer** entry at the top of the Device Manager list and clicking **Properties**, you can view devices by resource: for example, click the **Interrupt Request** radio-button to see which IRQs are in use, and by which devices – useful information to have if you need to find a free IRQ to allocate to a newly-installed device.

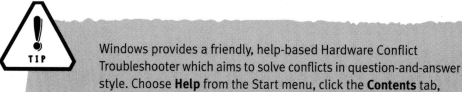

Windows provides a friendly, help-based Hardware Conflict Troubleshooter which aims to solve conflicts in question-and-answer style. Choose **Help** from the Start menu, click the **Contents** tab, then click **Troubleshooting**, following by **Windows 98 Troubleshooters** and **Hardware Conflict**.

Making resource settings

Assuming your computer has a Plug & Play BIOS, Windows will automatically allocate the resources for a Plug & Play device when you install one. On the Resources tab of a device's Properties page in Device Manager you should see that the **Use Automatic Settings** box is checked; this gives Windows the freedom to juggle resources around between different devices if you install more Plug & Play hardware, so this box is always best left checked.

With a Plug & Play BIOS, Windows will still try to allocate correct resources for a non-Plug & Play device, but these may not always suit the hardware itself. If they don't, you'll need to clear the **Use automatic settings** check-box and specify your own settings instead, according to the details given in the device's manual.

If neither hardware nor BIOS are Plug & Play compatible, the **Use automatic settings** box will be greyed out and you'll have to identify and set the resources manually.

Setting resources manually

Different hardware will require different resources, such as IRQ, DMA channel, I/0 range, and Memory address. The following steps explain how to carry out the common operation of changing the IRQ setting. The same procedure applies if you want to change the setting for one of the other resources – just select the resource you want to change in the **Resource Settings** window:

1. Highlight the offending device in Device Manager and click **Properties**.

2. Click the **Resources** tab, and highlight the **Interrupt Request** entry in the Resource Settings window.

3. Make sure the **Use automatic settings** box isn't checked; if it is, clear the check-box.

4. Click the **Change Setting...** button.

5. Change the interrupt setting in the **Value** box, keeping an eye on the lower box for an indication that you've picked a non-conflicting setting, as shown in the next screenshot.

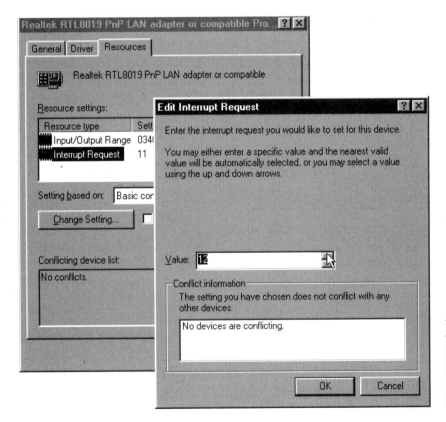

Assigning a different Interrupt Request to a device.

Of course, not only do you have to choose an IRQ that doesn't conflict with other installed devices, it must be one that your device can respond to, and some devices respond to a very limited number. You might be able to juggle IRQs for other devices to free-up a compatible one, but it's possible you'll have to replace the device itself with one with greater IRQ support.

If you can find an available IRQ that is compatible with your device, you may have to alter jumper or DIP switch settings on the hardware accordingly – check the device's manuals for details.

> **TIP** Some devices offer different preset configurations: before modifying any resources settings, take a look in the drop-down list titled **Setting based on**. A different configuration may give you the settings you need, or may let you change settings that were fixed in a different configuration.

Adding extra RAM

The most common upgrade of 1998 was extra memory, the result of a huge reduction in the price of RAM chips. It's a safe bet that memory will be top of the shopping list in 1999 as users upgrade from Windows 95 to Windows 98 and slam in the 32Mb RAM that makes it run most happily.

In most modern PCs, there are four or six RAM slots divided into banks of two. Depending upon your PC, the memory you have already may be in the form of SIMM chips or the more recent DIMMs. The big difference between the two types is that SIMM chips must be installed in matching pairs to fill a bank, so if you can only afford to add 16Mb memory you'll need to buy it as two 8Mb chips, whereas DIMM chips can be installed singly.

You'll also need to know how many 'pins' your computer's memory chips must have. For SIMM chips the norm is 72-pin; with DIMMs the standard is 168-pin, but always check your PC's manual before getting your chequebook out. Finally, of course, you need to decide on the capacity. RAM prices have recently tumbled to about 4% of their 1996 price, giving you a megabyte for about a pound, so 64Mb RAM has become a realistic target and should be enough for most uses. If you frequently open very large files or run a number of professional-level applications at the same time, you may want to play safe and go for a (still affordable) total of 128Mb.

RAM chips are extremely fragile and can be damaged by static electricity and careless handling. Always be gentle when touching these chips, and hold them only by their two short edges.

Memory chips are installed in the same way as expansion cards (see 'Fitting An Internal Device' earlier in this chapter): place the edge of the chip against the memory slot, and push gently while rocking the chip up and down. In most PCs the RAM slots have small plastic clips that slot into holes in the edges of the chip to hold it securely – if yours does, make sure that the clips are in place.

The good news about memory is that the physical installation is all that's needed. Provided you've installed the chips correctly (and it's not a foregone conclusion, even if a chip seems to be firmly seated!) your PC should find it and start using it immediately. When you start your computer, watch the screen carefully: as the initial tests take place, you should see that the total RAM displayed on the screen has increased. (If you use SIMMs, remember that two chips are needed in each bank: if one chip has been installed incorrectly, neither chip in that bank will be recognised.)

Chapter 16

What's New In Windows 98?

In This Chapter...

Using extra buttons and toolbars in Windows Explorer

Customise folders with background images and thumbnail views

Preview images and documents instantly in Explorer

Add dynamically-updated Web pages to the desktop

What's New In Windows 98?

At the time of writing, the computer world is going through a change as PC retailers start bundling Windows 98 with a new computer instead of Windows 95, and existing PC users think about making the same switch themselves. Although the two operating systems are very similar they're certainly not identical, and I've tried to cater for users of both in previous chapters. In this chapter, for Windows 98 users and Windows 95 users wondering whether to take the leap, we'll look at some of the changes and additions to the latest incarnation of Windows. (If you're a Windows 95 users with version 4 of the Internet Explorer web browser installed, you'll already have many of the new features mentioned in this chapter and elsewhere.)

New ways to explore

On the surface, the biggest changes to Windows 98 are noticeable in My Computer and Explorer windows, with redesigned '3D' toolbars and some handy extra buttons based on Microsoft's Internet Explorer web browser. (In fact, the resemblance to the browser is more than coincidental, as you'll learn in a moment.)

The new buttons are Back and Forward arrows that track your movements between drives and folders. Along with the established 'Up' arrow that takes you to the current folder's parent, the Back button opens the folder you were last looking at, and the Forward arrow lets you retrace your steps after using the Back button. Fans of the keyboard can step back and forth by holding Alt and pressing the left and right arrow keys. Tiny arrowheads beside the buttons can be clicked to show a menu of the recent folders you've visited: select a folder name from the menu to reopen it.

If you find that the arrowheads beside the Back and Forward buttons present too small a target to click, right-click on the button itself to open a menu.

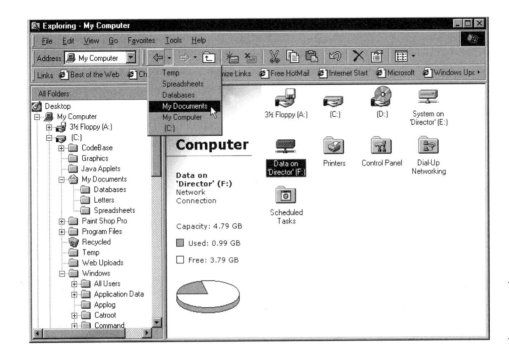

The new-look
Windows
Explorer

Another addition, which also owes its existence to the web browser, is the **Favorites** menu. For Internet use, this system has been used in browsers for several years, letting you store the addresses of Internet sites that you visit regularly and recall them with a couple of clicks instead of retyping long and complicated addresses. In Windows 98, you can use the same system to scurry between drives and folders on your own system too. Just click on a folder icon in any window and drag it up to the Favorites menu; as soon as you do so, the menu will open and you can drop the folder into the list, effectively making a shortcut to it. (Better still, you can drag around the shortcuts on this menu to arrange them in whatever order you like.)

A change of view

In Windows 95, it's possible to change the way icons are displayed within folder windows – large or small, List view or Details view. Windows 98 adds an extra raft of features that let you customise each folder individually, either for ease of use or just for the pure pleasure-factor.

The first of these is Thumbnails View, ideal for any folder containing image files (with extensions such as .bmp, .gif or .jpg), shown in the first screenshot below. To view thumbnail versions of the images in a folder, right-click inside the folder, move the pointer to **View** and choose **Thumbnails** from the submenu. The first time you select this option, Windows will create two new hidden files in the folder, which takes a few seconds; in future, the thumbnails will appear almost as soon as you open the folder. (If you don't have a Thumbnails option on your View submenu, select Properties and check the box marked **Enable thumbnails view**, then try again.)

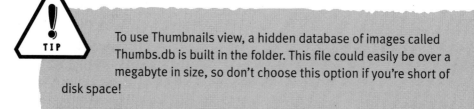

To use Thumbnails view, a hidden database of images called Thumbs.db is built in the folder. This file could easily be over a megabyte in size, so don't choose this option if you're short of disk space!

A second View option lets you do some pretty exotic things with a folder. Right-click in a folder-window and select the **Customize this Folder...** option, and a wizard will start to guide you through the simple process step by step. The simplest option, shown in the second screenshot below, is to choose a background image to be tiled behind your icons (you can also change the text-colour of the icons to make sure their labels remain visible). For increased exotica, you can style the folder like a page from the World Wide Web, adding clickable links, images and text, and even small programs and controls that start running as soon as you open the folder.

The Internet – wherever you are!

You've probably spotted a certain similarity between some of the new Windows 98 features mentioned above and the Internet's popular World Wide Web. This is quite intentional on the part of Microsoft: the thrust of the Windows 98 design is that you should be able to move between folders and documents on your own system or the Internet without running different programs or (in theory) seeing much difference between the two. As a result, Windows Explorer and the Internet

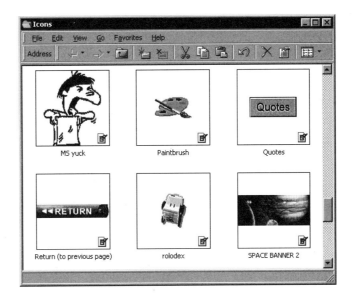

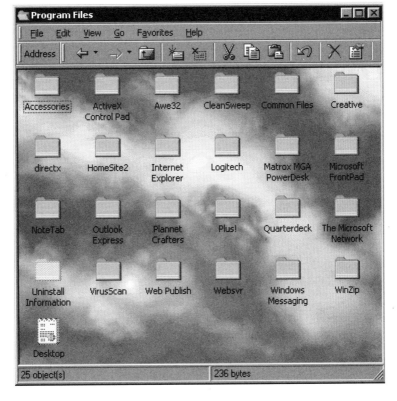

View images as thumbnails, or add individual backgrounds to your folders.

Explorer browser have actually become one and the same thing. As in Windows 95, My Computer and Explorer will display your drives, folders and documents, but their new talents allow them to display pages from the World Wide Web and even documents you've created in Microsoft Office.

Along with the Favorites menu mentioned above, Explorer now sports a Links toolbar which can be customized to give fast-access buttons linking you to your favourite web sites. You'll also notice a small vertical 3-dimensional bar at the left of each toolbar. This allows another handy piece of customization: by clicking on this bar, you can slide a toolbar left and right to position it, or even drag the entire toolbar up and down. By right-clicking on any toolbar, you can choose which bars should be displayed, and remove the text-labels from the buttons to make them more compact.

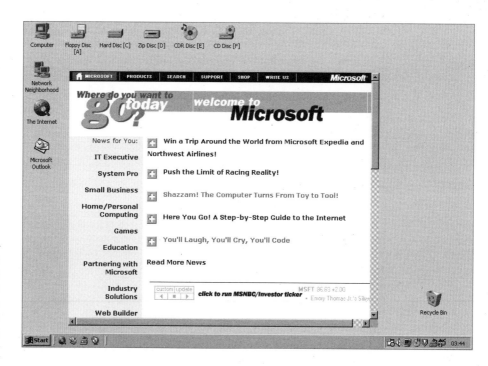

The Active Desktop displaying a page from Microsoft's web site

Another Internet-related feature is the new Active Desktop. By right-clicking the desktop and selecting **Customize my Desktop...** from the Active Desktop submenu, you can choose pictures or web pages to be displayed in small resizable frames on the desktop, as shown in the screenshot above. If you choose to display content from the World Wide Web, you can choose how often Windows should dial-up and check for the latest versions of these pages or (more practically for UK users, who still pay for local phone calls), choose **Update Now** from the Active Desktop submenu whenever you want to grab the latest editions.

> **TIP**
>
> To quickly remove all Web-based content from your desktop, right-click the desktop and click on **View as Web Page** to remove the check-mark. By switching this option off, you'll probably notice an improvement in the speed of your computer. Rather unwisely, Microsoft chose to switch this option on for everyone by default.

The multi-talented taskbar

The Taskbar has also had a facelift, allowing it to display the same type of sliding toolbars now found in Explorer and My Computer. Beside the Start button you'll find a Quick Launch toolbar containing shortcut icons to Internet Explorer and Outlook Express, along with a neat button that minimises all windows to return you to your desktop (or, combined with the Shift key, restores all windows). You can add shortcuts to other favourite programs or folders by dragging and dropping them onto the Quick Launch bar.

Sliding toolbars
on the Taskbar

By right-clicking the Taskbar, you can add more toolbars such as Address and Links bars for Internet access, or a custom toolbar containing shortcuts to any folder or file on your system. You can keep these toolbars out of the way while you work, leaving space to display taskbar-buttons for open windows. Whenever you need to access a toolbar, just double-click its name to make it slide open. To close it again, double-click its name a second time.

Taskbar buttons now have an extra role: clicking the currently-selected button will minimise the corresponding window.

Easy system management

Owning a computer is rather like owning a car: the potential benefits are immense, but to take full advantage of them, you've got to keep everything running smoothly. Because every piece of computer hardware relies on software in the form of drivers or system files to do its job properly, an accidentally-deleted file or a misbehaving software installation could cause problems.

Windows 95 includes a set of tools such as ScanDisk and Disk Defragmenter, covered in Chapter 14, which do a good job of spotting and correcting certain types of error, but you still have to remember to run them regularly. If you get a problem with a system file or a hardware driver, however, things aren't quite as simple, and you'll probably need to spend some time following the troubleshooting sections of Windows help.

Windows 98 takes a lot of the strain out of system management by automating it. Here are a few of the major system enhancements:

Task Scheduler – An updated version of the System Agent utility which was available with Windows 95's optional Plus! pack. Programs such as ScanDisk and Disk Defragmenter can be scheduled to run automatically at specified times, removing the need to remember to do it yourself, and a Disk Cleanup program can automatically delete unwanted temporary files and optionally empty your Recycle Bin.

Disk Defragmenter – A new version of the existing utility identifies the programs and files you use most often, and keeps these files grouped together on the hard disk to give even faster access to them.

Windows Update – Provided you have a modem and a connection to the Internet, this utility can examine your system and automatically install any Windows files that have been added or updated since your last visit. You'll find the Window Update icon on the main part of the Start Menu just above Programs.

System File Checker – A handy utility that can check your vital system files to make sure that none has been deleted accidentally, or replaced with an older version by a rogue program installation. If it finds a problem, the utility can restore the original file from your Windows CD-ROM. (If you can't find System File Checker on your Start Menu, choose the Run command, type **sfc** and press Enter, or create your own shortcut to **C:\Windows\System\Sfc.exe**.)

OnNow – This is a new technology, as opposed to a program. Provided your computer is recent enough to support it, OnNow enables your computer to start almost immediately. Rather than turning the PC on and off, this system effectively puts it to sleep by giving you an intermediate Standby mode (notebook computers have had a similar feature for years). If you use this feature, remember that your PC and peripherals are still plugged into the mains and switched on: to guard against damage from storms and electrical spikes, plug your PC and peripherals into a surge protector.

Quickfire Windows 98 additions

- If you delete a folder in Windows Explorer the entire folder is stored unchanged in the Recycle Bin and can be restored as easily as a single file with all its original contents recreated.

- Items on the Start Menu can now be dragged from one place to another, letting you organize them in any way you like. You can also right-click on a group icon and choose **Open** to open its contents in a window, or right-click any item at all to cut, copy or delete it.

- If you have one of those new-fangled mice with a wheel, you can use the wheel to scroll the contents of any window that displays a scrollbar, including lists of items in dialog boxes.

- Notepad's Edit menu now sports a **Set Font** option, allowing you to choose your preferred font and size for editing text documents.

- Paint can now save the pictures you create in the less disk-space-hungry GIF or JPEG formats.

- If you want to take a quick look at a file without opening its application to do so, you can right-click it and choose **Quick View** from the context menu. In the past, though, only a few types of file could be 'quick viewed'; in Windows 98, the Quick View utility option is available for many more files, including any file created with Office 97 and many types of graphics format. If you're not sure whether Quick View is installed, check to see if you have a folder called **Viewers** in your Windows\System folder. If you haven't, go to Control Panel's Add/Remove Programs applet, choose the Windows Setup tab and check the **Quick View** entry in the Accessories section.

- The display features of the optional Windows 95 Plus! pack are now included, allowing the contents of windows to remain visible as you drag or resize them, and High Colour icons to be used on compatible displays. You'll find these options on the **Effects** tab of the Control Panel's Display applet, where you can also change the icons used for My Computer, Network Neighborhood and the Recycle Bin, and switch menu animation on and off.

Part Three

Choosing & Using Software

In This Part...

Chapter 17

Selecting & Installing New Software

In This Chapter...

Points to check before buying software

Installing software – manual or automatic?

Removing unwanted software from your system

Using Windows' own add/remove option

Selecting & Installing New Software

In theory, you already know exactly what software you need. After all, you know *why* you need a computer, and it's the software you choose that determines what this machine can do. In reality, though, it rarely works out that way: we get so bogged down in the technicalities of picking the right computer that the reason for buying the PC in the first place often becomes a last-minute 'Oh yes, I need a word processor'. It's a fact of computer-buying life, but it's one to watch out for: for example, a single graphics application might cost nearly half the price of your PC, but you may never use more than a quarter of its features. Conversely, you might find you have to replace software soon after buying it because it can't do what you need.

The aim of the following chapters is to provide a basic introduction to some of the common types of software – what they do, how they do it, what's available and what's popular – to help you choose wisely.

Software-buying checklist

Before you splash the cash, it's vital to make sure you're buying the right tool for the job. It's a good start to know you need a word processor, but it doesn't narrow the field much: word processors range from simple £40 jotters to feature-packed £200 applications with advanced formatting and layout tools. Here are a few questions worth asking yourself before you make any final decisions:

Will it do what you need it to do?
The fundamental question that could save you both money and aggravation. Check this one carefully by reading reviews and comparing features with other applications. Try to get an in-store demonstration and a few minutes to explore it on your own.

Will it do more than you need it to do?

Given the alternative, it's better to buy something that does more than you need, but the heavyweight professional applications can swallow chunks of system resources, and you might find the plethora of toolbars and menus distracting.

Will Windows' own accessories do the job?

Another case for some experimentation. These add-on accessories aren't intended to rival full-blown applications, but if your word-processing requirements are limited to short letters, memos and faxes, you might find that WordPad could handle them for you comfortably.

Will file formats be compatible with your colleagues' applications?

For business users this can be an important consideration. If you need to pass the files you create to a colleague, make sure you can save files in a format compatible with your colleague's software. If you already use a particular application on your office PC, it makes sense to buy the same for your home or portable.

Can a different type of application do this job?

Modern word processors such as Microsoft Word and Lotus WordPro have built-in drawing tools that might make a separate drawing package redundant. A good spreadsheet application can make a very capable database. Draw up a list of the things you need to do with your PC and see how far you can reduce the number of separate applications required.

Would an office suite be a better buy?

If you need two or more heavy-duty applications, such as a word processor and a spreadsheet, you'll probably save money by buying an office suite (covered in Chapter 24) and get two or three more applications thrown in for good measure.

Will it run on your PC?

Take a look at the back or side panel of the software pack for the specifications needed to run the software. Above all, remember that these are minimum requirements: the program may seem rather sluggish if your PC matches those specifications exactly.

Is it available on CD-ROM?

If you have a CD-ROM drive and the software is available on CD-ROM, this is a much better buy than a bundle of floppy disks. Installation will be a lot faster and easier, and you might get a few extras that couldn't be squeezed onto a reasonable number of floppies.

Are you on the upgrade path?

If you bought an application and you now need something more powerful, find out if you qualify for an upgrade price rather than having to buy the full product. In many cases, if you have a competitor's product installed, or a 'lightweight' version of the product you want, you can save 35 to 50 per cent by buying the upgrade version. (But beware – this version checks your hard disk to make sure you weren't kidding before it goes very far!) These upgrade prices apply even if the original software was supplied 'free' with your PC.

Understanding version numbers

Software changes as fast as the hardware it's designed to work with, so software-producers add version numbers to the names of their products to help you ensure you're buying the latest version, or the version that works with your operating system. A new product will be called version 1.0; minor changes will lead to versions 1.1, 1.2, and so on. When a major change in design takes place they'll call it version 2.0. Very often the minor changes are the result of finding bugs (unexpected errors) in the previous release and putting them right.

Installing new software

Installation of software means making sure that all the files needed to run the program can be found by the computer when needed. This usually involves placing the files in particular folders on your hard disk, but a few programs are small and simple enough that you can run them from a floppy disk with no formal installation required. Other types of software, such as games or multimedia titles, may be several hundred megabytes in size and supplied on CD-ROM; copying this lot to your hard disk would be pretty impractical, so installation involves copying a few small files to your hard disk and leaving the rest where they are.

The most straightforward type of installation simply involves copying a few files around manually. For example, a small program supplied on a floppy disk, or downloaded from the Internet, may just need you to create a new folder on your hard disk, copy the program files into it, and create a shortcut so that you can start it easily.

Don't install more than one application at a time. If you install five in one session and your PC goes into a sulk next time you start it, it'll be no fun at all trying to track down the culprit. Install one, restart your computer, and check everything's okay before installing the next.

Automated installation

The more common type of installation, particularly with today's large applications, involves a semi-automated installation procedure. The software is supplied on a CD-ROM, or a set of floppy disks, and the installation is handled by a program often called Install.exe or Setup.exe which you'll find on the CD-ROM or the first of the floppies. Running this program will lead you through the procedure step by step, asking you questions as you go along. This may vary in complexity: some software will just ask if you're sure you want to install and then start copying the files to your hard disk when you say Yes; other programs will give you an opportunity to choose the drive and folder into which you want to install the software.

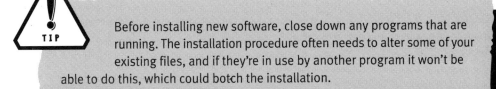

Before installing new software, close down any programs that are running. The installation procedure often needs to alter some of your existing files, and if they're in use by another program it won't be able to do this, which could botch the installation.

Larger software packages such as operating systems and top-level applications often require a lot of disk-space and include a collection of optional files, so they usually prompt you to choose between a Minimal installation (leaving out most of the optional utilities and accessories to conserve disk-space), a Typical installation (including the options most users will need), or a Custom installation. The Custom installation allows you to choose which elements of the software you want to install, usually gives a brief description of each one, and keeps a running tally of the disk-space required as you check off the items you want.

> **TIP**
>
> For all but the computing novice, it's worth taking the Custom option and choosing which elements you want installed. But whether you do this or not, you can run the Setup program again in the future and add or remove elements easily.

The necessary files will then be copied to various folders on your hard disk, and changes may be made to your system files so that the computer is made aware of this new software's arrival and the whereabouts of its files. In some cases, you'll have to restart your PC after installation so that the computer can read these updated system files into its memory. You may also be asked whether you'd like icons to be added to your program groups: if you agree to this, you can delete the icons at any time if you change your mind; if you turn down the offer, you can still add the shortcuts manually.

Uninstalling software

'Uninstalling' software means removing it (and, in theory at least, all traces of it) from your computer. The method of doing this will usually reflect the method of installation: if you created a new folder and copied the files into it yourself, uninstallation is as simple as deleting the files you copied and deleting the folder. If you created an icon for the program on your desktop or elsewhere, you'll need to delete that too.

Most software that has its own installation program, as described above, usually has an automated method of uninstallation too. This may involve running the Setup program again and clicking a button marked Uninstall, or you may find an uninstall program in the folder that the software was installed into. This program should remove any files that were copied to your hard disk as a part of the installation, and reverse any changes made to your system files (again requiring you to restart the computer).

It may or may not remove the icons it added to your program groups, and it usually won't delete any folders it created. This last point is actually good news: you might have saved documents of your own into these folders which you wouldn't want to lose. Deleting a folder deletes its entire contents including any subfolders, and any files in those subfolders.

Never uninstall a program by just deleting its folder unless you created that folder yourself when you installed it. You'll usually be leaving other files scattered elsewhere on your system, along with settings that cause your system to act strangely.

Let Windows uninstall it for you

Most of the software you install that was designed for Windows 95 or 98 will add itself to a list of programs on the Install/Uninstall page of Control Panel's Add/Remove Programs applet, shown in the next screenshot.

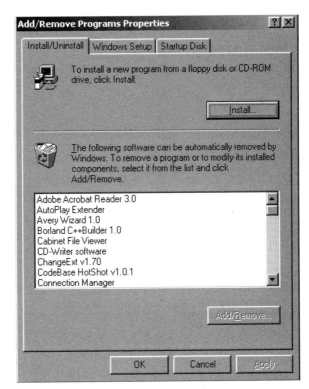

Select the program to be removed, and click the Add/Remove button to kiss it goodbye.

Despite the name of the page and the details on it, there's no need to use this page to install software – just follow the instructions included with the software itself. But if you need to uninstall the program, and you can't see an uninstall option for it anywhere else, take a look at this page to see if the program is logged there. If it is, click its name in the list, then click the **Add/ Remove** button and follow any instructions that appear

Chapter 18

Get Writing with a Word Processor

In This Chapter...

The big differences between typewriters and word processors

Finding your way around a long document

Apply formatting to text and paragraphs

Get it word perfect with spellchecker and thesaurus

Get Writing with a Word Processor

It sounds like something that could only have been named by a committee, but a word processor is actually one of the simplest types of program you'll come across. Essentially, a word processor is the computer equivalent of a typewriter, letting you type and print text-based documents, but the differences between the two are immense. How many typewriters let you change the size, colour and style of the typeface, insert drawings and pictures, or add a few lines to page 20 while you're writing page 54? Better still, there are no ribbons to change, and you don't need to cover your screen with correction fluid!

Word-processor basics

When the program opens you'll see a wide expanse of white space in the middle, which is your 'paper', and you can start typing immediately. A flashing vertical line (known as the cursor or insertion-point) indicates where you are in the document – any text you type will appear immediately to the right of this line. You can move the insertion-point to anywhere in the document using the arrow-keys, or by clicking the left mouse-button. Whenever the mouse is positioned over the 'paper', it turns into a shape called an I-beam (shown in the next screenshot) to help you position the insertion-point more easily between two adjacent characters than the ordinary pointer would allow.

Another important difference between a typewriter and a word processor is that you don't need to press the keyboard's carriage-return key (Return or Enter) when you reach the end of a line. Instead, the text 'wraps' automatically onto the next line, and carriage-return keys are used only when you want to start a new paragraph or insert blank lines.

Finally, of course, a word processor doesn't commit you to anything you've typed. You can make all the spelling mistakes you want and sort them out later; if you change your mind about the order of the paragraphs you can use Cut and Paste to

Text-editor

A text-editor (such as WIndows' Notepad) is like a word processor without any flashy features, used to create plain text (*ASCII*) files that have no font-styles, formatting or layout detail. Text-editors work with files with a .txt extension and are useful for creating short notes, memos and so on, being quick and easy to use. In effect, all word processors are text-editors – any word processor will be able to open and save files in this format.

rearrange them. Most importantly, you can use a huge range of features to format the document, including fonts, tabs and paragraph alignment, line spacing, and text-colours. A top-level application will also include options to create graphs and tables, add logos and graphics, place text in shaded, boxes, and so on.

● *Common editing facilities found in word processors are explained in Chapter 11.*

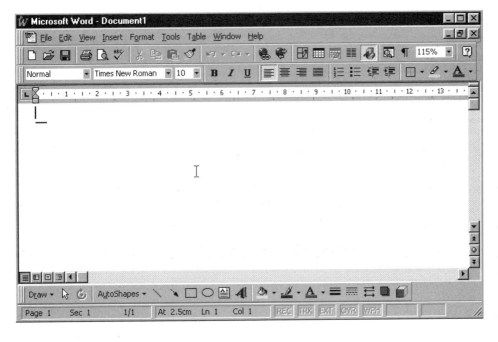

Microsoft Word ready for work, with the cursor in the corner of the document window and the I-beam in the centre.

Moving around a document

As you type text into your word processor and your document gets longer, the text scrolls upwards and gradually disappears off the top of the screen as if you'd threaded an everlasting roll of paper into your typewriter. The text is still there, of course, and you can move backwards and forwards through the document to view or edit your work any time you like. Here are some of the methods for doing this:

- Use the arrow-keys to move around one character or line at a time, or in conjunction with Ctrl to move back and forth one word at a time.

- Use the PageUp/PageDown keys to move up and down one screen at a time. A 'screen' will be smaller than a complete printed page.

- Use the Home and End keys to move to the beginning or end of a line, or together with Ctrl to move to the top or bottom of the document.

- Use the scroll-bar on the right of the screen to bring a portion of the document into view, then click the mouse at the position you want the insertion-point to appear.

JARGON BUSTER

Headers and footers

Small margins at the top and bottom of each page in a document that might contain the name of the document, or chapter titles. You would normally enter these once, perhaps with different entries for odd- and even-numbered pages, and they'll be automatically added to every page when you print the document. Page numbers can be inserted in the same way and the software will keep them updated as you add and delete text.

Working with fonts & formatting

Many word-processing, spreadsheet, database and presentation applications have a toolbar like the one shown in the next screenshot containing the primary text-formatting options. From this bar, you can select a font from the dropdown list-box, choose the size of the font (measured in 'points') from another list-box, and pick styles and effects such as bold, italic, underlined and coloured text in any combination from buttons that can be toggled on and off. In some high-level applications, there may be extra buttons on the toolbar or a Format menu offering even more text-formatting options.

The standard text-formatting toolbar.

These controls are very simple to use: if you're typing a document in a word processor and you know the next portion of text you want to enter should be Times New Roman, 12-point, and bold, just select the font and point-size from the two drop-down lists, click the **B** button, and start typing. To type a word in 'normal' print (i.e. not bold), click the **B** button again to turn it off. (If you don't want to use the mouse, you can usually switch bold, italic and underlining on and off using the hotkeys **Ctrl+B, Ctrl+I and Ctrl+U** respectively.)

JARGON BUSTER

Point-size

Points are the units of height-measurement for fonts, in which 72 points equals one inch. (This would often be abbreviated to 72-pt.) Body-text, the typographer's name for standard paragraph-text, is usually 11-pt or 12-pt.

You can also edit text you've already typed in just the same way. Let's say you want to underline a section of text – first select the portion of text you want, then click the **U** button. You can change the font or point-size (or both) for selected text by choosing from the drop-down list-boxes.

Bold	~~Strikethrough~~
Italic	Superscript Superscript
Bold-Italic	Subscript Subscript
Drop Cap	<u>Underline</u>

Some of the common, and not-so-common, text-formatting features you can use with TrueType fonts.

Setting margins & alignment

One of the fundamental needs in document-formatting is the ability to set page margins. When you first start your word processor, the margins will be preset to defaults, but these are easily changed and the changes are saved together with the document. Margins are usually set from a Page Setup... entry on the File menu, and contain boxes for Top, Bottom, Left and Right into which you type a size for each margin in centimetres. You can usually type in a size for the header and footer too, and some top-level applications let you specify different inside and outside margins for documents that are to be bound, such as books and reports.

As well as changing the settings for the whole document, you can set margins for individual paragraphs. With the insertion-point placed somewhere within the paragraph you want to change, open the **Paragraph** dialog, which is usually found on the Format menu. Here are a few of the options you might find, and what they mean:

Indent – The distance in centimetres that the selected paragraph (or its first line) should be moved from the left and right margins.

Spacing – Changes the spacing between paragraphs. You'll have simple options like **double-spaced**, and you might also be able to specify exact spacing in **points**.

To make sure your document-layout looks okay before printing, choose **Print Preview** from the **File** menu to view one or more complete pages on the screen.

Left-Aligned – This is the usual alignment option, in which each line of text will follow the line of the left margin and be ragged at the right. Your application will left-align your text automatically. (Instead of opening the **Paragraph** dialog, you can often just use the hotkey **Ctrl+L**.)

Right-Aligned – Text will follow the line of the right-margin and be ragged at the left (used only for effect, usually for single lines, dates and addresses). The usual hotkey combination is **Ctrl+R**.

Justified – Each line of the paragraph will be forced to follow both the left and right margins to give a completely 'square' look; spaces are added between words to make the lines the correct length. Justified text can be difficult to read and is now used just in short bursts for effect, or to prevent narrow columns of text looking messy. You can usually press **Ctrl+J** for this one.

Centred – This places the paragraph centrally between the left and right margins, and is used mostly for headings or unusual effects. The common hotkey is **Ctrl+E**.

Widows and orphans

Many word processors have an option to prevent widows and orphans in their paragraph-formatting dialogs. A widow is the last line of a paragraph printed by itself at the top of a new page; an orphan is the first line of a paragraph printed at the bottom of a page.

Using the spellchecker & thesaurus

These two common features are being built into word processors more and more often, but it pays to check whether they are included before buying – although users may regard them as essentials, some software producers still don't! The thesaurus is a doddle to use: any time you're stuck for a word, type a word with a similar meaning, then start it up and see what suggestions are listed. If nothing suitable appears, look up one of the suggestions to see some of its synonyms. When you find what you want, there should be a Replace button that will enter it into your document.

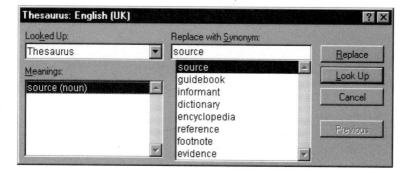

Ever needed a
synonym for
'thesaurus'?

Much as you'd expect, the spellchecker checks your spelling by looking through the document and prompting you when it finds a word not listed in its own dictionary. You can take the spellchecker's suggested word, edit the word yourself or add the word to your own user dictionary which the spellchecker uses in tandem with its own. The effectiveness of a spellchecker depends largely on the size of its dictionary, but it's important to make sure it can distinguish between American English and UK English. Some spellcheckers come with a bundle of foreign language dictionaries, which might prove useful.

TIP

When you start using a new word processor, create a document containing your name and address, and those of friends and colleagues, lists of technical terms and jargon you use regularly, and so on, and then run it through the spellchecker to add these to the user-dictionary. It makes the spellchecking of documents a much quicker process when you're trying to get some work done!

Creating mailshots with Mail Merge

The Mail Merge options included in all but the most basic word processors can be a huge time-saver for business-users, letting you create personalized mailshots automatically by merging customer details from a database, spreadsheet or personal organizer into a letter. The routine involves typing a standard sales-pitch letter, but instead of typing the recipient's name at the beginning you type something like 'Dear <<Title>>, <<Surname>>', where the bracketed entries are the names of 'fields' in the database which are usually entered via a menu option. (This type of document is known as a form letter, and the fields are usually entered by clicking a button and choosing the fieldname from a list.)

You then simply select the database you want to use and direct the word processor to merge the two items. The field-references in the letter are replaced with the contents of those fields from the database, producing letters that look as if you've typed every single one personally!

- *Turn to Chapter 20 for more on setting up databases of client details.*

Hot features in top word processors

Here is a brief look at a few of the clever features found in some of the more advanced word processors:

Styles – Type and format a heading, for example, choosing a particular font, size, colour, alignment and so on, and assign it a style-name such as 'Chapter Title'. You can then select any other text you type and apply this style to it with a single click rather than carrying out all that formatting each time. If you need to change a style, all the text in your document that uses the same style can be updated automatically.

Columns – Split your page into multiple vertical columns, newspaper-style.

Drawing tools – Switch on the drawing toolbar and add pictures, logos and designs to your document without the need for a separate draw or paint program.

Frames – Traditionally the domain of desktop publishing, you can place text or drawings into frames and drag them wherever you want them in the document, force text to flow neatly around them or even place them behind the text like a watermark.

AutoCorrect – Automatic correction of words you commonly misspell. Enter your incorrect spellings into a list together with their correct spellings and the application will keep watch for these as you type and correct them automatically.

Group support – If you work on documents in a team, your colleagues can enter their own corrections and annotations without removing the original information, letting you choose whether to incorporate their suggestions or not.

Indexing – Automatic creation of indexes, tables of contents and cross-references which can be updated with a mouse-click or two as the document's contents change.

Web page design – Save ordinary documents in a format that can be published on the Web, or work from custom templates that include preset graphics, layouts and colour schemes.

Choosing a word processor

Top of the heap in the word-processor world are Microsoft Word (the long-time best seller) and Lotus WordPro. Either of these will require a bare minimum 16Mb RAM to run under Windows, and 32Mb is a more realistic minimum. To use them in conjunction with other heavyweight applications such as spreadsheets or presentations, 64Mb RAM will help things to run faster and more smoothly. Sitting well behind these two in the popularity stakes, though still with adequate features, is Corel WordPerfect. If you want to use Mail Merge, make sure the word processor can handle it, and check which formats it supports for importing records to be merged – you don't want to find yourself in the position of retyping your whole database into a different program if you can avoid it!

Before buying a word processor, take a look at Chapter 24 – you might be able to save money by buying an all-in-one office suite or an integrated application.

Chapter 19

Crunch your Numbers with a Spreadsheet

In This Chapter...

A few typical spreadsheets uses

Quick start: getting to grips with a spreadsheet

Use formulas and functions to make your calculations

Apply formatting to make your spreadsheets more attractive

Crunch your Numbers with a Spreadsheet

It sounds like something technical that you'd run a mile to avoid using, but a spreadsheet is just a collection of boxes used to keep track of numbers. The numbers can be anything you like – your car mileage, the state of your bank account, a home-insurance valuation. But a spreadsheet lets you do much more than create lists of numbers: its speciality is to add, subtract, average, and generally crunch those numbers in any way you want them crunched, and to update the results automatically whenever you change or add an entry.

Why use a spreadsheet?

The primary use of a spreadsheet program is to enter lists of numbers and perform calculations on them; for example, you might use a spreadsheet to log sales of a product, budget your money, manage your income tax accounts, or chart the progress of your favourite football team. Once the numbers are entered, the spreadsheet can perform anything from simple addition of figures to a complicated statistical analysis of a selection of these numbers – the kind of stuff that would take hours with a calculator and years off your life!

However, spreadsheets are more than just number-crunchers – you can view these figures as colourful charts and graphs (shown in the next screenshot), import them into word-processed reports or presentations, and create finished documents such as invoices and receipts by adding company logos and graphics. In fact, you don't have to use numbers at all – the spreadsheet's Find and Replace facilities mean that you can use it as a database for any text-based information you want to keep track of too.

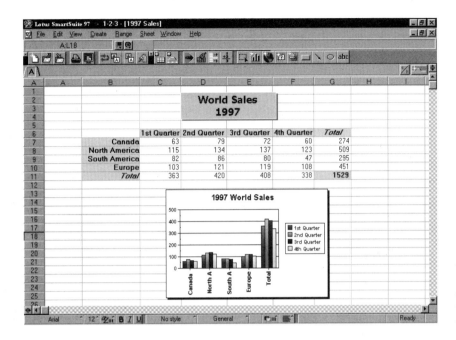

Figures and
chart in Lotus
1-2-3

Finding your way around

On first opening a spreadsheet you're presented with a large grid of boxes; each of
these boxes is a 'cell', and it's into these you'll enter text, figures and formulas. Each
cell has its own 'address', consisting of a column-letter and a row number. For
example, the cell in the top-left corner of a worksheet is called A1.

JARGON
BUSTER

Worksheets

A spreadsheet application usually lets you create lots of sheets all
in the same file, each of which is called a worksheet. You'll see tabs across the
top or bottom of the window marked Sheet 1, Sheet 2, and so on. Click on a
tab to switch to it, or double-click to give it a more informative name; for
example, you might keep your year's accounts in a single file with separate
worksheets named 'January', February' ...

When you start up the spreadsheet application you'll see a thick box around cell A1 – this is the cell selector and lets you see where you are on the sheet (rather like the flashing text-cursor in a word processor). You can move to a different cell using the keyboard's arrow-keys or by clicking a cell with the mouse. If the cell you select contains an entry, this entry will be displayed in the formula bar just above the column-headers, shown in the screenshot below. Here's a quickfire list of things you should know about spreadsheets:

The all-
important
formula bar.

C6 ▾ ✗ ✓ *fx*	=SUM(C2+C3+C6)				
A	**B**	**C**	**D**	**E**	**F**
1					
2					

- To enter text in an empty cell, move the selector to it using the arrow–keys or by clicking it, and start typing. When you're done, you can press **Enter** to confirm, or click the ✔ button on the formula bar, or move to a different cell.

- To delete an entry in a cell, click the cell and then hit the **Delete** key.

- To cancel an entry you've typed wrongly, click the ✗ button on the formula bar. You can then either type in something different or hit **Enter** to finish and leave the cell blank.

- To change an entry in a cell, just click it. If it contains data you entered yourself you can replace the data by typing something new – there's no need to delete the original data first. If the cell contains the result of a calculation, the function or formula you used will be displayed in the formula bar and you can edit it there.

- You can select a whole column for editing by clicking its letter-button, or a row by clicking its number-button.

- Select a group of cells by clicking in one cell and dragging to highlight the cells you want to work with.

- Select cells scattered around the sheet by holding **Ctrl** and clicking on each cell you need.

- You can use Cut, Copy, and Paste to move or copy the contents of cells from one part of the worksheet to another, or to a different worksheet. You can also paste (embed) them into a different type of document such as a word-processor report, or link them so that the word-processed document always shows the latest changes to the cells.

The usual way to begin creating a spreadsheet is to enter a list of names or labels in column A and along row 1 (making the columns wider if necessary) and then to enter all your values in the appropriate cells. Spreadsheets are intelligent – they can tell the difference between words and figures without you having to do anything special. However, if you intend certain figures to be dates or currency, you will need to format the selected cells correctly so that the spreadsheet knows to treat them that way: in most applications, you'll be able to click a button on the toolbar to set the most common number formats, or select them from a Format menu.

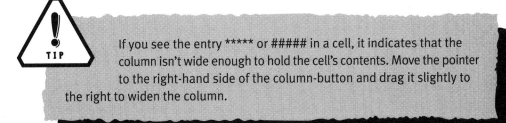

TIP

If you see the entry ***** or ##### in a cell, it indicates that the column isn't wide enough to hold the cell's contents. Move the pointer to the right-hand side of the column-button and drag it slightly to the right to widen the column.

The next step is to enter the formulas needed to make the necessary calculations. Check the results of formula-cells carefully to make sure they're doing what you want before you start to rely on their output – it's easy to miss out a data-cell you meant to include or enter the wrong symbol by mistake. Finally, add any formatting you want to make the whole thing look good.

Formulas – doing the maths

Getting all the data into the spreadsheet (and making sure you've typed it correctly!) is a good start, but it's still just lists of numbers – this is not particularly clever, and could be done in a word processor. The 'clever' comes in the form of instructions entered into a cell that tell the application what you want to know about particular sets of figures. These instructions are known as formulas and consist of cell addresses and the standard mathematical symbols + (add), – (subtract), * (multiply) and / (divide). A formula will always start with the = (equals) sign to indicate to the software that what you're entering is a formula rather than more data.

As an example, let's say you've entered a pair of numbers into cells A1 and A2 and you want to add them together. Click in A3 and type:

=A1+A2

and press Enter. The formula you just entered will vanish to be replaced by the result of that calculation. Any time you click on A3 the formula you entered will be displayed in the formula bar, but A3 itself will continue to show the result. If you now change the number in A1 and press Enter, the total shown in A3 will immediately update – the application doesn't care *which* numbers are in the cells, it just knows it's got to add them together.

Instead of typing the cell-addresses into the formula, you can just click the cell you want each time. (You've still got to type the mathematical symbols though!)

Make sure you enter the separate calculations into a formula in the order you want the application to perform them. For example, **=A1*B1+D4** would multiply A1 and B1 and then add D4 to the total, whereas **=A1*(Bl+D4)** would multiply A1 by the sum of B1 and D4. You can use as many parenthesized entries in a formula as you like.

Making the maths easier with functions

Although all formulas involve typing to some degree, there are ways to minimize the amount of keyboard-bashing you've got to do. Typing **=A1+A2**, as in the example above, isn't too painful, but what if you had entries stretching down to

A38 that needed to be added together? All those numbers, all those + signs! For this reason, spreadsheet applications include functions, predefined formulas that make the whole thing a lot quicker. Some of the most-used functions will be represented as buttons on the toolbar; other more exotic functions will be selected from a dialog such as Microsoft Excel's Function Wizard.

The most commonly-used function is SUM, which adds together the contents of cells, making it unnecessary to enter + signs. You can use the SUM function by typing =**SUM** in an empty cell, or by clicking the toolbar button marked Σ and then selecting the cells you want to add together. Here's a few examples:

- To add A1 to A38, type =**sum(a1:a38)** and press **Enter**. You must enter the parentheses, and make sure you don't enter any spaces. Sets of sequential cells like this are referred to as a 'range'. A range can cover multiple columns and rows; for example, the range **(a1:c16)** would cover A1 to A16, B1 to B16 and C1 to C16, a total of 48 cells. To select this range, you'd click in A1 and drag the pointer diagonally to C16.

Save yourself the Shift-key hassle of typing in the separating colon – you can usually use a dot instead and the software will understand what you mean and convert it to a colon for you automatically.

- Another way to total A1 to A38 with no typing at all is to click the Σ button, click in cell A1 and drag the pointer down to A38 to highlight all these cells (although A1 will remain unhighlighted) then press **Enter**.

- To total cells scattered all over your spreadsheet, such as A3, C19, B7 and D11, click the Σ button, then hold **Ctrl** and click each of these cells in turn. After clicking the last one you want to select, release Ctrl and press **Enter**.

- To total the entire contents of a row or column, click the Σ button then click on the header-button for that row or column. Once again, you can select multiple headers in this way if you hold **Ctrl** as you click each one.

TIP

If you total an entire row or column by clicking the header-button, make sure the cell into which you're entering the formula isn't in the same row or column: it'll try to add itself to the calculation and end up going around in circles (known as a 'circular reference').

A spreadsheet example

The screenshot below shows the quarterly income generated by two sales teams, and the expenses incurred by each team over the year. Rows 8 to 11 contain some of the calculations you might want to make from data such as this. Let's look at the formulas and functions you'd enter to arrive at these results.

D11		=SUM(B8:C8)	
	A	**B**	**C**	**D**
1		Sales Team 1	Sales Team 2	
2	1st Quarter Income	50,000	62,000	
3	2nd Quarter Income	45,000	75,000	
4	3rd Quarter Income	65,000	40,000	
5	4th Quarter Income	30,000	37,000	
6	Expenses	28,000	36,000	
7				
8	Total Income	190,000	214,000	
9	Total less Expenses	162,000	178,000	
10	Average per Quarter	47,500	53,500	
11	Total Company Income			404,000
12				

Typical spreadsheet data and calculations.

- To calculate the Total Income for Team 1 in B8, use the function **=sum(b2:b5)**. The total income for Team 2 in C8 would be calculated with **=sum(c2:c5)**.

- Calculate the Total less Expenses for Team 1 in B9 using the formula **=b8-b6**. To do the same for Team 2 in C9, you'd type **=c8-c6**.

- You could calculate the Average Sales per Quarter of Team 1 (cell B10) with the formula **=(b2+b3+b4+b5)/4**, but you should have a function that does this more easily: type **=average(b2:b5)**. For Team 2 in C10, enter **=average(c2:c5)**.

- The Total Company Income in D11 is calculated with the function **=sum(b8:c8)**.

Defining ranges for quick reference

Entering SUM functions in the example above is pretty easy – there are only two sales teams and the data is broken down into quarters. But imagine what the spreadsheet would look like if you had 30 teams and you were tracking their performance weekly – 30 columns by 52 rows of data! To set up calculations based upon each team's performance in particular months would involve a lot of careful typing or mouse-dragging to enter the correct ranges.

To make it easier and quicker to work with large amounts of data, spreadsheet applications allow you to assign a name to a bunch of cells you've selected in advance (look for the Name entry on the Insert or Range menu). For example, you might select the cells relating to Team 1's sales in March and assign them the name T1Mar. You can then type this name into your formulas and functions rather than having to work with individual cells.

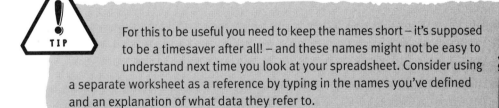

For this to be useful you need to keep the names short – it's supposed to be a timesaver after all! – and these names might not be easy to understand next time you look at your spreadsheet. Consider using a separate worksheet as a reference by typing in the names you've defined and an explanation of what data they refer to.

Adding colours, formatting & graphics

Although the spreadsheets you create are obviously supposed to be functional, spreadsheet applications include formatting facilities to make them look more attractive than just a plain grid of black text. In fact, formatting adds to a worksheet's functionality – for example, if all the cells containing the results of calculations are in bold type, or have a coloured border around them, you can find the information that matters a lot faster. You'll find all the formatting options in dialogs reached from a Format or Style menu, but some of the more common features will usually be gathered together as buttons on a toolbar.

Let's start with a quickfire list of the cell-formatting options. These are applied to the selected cell or cells; for example, to increase the font-size of several cells there's no need to format each cell individually – just drag over the range with the pointer, or click all the cells you want to change while holding **Ctrl**.

Text formatting – You'll have similar text-formatting options to those found in a word processor. You can change the font and size, underline text, or add effects such as bold, italic, or colour. In addition, you can often rotate text by 90°, or place the characters vertically in a column.

Cell shading – You can change the background of selected cells from the default white to one of a range of more interesting colours. This can be handy for distinguishing different types of data; for example, in a sales-related sheet you could use a different background colour for cells relating to each of the four quarters of the year.

Borders – You can insert lines of various colours and styles around a cell or a group of cells. Each of the four edges of a cell can be a different colour.

Text-boxes – It's usually possible to create a text-box into which you can type a heading for the worksheet and move it to wherever you want on the sheet. In this way you could create forms such as invoices with separate text-boxes for your company name, company address, client details and so on.

Graphics – You can usually insert graphics files into spreadsheets and position them where you want them, perhaps to add your company's logo to the top of a form.

Apart from the standard cell-formatting features, you may have other options that can be applied to the whole sheet:

● You can remove the column and row header-buttons from the sheet, as well as the dotted gridlines.

- Top-level spreadsheet applications offer a range of preset styles that include cell-shading borders, text colours and formatting which you can apply to your worksheet once you've finished adding all the data and formulas you need.

- Most applications include preset templates such as invoices, purchase-orders, and budgets. All you need do is insert personal or company details and add your data.

TIP

The column and row header-buttons and gridlines are included just for guidance – whether you choose to 'hide' them or not they won't be printed when you send your worksheet off to the printer. This is a good reason for putting borders around blocks of cells using the formatting tools.

Creating charts & graphs

In the case of business presentations or printed reports, it's often far more meaningful to illustrate the point you're making with a chart than to provide reams of figures. A well-chosen chart can convey the information that matters with little more than a glance. To this end, spreadsheet applications build in features that can create charts and graphs from your worksheet (or a selected portion of it) quickly and simply.

Select the cells you want included in the chart, click the dedicated button on the toolbar, drag the pointer diagonally over an empty section of the worksheet to create a box for the chart and that's about all there is to it. In Microsoft Excel the ChartWizard will appear and offer you simple choices about style and layout options. In Lotus 1-2-3 you can double-click the chart to bring up the customization dialog.

As long as the chart remains on the worksheet, any changes to the data within the cells will be reflected by the chart. In the same way, as the values in the cells increase, the chart will automatically increase its scale.

Choosing a spreadsheet

The undoubted king of spreadsheets, in terms of popularity and user-base, is Microsoft Excel, which has become the spreadsheet standard in corporate computing. Although most users will barely scratch the surface of its capabilities, it's was easy to work with as many 'lighter' applications. Its two competitors are Lotus 1-2-3 and Corel's Quattro Pro, which can't match Excel's market-share but still offer similar features and power.

Top-level applications such as these will need 32Mb RAM to run at a reasonable speed, with 64Mb a better bet if you expect to run another application such as a database or word processor alongside it. For heavy-duty use (large, formula-laden sheets), a faster-than-average processor is an advantage. A 17-inch or larger monitor will let you see more information at once, lessening the need to scroll through the window contents.

Excel, 1-2-3 and Quattro Pro are all bundled in office-suites – Microsoft Office, Lotus SmartSuite and Corel Office Professional respectively (see Chapter 24). If you need two or more office-quality applications, it's worth considering a suite. All three companies mentioned here also include a spreadsheet in their integrated (Works) applications that can satisfy all your number-crunching and formatting requirements without terrifying you with complex options you feel you're supposed to be using.

Chapter 20

Databases – Instant Storing & Searching

In This Chapter...

Design a template form to present your information

Add records to build your database

Choose how to view the information you enter

Retrieve the information you need fast with queries

Databases – Instant Storing & Searching

You've worked with databases – a phone book is a prime example. Most of us keep a book of names and numbers by the phone and flick through it when we need to call someone. The principle of a database is straightforward enough – an expanding collection of information – but the difficult trick is to find that one tiny piece of information you need quickly, and this is where the computer's ability to search vast amounts of data quickly really pays dividends.

But the computer database can do much more than simple storing and searching. Want to see your phone numbers displayed in numerical order? Easy (though perhaps not useful!). How about a list of all the people you know aged over 35? No problem. As long as you provide the information to begin with, the database can search, sort, store and organize it in any way you choose.

Different flavours of database

Almost any text-based application you use could be thought of as a type of database: provided it will let you save and edit files, and it has a Search or Find option, you can use it to store and retrieve information. However, your options for sorting and searching will be very limited. An application that dares to call itself a database will let you view the information you've entered in a variety of formats, and conduct searches for all the entries that meet your criteria. Databases work with information in three different ways:

Freeform databases – Data can be entered anywhere, and in any order, rather like a jumble of papers on a desk. When you search for particular information, the whole database will be searched for any instances of the word or number you requested.

Flat-file databases – The standard type of database. Information is entered in an organized way, using field-names. As a result, you can retrieve the information in an organized way too.

Relational databases – The relational database still uses fields to sort particular types of information, but the application can work with multiple databases and can find and present information spanning all these databases. Many relational databases are programmable – if you understand the language you can build your own database applications tailor-made for specific information and uses.

Files, records & fields

There are three separate elements to a database:

Fields – A field is a single piece of information such as someone's first name, or phone number. A field consists of a field-name, such as **Address**, and a blank box into which you'd type the corresponding information.

Records – A record is like a single card in a Rolodex or card-file with multiple fields, perhaps containing all the relevant information about a single person. A single database might contain hundreds or even thousands of records.

Files – A database file holds a collection of records in the same way that a spreadsheet file can contain multiple tabbed worksheets.

The first step: constructing a form

There are two distinct steps to creating a database. The first is to create a form that contains all the fields you need on each record, such as names, addresses, phone numbers, and so on. When the form is complete, you'll use it as the template for entering all your information.

In recent applications you can choose from a range of preset templates designed for different uses such as employee records, music and video collections, mailing lists, recipes, and all kinds of exotica. You can then alter the field-names if you need to, add and remove fields, and the first part of the job is done.

If your database application doesn't offer preset templates, or you can't find one that works for you, you can create your own by starting from a blank sheet and adding fields to it. As you add a new field-name, you'll see a box appear beside it into which you'll later type the relevant information – in most programs you'll have to specify how many characters you should be able to enter in each field.

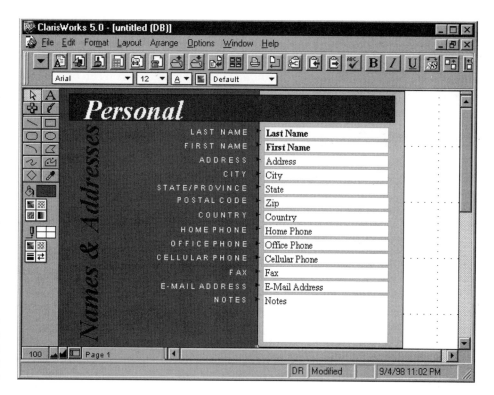

A simple database in ClarisWorks

Split your records into as many fields as possible to make searching for information easier: for example, if you create three separate fields for day/month/year of birth it'll be easy to find details of anyone born in 1964. If you want to use your database for mail merges (see Chapter 18), make sure you've split the information into the fields you'll need to enter in the form letter: for example, using separate fields for Title, First Name, Middle Initial, and Last Name will let you extract just title and last name, so that your mailshots can begin 'Dear Mr Wilson' or 'Dear Mrs Jones'.

You can move the fields around the sheet by dragging them to create a sensible and attractive layout, and apply various types of colour and style formatting to personalize the database. In many applications you can import pictures (perhaps to include photographs of your employees on their records), and add simple selection-buttons for either/or fields such as Male/Female or CD/Tape.

Protection

Databases often use two types of protection (neither of which is designed to stop them having lots of little databases, in case you were wondering!). Form protection prevents you accidentally messing up field-names and layout that you've carefully entered in your template. Data protection keeps safe the information that you've entered into the records themselves. Turning on one of these forms of protection is known as 'locking' the form or data, and it's well worth doing even though you'll have to unlock the data every time you want to enter something new.

Filling in the blanks to create records

The second step in creating a database is to actually enter the information into your fields and build up a set of records using the template form you've just created. When you've typed information into one field, press **Tab** to move to the next, and so on until you've completed the first record. You can then click a button on the toolbar to add a new record and start filling the blanks in that. In most applications, the status bar at the bottom of the window will keep you informed about how many records you've created, and usually has buttons to let you step forwards and backwards from one record to the next, or jump to the first or last.

In some cases, if you already have the information entered in another type of file, you may be able to import it. For example, if you've been keeping a block of information in a spreadsheet, your database application may be able to lift the information straight from the spreadsheet by matching column or row headings to field-names. If that doesn't work, you'll probably still be able to save some typing by dragging the text from the spreadsheet to the database.

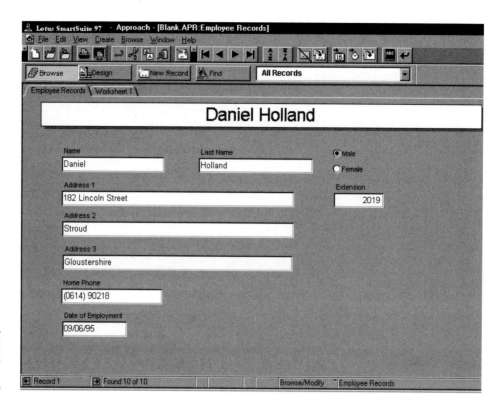

A single record
in Lotus
Approach.

Sorting records – choose your views

When you add new records to a database they remain in the order you entered them, so as you browse through the records using the buttons on the status bar you won't see any particular order to them. In fact, in some basic applications the only way of organizing records in alphabetical order is to actually insert them alphabetically. However, more advanced applications make this a lot easier by providing comprehensive sorting options: simply choose an alphabetical or numerical field to sort by, choose whether to view the records in ascending or descending order, and the software will juggle your records around for you.

Most databases can also present the records in a 'list-view' that looks and functions very like a spreadsheet, with each field having its own column and each record being in its own row. This can be useful for viewing and comparing a large number of records at once or making quick changes to the same field on every record.

Running queries to find information

One of the most common things you want to do with a database is to look at one particular record. Select the **Find** option from a menu or toolbar and you'll see a blank copy of your form layout. Type details into as many of the fields as necessary to locate the record you want; for example, if you want to see the record of an employee called John you'd type **John** in the First Name field; if you have several employees called John you'd fill in the Last Name field as well.

The database really comes into its own when you need to perform more complicated searches (known as queries). Instead of typing fixed entries into the fields you can use a variety of wildcards and symbols to find records that meet a number of criteria. The common wildcards **?** and ***** can be used to replace single or multiple characters respectively (so entering **J*** in the First Name field would find the record of anyone called John, James, Jim or Jan; entering **J??** would find Jim or Jan). The other symbols you have available will vary according to the application you're using but here are a few of the common ones:

Query format	Result
< 75	Finds records with any value lower than 75 in this field.
≥100	Finds records with values greater than or equal to 100 in this field.
75...100	Finds records with any value between 75 and 100 in this field.
Jim, Jan	Finds any records with Jim or Jan in this field.
Jim&Jan	Finds any records with both Jim and Jan in this field.

Choosing a database

At the top of the tree are the programmables, the list headed by Borland Paradox and Microsoft Access. Both combine power with ease of use, but unless you really need a professional-level application you'll be paying extra for features you're unlikely to use. Access is bundled with the more expensive Microsoft suite, Office Professional, but is not included in the Standard and Small Business editions.

Both Lotus Approach and Claris FileMaker Pro offer similar features to the big guns, with hoards of templates and preset applications at a lower price. Both are relational. Approach is included as part of Lotus SmartSuite (see Chapter 24).

Each of the major integrated Works applications includes a basic flat-file database suitable for the casual or less demanding user. Simple preset templates are included but querying and sorting features are usually limited.

Do you need a database at all? If you have a spreadsheet application you can create a great-looking, and totally searchable, database on a worksheet. If flashy presentation doesn't matter, you could even create a free-form database by typing details into a word processor document and using the Find and Find Next features to search for what you want. You won't be able to use advanced querying and sorting, but if you simply need to keep lists of information and find an item from them fast, either option will let you do that with ease.

Chapter 21

Get Artistic with Graphics Software

In This Chapter...

Ready-made graphics from clip-art libraries

Use paint programs for photo-quality artwork

Construct pictures layer by layer with a draw program

Create special effects with filters and WordArt

Get Artistic with Graphics Software

When it comes to adding artwork to text-based documents, or creating stand-alone graphics, there's very little you can't do on a PC. In this field of computing more than most others, the variety of software available is immense and the features you'll find cover most points between 'incredibly basic' and 'full multimedia capabilities'. But this is also an area in which the computer can do little to automate the creation process – an expensive graphics package won't make an artist of you if there's no raw material there to start with, it'll just give you more to learn about while you're struggling! So, as a gesture of support to the artistically-challenged, before we examine graphics programs themselves, let's take a look at another way you can add attention-grabbing graphics to your documents.

Easy art – clip-art collections

One of the main funds of graphics is the clip-art collection. Clip-art is a term used for pictures created by somebody else and sold (or given away) in collections, and many office suites and integrated applications come with their own library of clip-art (sometimes termed a 'gallery' in a burst of self-indulgence). The clips are usually grouped into categories such as Travel, Buildings, People, Sport, and so on, to make it easier to find what you want among the hundreds or even thousands of pictures in the collection, and there's usually a bunch of utilitarian signs and symbols such as maps of the world, road-signs, backgrounds, decorative borders, etc.

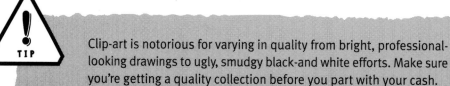

TIP Clip-art is notorious for varying in quality from bright, professional-looking drawings to ugly, smudgy black-and white efforts. Make sure you're getting a quality collection before you part with your cash. Remember, some of the best stuff will be on the back of the box, so if you don't like that, it's odds-on that you'll hate the rest!

How you work with clip-art will depend how it's organized: most of the many collections available on CD-ROM will have a viewer program included which loads the clips in the category you choose. When you've selected a clip, just use **Copy (Ctrl+C)** to copy it to the clipboard and **Paste (Ctrl+V)** to paste it into your document. Applications such as Microsoft Office and Microsoft Works come with their own clip-art collections and viewers to which you can add your own images to keep all your graphics and multimedia files catalogued.

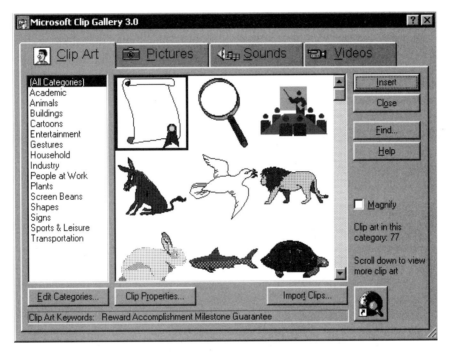

Cataloguing and inserting clip art with Microsoft ClipArt Gallery.

Do-it-yourself graphics software

If you prefer to create your own designs and images, there are inordinate amounts of software available, ranging from full-blown graphics suites and applications to smaller editing and retouching utilities, plus additional tools and filters to create effects. These fall loosely into two categories: paint programs and draw programs.

Paint programs

Let's start with the simplest. The Windows operating systems give you Paint, a basic example of a paint program with tools for drawing lines, squares, circles and freehand shapes, choosing colours, and erasing any part of the picture that didn't turn out quite as you intended it to. Paint works only with uncompressed bitmap (.bmp) images which makes the finished image-file considerably larger than the more popular compressed formats (.gif and .jpg) offered by other applications.

As a scratch-pad for ideas or uncomplicated diagrams, Windows Paint does the job, but as a serious graphics application it doesn't come close. Professional-level applications can cost hundreds of pounds, but at the cheaper end of the market you'll still get all the tools you need to create some stunning results. One example is the massively popular Paint Shop Pro from JASC (shown in the next screenshot). Like most graphics applications, Paint Shop Pro lets you edit multiple images at once and save them in any popular graphics format. You'll find similar drawing tools to those in Windows Paint, but with far greater capabilities: lines and joins can be smudged and blurred, irregular shaped areas can be selected for editing or copying, and a range of colour tools make it easy to swap colours in an image, apply tints, or adjust brightness and contrast.

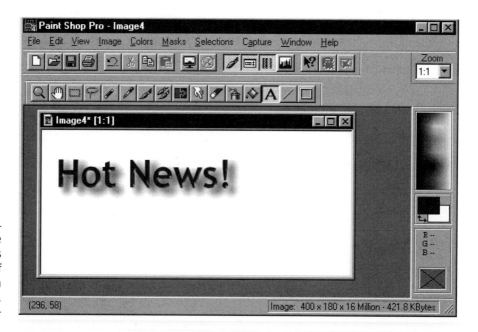

Comprehensive drawing tools and a range of special effects in Paint Shop Pro.

Although almost any graphics application will have scanner support that lets you scan an image straight into the program from a magazine or brochure, more expensive applications such as Adobe PhotoShop are designed for photo editing and manipulation, and often include an exotic collection of tools for retouching scanned photographs. Most will also have a range of built-in filters that let you emboss or posterize an image, add shadows, or apply deformations to photographs or to your own artwork, for example.

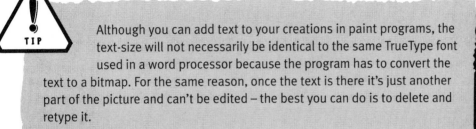

TIP

Although you can add text to your creations in paint programs, the text-size will not necessarily be identical to the same TrueType font used in a word processor because the program has to convert the text to a bitmap. For the same reason, once the text is there it's just another part of the picture and can't be edited – the best you can do is to delete and retype it.

Draw programs

Rather than working with photographs and creating photo-quality artwork, draw programs offer a slightly different method of creating drawings and pictures from scratch. Although you can create similar results in a paint application, draw programs offer much greater editing flexibility and are more forgiving to work with.

Draw programs load, create and save 'vector graphics' formats. Each element of the picture is a separate shape, such as a circle, square or freehand outline which can then be filled with colour, and each of these shapes remains an individual object. You can click on any object and drag it somewhere else, rotate it, or change its shape, without affecting any other part of the picture. The result of this object-oriented approach is that you can build complex pictures from the ground up by layering one object over another.

Because draw programs work with vector graphics formats, any object in the picture can be resized using the grab-handles that appear when you click the object, as shown in the screenshot below. Here's a few of the features you'll find in a draw program:

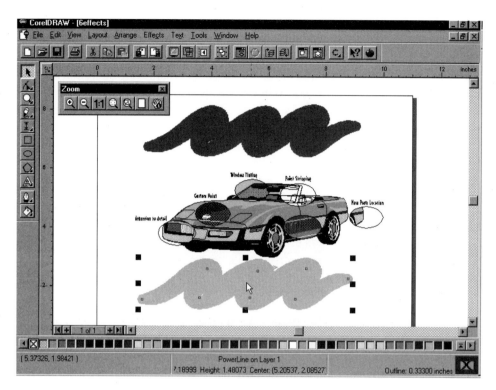

The popular and
powerful
CorelDRAW.

Send Forwards/Backwards – Because pictures are created by layering smaller sections, it's sometimes necessary to move items in front of or behind other items. These options are usually coupled with Send To Back and Bring To Front.

Grids and snapping – To help in precise drawing you can add a grid overlay to the 'canvas'. Snapping is a useful option to ensure that objects (especially squares) are perfectly aligned with each other by forcing them to jump onto the nearest gridline as if magnetized.

Full text-editing – Because these are not bitmapped graphics, text can be entered and edited freely as if in a word processor. Some draw programs even go so far as to include proofing tools for text such as a spellchecker and thesaurus!

Object grouping or linking – You can create groups of two or more objects in a drawing that will respond as a single object when cut, copied, moved or resized. This is usually done by using a selection tool to draw a dotted-box around the objects you want to select, but another option is often to hold Shift and to click each object separately.

Graphics filters & effects

Together with complete graphics creation applications, you can also find smaller utilities aimed at creating advanced effects or just having fun. A popular example is Kai's Power Goo, which lets you do unwholesome things to photos with tools such as smear, smudge and bulge, or even combine pieces of one photo with another. The results can be saved as a single image, or you can create multiple cartoon-like 'frames', and save the finished masterpiece in .avi video format.

For the more serious graphic designer, most graphics applications support filters. These are software add-ons, available from a variety of companies, that add extra processing and effect options to your application. Once installed, you can select the filter you want to use from a drop-down menu. Popular filter collections are Alien Skin's Black Box and Kai's Power Tools.

One final oddity in the field of graphics is WordArt, which lets you do weird things to perfectly innocent text while it's looking the other way. WordArt is a Microsoft applet that comes bundled with both Office and Works, although Serif TypePlus has similar capabilities as a stand-alone program.

You can insert a piece of WordArt into a document by selecting Insert/Object and choosing Microsoft WordArt from the list. A new toolbar will appear together with a small text-box. Type your chosen text into the box and then start getting creative. From the drop-down lists you can choose a font and size, and apply one of various shapes to the text. Toolbar buttons let you add outlines and shadows to the characters, stretch or compress them, tilt or swivel them, and add coloured or patterned fills.

Choosing a graphics application

The market-leader in draw-programs is CorelDRAW, though to refer to it simply as a draw program is a bit unfair – in addition to its drawing facilities, CorelDRAW can handle 3D image rendering, 3D animation. multimedia presentations, frame-by-frame video editing and includes sound and animation clips together with a 25,000-strong clip art library. If you're serious about computer-graphics, this package is worth its serious price-tag. Giving CorelDRAW a run for its money are Macromedia Freehand and Adobe Illustrator.

At the cheaper end of the draw-programs market are Serif DrawPlus and the modestly-titled but fuller-featured Corel Graphics Pack.

JASC's Paint Shop Pro is a hugely popular paint program, offering advanced editing and creation tools with a good array of filters and special effects. Adobe PhotoDeluxe is slightly less versatile, but more beginner-friendly. In the higher price bracket, Adobe PhotoShop is widely regarded as the 'must-have' graphics application.

To create and work with images of any format and enjoy bearable results you'll need a display that can handle at least 256 colours, but if you're working with photographs or you want to create photo-realistic artwork you'll need a 64-thousand colour (High colour) or 16.7-million colour (True colour) display. For intensive work with large graphics, 64Mb RAM should be regarded as an absolute minimum.

Chapter 22

Document Publishing with DTP

In This Chapter...

Add text and graphics to your pages

Arranging frames and linking text frames

Tips and tricks for successful desktop publishing

Can your word processor handle DTP?

Document Publishing with DTP

Desktop publishing packages (or DTP in geek-speak) are the applications that bring you newspapers, magazines, books, brochures, flyers and so on, the common link being an amalgamation of text and graphics in the same document. The main curiosity of DTP software is that text-editing and image-editing facilities are usually poor. This isn't as paradoxical as it seems; rather than aiming to replace the word processor and paint or draw program, DTP's role is to act as a receptacle for previously composed text and graphics, and to provide the necessary tools for final formatting and layout to construct a finished document.

Getting started with desktop publishing

The first move is to write your text. This can be done in a simple text-editor such as Notepad, but make sure you turn on the Word Wrap option – if you don't, you'll be tempted to insert carriage-returns at the end of a line to keep from scrolling too far across the screen, and these will appear as separate paragraphs in the DTP document. Preferably, use a more advanced word processor with a spellchecker so you can be sure the text is correct before you copy it to the DTP page, but save it in plain text (.txt) format.

JARGON BUSTER

Story

Text you import into a DTP document is referred to as a story, and a document can contain as many different stories as you want, just like a newspaper or magazine.

If you need to create graphics (other than basic lines, rectangles and circles), do these too but make sure you save them in a format your DTP program can open.

Adding your text to the page

The big difference between DTP programs and basic word processors is that text and graphics are placed in frames, which are rectangular dotted-line boxes. Text requires a text-frame, pictures need a graphics-frame. The tools for drawing these frames are frequently used so you'll normally find buttons for them on the toolbar.

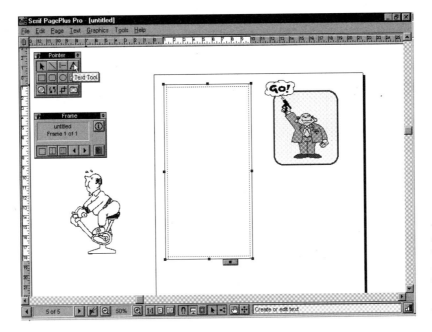

A text-frame, waiting for text, and a graphic waiting on the paste-up board.

To import your text, create a text-frame like the one shown in the screenshot above. You can create a single-column frame or choose to split the frame into two or more columns across the page and the text will be flowed from one to the next automatically. Then select the **Import Text** command and find and double-click the text-file you created. If your frame isn't large enough to hold all the text, move the pointer on to one of the grab-handles and stretch it.

If you're importing an especially long story, create a number of text-frames and link them together using the Link option. When frames are 'linked', the software knows it can use these frames for that story and will automatically flow the text from one frame to the next. If you have only one small frame and a very long story, it'll seem that most of your text has vanished until you create more frames!

Paste-up board

When you look at your DTP document in full-page view, the space you see around the document is known as the paste-up board. You can use this space to store imported stories and graphics to help you keep track of what you want to add, and drag them into the document itself when you're ready for them. In the same way, you can drag sections out of the document and onto the paste-up board if you want to rethink a layout.

As it appears in your document, the text looks pretty dull (and in full-page mode it looks tiny too). The next step is to zoom in so that you can read the text comfortably and to begin the formatting. The formatting options are similar to those found in any word processor – fonts, sizes, colours, bold, italic, and so on – but there are fewer shortcuts to selecting text. Although it's possible to type all your text directly into the document, it's this lack of flexibility that makes the import method preferable. In some DTP applications, you can double-click a block of text and format it in a fairly normal-looking window instead.

Importing pictures & graphics

You'll usually have an Import Picture option on the File menu for bringing in graphics in a similar way to importing text. First you'll have to create a graphics-frame for the image: in some applications the imported image will expand or contract to fit the size of the frame and look pretty distorted until you resize it; in others, the box will be automatically resized to fit the image. The idea of having separate text- and graphics-frames is a good one: you can move a graphics frame on to a text frame and (in most applications) the text will shift out of the way automatically and skirt around it, as in the next screenshot. This is known as text-wrapping; in most cases the application will handle it automatically, but in others you'll have to make the settings for each graphic yourself. You can usually choose whether the text surrounding the picture should form a square edge to it or follow its contours, and you may have extra options to let you choose how much space there should be between picture and text.

JARGON BUSTER

Serif and sans-serif fonts

In a serif font the characters have small hooks or ornaments (called serifs) which add a slightly informal air to the text; this sort of font is commonly used for block text. Sans-serif fonts don't have these ornamental flourishes and are mostly used for headings.

Drawing tools are usually basic, but you'll have the full range of colours to work with (including 'Clear' to make text or a graphic object transparent) and a few DTP applications support the Pantone colour-chart for precise colour-matching.

NewsLetter

"Of course" said Sharon in a disappointed voice "it's entirely possible that nobody will recognize me. After all..." she eyed the cartoon rabbit quizzically "...I'm merely a thinly disguised pastiche on one of literature's most famous women." She walked towards the grassy knoll in the center of the grounds, still wondering where on earth she'd seen the rabbit before. He wasn't wearing a top hat this time. And shouldn't he have been a real live rabbit? It made little difference to the puzzle...

"What did you say your name was?" she demanded irritably. "I didn't actually introduce myself" replied the rabbit tearfully "but as you ask, I'm Roger, and I'm looking for Jessica."

Sharon twisted her ponytail absently. She didn't know a Jessica... But she did know a

Sandy, worse luck. They had been best friends at Rydell High until Sandy stole her boyfriend. Danny was such a rat! She sighed in remembrance. It was a world away from this mysterious garden and the cartoon rabbit. (How did she get here? Last thing she remembered she'd been in a Chrysler, as big as a whale, heading down the Atlanta highway, looking for a love getaway.) She was puzzled by the rabbit's reply. "Two what? Are there more rabbits in this garden?" She thought of Lenny. If only he could be here. He liked Rabbits, and loved hearing George talk about them. "Of course" said Sharon in a disappointed voice "it's entirely possible that nobody will recognize me. After all..." she eyed the cartoon rabbit quizzically "...I'm merely a thinly disguised pastiche on one of literature's most famous women." She walked towards the grassy knoll in the center of the grounds, still wondering where on earth she'd seen the rabbit before. He wasn't wearing a top

Some of the formatting options available, including text-wrapping and drop-shadows.

Hints for successful DTP-ing

When laying out your document it's important to keep your eye on the ball.
Although you can do all kinds of clever stuff with rotated text, coloured boxes and
frame-outlines, text-wrapping and so on, a page overloaded with interesting effects
becomes very difficult to read – in other words, less is more! That being said, here
are a few tips and effects you can use:

- Place headlines or pictures in a box with a thin black outline and add a drop-
  shadow to it by placing a grey rectangle underneath it shifted slightly
  downwards and to the right or left. This has the effect of pushing the text-box
  towards the reader.

- Add shadows to text by making a copy of the text frame, changing the colour
  of the copied text and placing this behind the original but slightly off-centre.

- Place a small amount of justified text inside a circle (created using the circle-
  tool) and use text-wrapping to wrap it to the inside edges of the circle. You
  can heighten the effect by making the circle and its border clear so that all you
  can see is the text itself.

- Choose your fonts carefully and try to stick to a maximum of four in a
  document. A serif-font such as Times New Roman makes an easy-to-read
  body-text typeface; headlines often work well with sans-serif fonts such as
  Arial, but a more fancy font adds an informal air if it doesn't appear too often
  on the page.

- In brochures intended to sell a product, rotate pictures of the product a few
  degrees (between 6° and 10° should do it) rather than keeping them square on
  the page, to make them look friendlier and more appealing. Use the Crop tool
  to remove any large expanses of distracting background, and use a paint or
  draw program to improve photographs (by adding the clear blue sky always
  found in holiday brochures, for example).

- If you want each page to follow a similar layout (for example, four columns
  with your company logo at the top), you can create a master page with each
  item in position which will be used as a template for each document-page to
  save you repeating all the same moves for each page.

Leading and kerning

Two typesetting terms that pop up a lot in DTP. Kerning is adjusting the space between two characters. This is often used in headlines to tidy up irregular-looking spacing, but you can use it to great effect to give a headline or subhead a much tighter look. Leading (pronounced 'ledding') is the vertical distance between lines of type (measured in points).

DTP versus word processor

Modern word processors are becoming more like desktop publishing programs all the time: you can flow text into columns, create drawings, import graphics, place pictures or text into frames, put the frames anywhere on the page, and much more. So why not just use a word processor instead?

In fact, there's no reason why you shouldn't. If you've already got an application like Microsoft Word or Lotus WordPro that includes drawing tools and frames, you can create remarkably sophisticated documents by placing everything into frames and moving these where you want them. Here's a few of the major differences and additions you'll find in a dedicated DTP program – if these don't matter to you, and you've got a good word processor already, stick with it.

Grouping – Once you've placed multiple frames, pictures and objects where you want them and juggled around with the Send To Back and Bring To Front commands to layer everything correctly, you can group these items together as one to ensure you can't move one frame accidentally and ruin all your careful work. Word processors treat frames and drawing-objects as separate items.

Snapping – Precise alignment of frames is made simple with snapping which forces the edges of a frame to jump to the nearest gridlines. You may even be able to type in exact co-ordinates and sizes for each frame.

Stacking – You can stack as many frames and objects as you like one on top of the other regardless of their contents. A word processor will give you little choice about how different items can be stacked and which will remain visible.

Crop and Rotate – DTP programs allow you to crop pictures – chop out unnecessarily large areas of background and so on. They will also allow you to rotate frames a degree at a time (watch out for programs that allow rotation only in huge 90° increments).

Choosing a DTP application

At the professional end of the market, you'll find Quark Xpress on most publishers' computers. (These computers are usually Apple-Macs, but Quark Xpress actually runs faster on a PC of comparable specifications!) Slightly cheaper is Adobe PageMaker.

There's a huge price difference between the best and the rest: in the more affordable price-bracket are Microsoft Publisher, and the amazingly full-featured Serif PagePlus. The Serif Publishing Suite bundles PagePlus with DrawPlus and TypePlus (mentioned in the previous chapter) as a self-contained graphics and DTP package, and is well worth a look.

Successful DTP is harder to achieve on a standard 15-inch monitor: ideally you want as much as possible of your page to be visible while you work on it, without zooming out so far as to make the text unreadable. If you expect to do a lot of DTP work, regard a 17-inch monitor as the minimum and a 20-inch monitor as a safer bet.

As with any graphics-related application, the more RAM you have the better. You could find the going a bit slow with less than 48Mb.

Chapter 23

Multimedia & Business Presentations

In This Chapter...

Working from preset styles and templates

Inserting text, graphics and animation effects

Arranging slides to create a complete presentation

Advanced effects and control with multimedia authoring

Multimedia & Business Presentations

Presentations are not far removed from the desktop publishing documents we looked at in the previous chapter. The same combination of text and graphics is there, but presentations are primarily meant to be shown on screen rather than printed on paper, so visual impact takes priority. Text tends to be in the form of headings, subheadings and bulleted lists or very short paragraphs. The name 'presentations' gives a clue to the main purpose of this software: any time you have to get up in front of a bunch of people and announce a marketing strategy, explain a business plan or introduce a new product, you can create a new presentation that includes all the charts, graphs and pictures you need to show in the correct order.

Making a start with business presentations

Presentations are multiple-page files, with all the pages usually following a similar colour-scheme and style. The pages are called slides and the finished presentation is often referred to as a slide-show. You can print out all the slides on paper as handouts for your audience, or convert them to transparencies for overhead projectors or 35mm slides for slide-projectors.

There are several ways to start work on a new presentation. You could start with a completely blank sheet, but unless you're both artistic *and* patient this isn't a favourite option. Method two is quite the reverse: programs such as Microsoft PowerPoint include whole presentations designed for particular uses (such as 'Communicating Bad News', with a mournful black background). All the slides you need are prepared and arranged in an order that should get the point across clearly. Just select the one that fits, read the tips and explanations on each slide and then replace them with your own text.

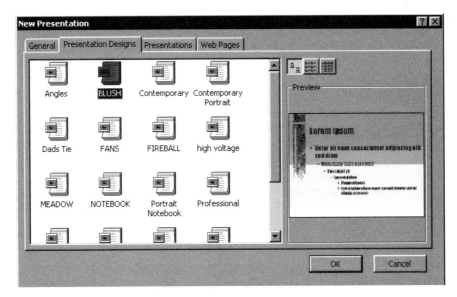

Choosing a style template for your presentation.

The third, and usual, way to begin is by choosing a style template for the presentation from those included with the program. There's usually plenty to choose between and most applications include a preview window like the one shown in the screenshot above. If you later decide you don't like the choice you made here, you can apply a different style to your slides with just a couple of clicks.

> **TIP**
>
> Although the finished slide-show will often be shown full screen, it's usual to work with a smaller representation of each slide (roughly 50 or 60 per cent) so that you can see the complete layout and still reach all the application's editing tools. At any time you can test a single slide, or the slides you've added so far, to make sure the layout looks okay.

Once you've selected a style for the presentation, you'll usually see another dialog asking you to choose a layout for the first slide. Every time you want to add another slide to the presentation the same dialog will appear. The first slide would normally be a title-slide, but other options might contain mixtures of charts, tables, bulleted lists, clip-art and so on. You can also choose a blank slide that follows the selected style but has no layout detail.

Adding text & graphics

If you pick a slide with a predefined layout, you'll see several boxes that say 'Click here to add a title' or 'Click here to insert clip art', and it really is as simple as that! Just click and type in the text you want, or choose a piece of clip art from the library when it appears, and then move onto the next slide.

Although you'll rarely see a slide that says 'Click here to add a movie' you can add almost any type of sound, animation or video file you want to by using the Insert menu. In some programs the file can be set to play as soon as its slide is displayed; in others you'll have to click or double-click its icon to play it.

Many presentations tools are similar to those you'd find in a DTP application: if you want to add more text to a slide just create a text-box and start typing, and you can also add simple shapes and drawings.

Adding effects & transitions

Any item on a slide is referred to as an object, whether it's a text-box, drawing, chart or clip art. Each of these objects can have its own animation settings. First, you can choose which objects should be on the slide when it first appears, which should arrive later, and in which order they should arrive. These are known as 'build' settings (because you're gradually building the slide) and one of the most fun aspects of builds is choosing how the objects should arrive. For example, you might choose to have each item in a bulleted list sliding on to the screen separately one after the other, accompanied by the sound of screeching tyres. Or you could choose to build the slide's title by making the letters appear one at a time to the sound of a typewriter.

If you want to add different effects to each line of a bulleted list, you'll have to place each line in a separate text-box. Otherwise the effect you choose will apply to the whole list.

In programs designed for creating business presentations, your build choices will be limited; for example, you won't usually be able to specify a delay in seconds before an object appears, or choose how long it will take to fully appear. Similarly, you won't be able to specify how long it should stay on the screen and how long it should take to disappear. However, you'll usually be able to make sure the next object doesn't appear until you click the mouse.

Preparing the slide-show

Once you've created all the slides you need for your presentation, the final step is to turn them into a working presentation. If you used a preset 'fill-in-the-blanks' presentation most of this work has been done for you. You might even have been so well prepared that you created the slides in the correct order, but there's still a couple of things you might need to do.

You'll usually be able to switch to a different view that shows thumbnails (tiny pictures) of each slide, similar to the one shown in the next screenshot. To rearrange the order in which they'll be shown, just click on one and drag it to where you want it in the list. This is also the place where you'll fine-tune the running of the show; you can choose how long each slide should remain on the screen, or opt to change slides with a mouse click, and choose transitions for each slide – special effects such as fades, wipes and dissolves – that determine how each slide should replace the previous one.

Business presentation packages also have pages for speakers' notes to help you plan the entire presentation as you go. With the notes printed out, you can run the slide-show to time how long you need for each slide, and have these timings automatically entered.

Running the show

One of the useful features of slide-show creation is that you can plan contingency actions. However carefully you think you've skirted it, some bright spark is sure to ask the question you didn't want to answer. Business presentation programs allow you to hide slides (that is, leave them out of the slide-show) and bring them in only if you need to. By the same token, someone is sure to ask a question about something you dealt with four slides back, so it helps to be able to return to that slide easily.

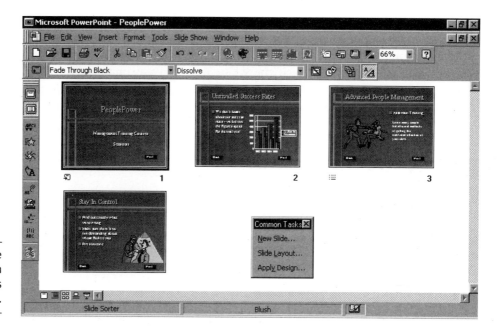

To make this possible, business presentation programs have a small control-bar (either permanently displayed or optional) that allows you to pause the slide-show, move to the next or previous slide, or choose a slide from the list. You may have other options such as drawing on the screen as if it were a chalkboard, and adding notes about points raised during your presentation. If your presentation is supposed to be completely self-contained you can choose to hide the pointer. This can be useful for presentations intended to run continuously and without supervision, perhaps on a PC sitting in the entrance hall of a trade-fair.

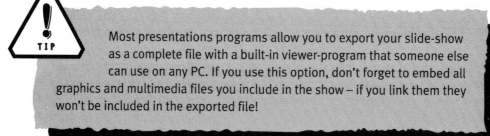

Most presentations programs allow you to export your slide-show as a complete file with a built-in viewer-program that someone else can use on any PC. If you use this option, don't forget to embed all graphics and multimedia files you include in the show – if you link them they won't be included in the exported file!

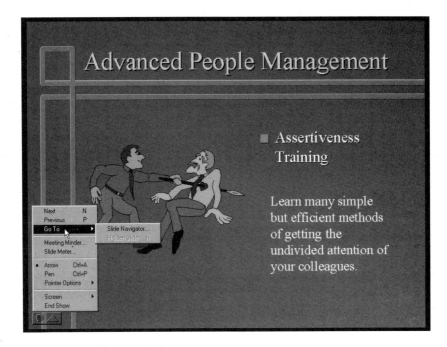

Using the mouse to control a business presentation.

Multimedia authoring

A separate, and rather more expensive, branch of presentation software is the multimedia presentation program, and the process is grandly referred to as multimedia authoring. Most of the creation methods are identical to those covered above, but the slide-shows created are not intended for business presentations so there's rarely any support for speakers' notes, rehearsals and so on. Here's a quickfire list of just a few extras you *will* find in a full-featured multimedia presentations program:

Full multimedia support – Not only can you add sound, MIDI and video files to these slides, you can choose exactly when they play and for how long.

Button controls – You can add clickable buttons to slides that might give you a choice of slides to view next, play a multimedia clip, run a program, or reveal some other object not yet visible on the page. A single button might even start several of these actions at the same time. In some programs a button doesn't even have to look like a button – you could use a piece of clip art instead, or nominate several different areas of a large graphic to act as buttons.

Advanced builds – Any object on the slide can have its own builds. You can choose exactly when the build begins and ends, and you can 'unbuild' a slide by removing objects after a specified time using different effects to produce fully animated presentations.

Timeline – The timeline is a common fine-tuning tool. Each object on the slide has its own line on this page calibrated in seconds according to the length of time the selected slide will remain on the screen. By placing markers at different points along the line you can choose exactly when an object's build should start and end (or when a media clip should play) and when the object should begin to disappear. Instead of having to specify an order for the different objects to appear, you can ensure that particular things will happen at exactly the same time.

Multimedia presentations are commonly used on the CDs attached to magazine covers to let you see the contents of the CD and install software with a single click. Just starting to appear, though with limited popularity so far, are CD-ROM-based magazines that use multimedia presentations instead of paper and let you click buttons instead of turning pages.

You can export multimedia presentation files as stand-alone programs, as you can with business presentation packages, so the possibilities for use are endless: if you're a musician or artist you could mail out multimedia CVs; if you're selling software you could create interactive demos or tutorials for your program; if you're running an exhibition you could create an interactive map of each floor of the building to help people find their way around.

Choosing presentations software

In the business presentations sphere, Lotus Freelance and Microsoft PowerPoint have got it pretty sewn up between them; both are well-featured, reasonably priced and bundled with their respective office suites. They offer good-quality preset presentations and templates together with ease of use, and both applications can also publish slides directly to the Web in HTML format (turn to Chapter 35 for more on HTML).

Multimedia authoring packages can cost as much as a couple of multimedia notebook PCs with all the trimmings. Top of the heap is Macromedia's

Authorware, aimed at professional users. At the SoHo (Small office/Home office) end of things, the top choice is Gold Disk's accurately-named Astound. Similar in style is Macromedia Flash, a simple-to-use application for creating interactive multimedia animations to publish on the Web.

You'll need 32Mb RAM to cover a simple business presentation running under Windows 98, but think in terms of over 64Mb minimum to run a multimedia authoring program, or a business presentation containing animations, sound, and other multimedia elements. More RAM will ensure sharper builds and transitions, and help to ensure that actions intended to occur at the same time (such as transition, a sound clip and an animation) really *do* happen together.

Chapter 24

Office Suites – The All-In-One Solution

In This Chapter...

Pros and cons of office suites and works applications

Applications and requirements for the top office suites

Features of the popular works applications

Office Suites – The All-in-One Solution

After reading the last few chapters you may have built up a list of two or three or more types of software you want. If so, this is a good time to pause and consider another option – the integrated application or office suite. Instead of buying a bundle of separate software titles, you might be able to buy a single package that contains everything you need at a significantly lower price.

What's the difference?

Office suites are often recognizable by the use of the word 'Office' somewhere in their names (and an extra digit in their prices!). They are collections of fully featured applications, all of which are also available separately. The main selling point of office suites is that the total package costs a lot less than you'd spend buying each item individually, and a few extras are thrown in for good measure. Office suites have added features that help you organize your work, share information between the different programs, and start or switch between each application easily.

Works applications are also known as integrated applications, and often include the word 'Works' in their names. Works software consists of a single all-in-one application that fulfils the same role as an office suite in a smaller, cheaper package with fewer features. These are primarily aimed at non-professional users.

Office suite pros & cons

The main plus-point in buying an office suite is price: if you need two or more professional-level applications you'll probably save money by buying the suite and gain another couple of applications and a few handy extras into the bargain.

The second benefit is that each application will be carefully integrated – throughout the suite, the menus and toolbars follow a common layout to make the learning easier. This integration also helps you work with several applications at once; for example, you can quickly import names and addresses from the database into the word processor to create a mail merge, or copy a chart from the spreadsheet into a business presentation.

On the negative side, office suites are huge beasts: a typical installation will take up over 100Mb of hard-disk space, and the power of these applications requires a lot more resources than a works package. If you only need one top-level application (such as a good word processor) and you can make do with simpler spreadsheet and database features, there's no point in wasting money and hard-disk space on the full suite.

Works applications pros & cons

There are several simple reasons for the popularity of works software: the package is compact, light on disk space and resource requirements, easy to use, and gives great visual results. As with office suites, each element is tightly integrated with all the others and uses common tools and menus. Although a works package is a single application, it has a multiple document interface (MDI) so it's easy to have a database open in one window and a spreadsheet in another to compare or copy information between them. Finally, integrated applications are between a quarter and a third of the price of an office suite.

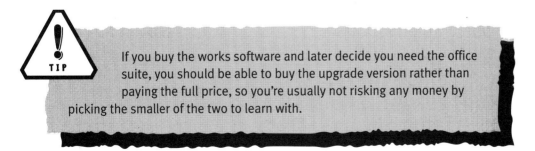

If you buy the works software and later decide you need the office suite, you should be able to buy the upgrade version rather than paying the full price, so you're usually not risking any money by picking the smaller of the two to learn with.

There's not much to be said against works packages – because they're cheap it's not really a disaster if you decide you need something more powerful six months later. Indeed, you may decide you just need to buy a more powerful word processor, but continue to use the other elements of the works application. However, you may want to consider the issue of compatibility: if you use an office suite at work, you won't usually be able to open the same files in your integrated application.

Which office suite?

The two big players in the office suites league are Microsoft Office and Lotus SmartSuite. In both, the applications provided are powerful and feature-filled, but generally manage to be easy to understand and use. Here's a closer look at what each contains:

The Microsoft
Office shortcut
bar.

Microsoft Office

This is the top-selling office suite, which helps to explain why most of its constituent applications also hold the top spot. The current version, Office 97, is available in three flavours: Small Business Edition, Standard, and Professional, aimed at different types of user with varying requirements.

All three editions contain Word (word processor), Excel (spreadsheet), and Outlook (personal organizer). The Small Business Edition also includes the Publisher desktop publishing package and Financial Manager for preparing financial reports, forecasts, and accounts. The Standard and Professional editions also include PowerPoint (business presentations), and the Professional edition also adds Access (programmable, relational database) to its list of applications.

Each program can be accessed from the Shortcut Bar (shown in the screenshot above) if you choose to install it. This docks at one edge of the screen and works just like the Windows Taskbar. You can add your own shortcuts to any program or folder as buttons on the bar, and choose whether the bar should slide out of the way when not in use. Another addition is Binder, which lets you group collections of related documents together in one file and switch between them in a single window. You can also install Camcorder, a clever little program that can record all your mouse movements, key-strokes, and screen actions, and play them back as a movie – ideal for creating software tutorials or demonstrations. You'll need 40 to 60Mb of disk space to install the Standard version, and a minimum of 32Mb RAM. To work with two or more Office applications at the same time with reasonable speed, 64Mb RAM is a more realistic target.

Lotus SmartSuite's SmartCenter bar with drop-down 'drawers'.

Lotus SmartSuite

SmartSuite comes in one all-in version. Applications include WordPro (word processor), 1-2-3 (spreadsheet), Freelance (business presentations), Organizer (personal organizer), and Approach (programmable, relational database). In a similar vein to Microsoft's Camcorder, SmartSuite includes ScreenCam, along with a separate ScreenCam Player.

SmartSuite has a similar Shortcut Bar to that used by Office, which follows a file-cabinet metaphor: various 'drawers' open to display shortcuts to applications, shortcuts to documents, help-file icons, an address-book, and an appointments calendar. Another quick-start option is SuiteStart, which places icons for each application in the Windows Tray.

A typical installation of Lotus SmartSuite will swallow 110 to 120Mb of hard-disk space, similar to the space required by Office 97's Professional edition. For anything other than occasional use, 48Mb RAM will keep everything running without irritating pauses.

Which works application?

The two leaders in this field are Microsoft Works and ClarisWorks. Once again, Microsoft's offering is the biggest seller by virtue of being bundled with most new PCs as part of the ubiquitous 'free software' package.

Microsoft Works

When you first start Works you're presented with a simple dialog from which you can choose the type of document you want to open or create. Works includes a word processor, spreadsheet, draw program and flat-file database, all of which are easy to use and give good results.

Like all office suites and integrated applications, Works offers a huge collection of templates that you can use to get started on particular types of document, or you can use a WorksWizard, which asks you simple questions about the design, layout, and content of the document you want to create and puts it together for you. You also get several extra applets including WordArt and Draw to add graphics to your documents. Works will run quite happily with 16Mb RAM under Windows, although 32Mb will give improved speed, particularly if you have several documents open at the same time.

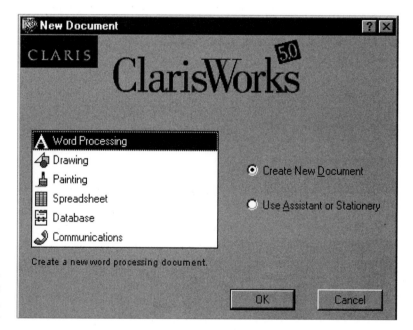

Starting work in
ClarisWorks.

ClarisWorks

As with Microsoft Works, running the application will present you with a dialog to choose what type of file you want to create. Either double-click a document type or check the 'Use Assistant' box to work from one of a range of templates. The usual four components are included – word processor, spreadsheet, flat-file database, and communications terminal – but the inclusion of the two graphics elements makes for great flexibility. In general terms, the features included are superior to those found in Microsoft Works, and the Paint component could teach Windows' Paint a thing or two. ClarisWorks also supports simple slide-show presentations, which can use any type of information the package can handle. Despite its increased capabilities, ClarisWorks will grab even less hard-disk space than Microsoft Works.

Choosing office suites & works software

If you need two or more powerful, full-featured applications, an office suite is a sensible and cost-effective choice. It'll take a large chunk of disk space, but if these are the applications you'll spend most of your time using this shouldn't matter too much. Make sure you've got a bare minimum of 32Mb RAM to keep things moving at a reasonable speed.

Microsoft Office is the clear winner in terms of popularity and sales, and it's neat, fast and easy to use. However, if you need a database you'll have to pay extra for the Professional edition (or buy one separately). Lotus SmartSuite grabs extra points for including a high-quality database as standard, but tends to be slower in use than Office. Corel Office Professional rivals SmartSuite in price and features, and is worth considering if you require a suite including database facilities at a more reasonable price than Microsoft can manage.

Integrated applications are far more streamlined in terms of disk space and RAM requirements, and are ideal for anyone who needs to produce quality results quickly and simply. ClarisWorks is a great, flexible package and is also available in a ClarisWorks for Kids version. Microsoft Works comes in a good second, and even if it came bundled with your new PC it has the benefit of getting you onto the upgrade path for Microsoft Office if you have a sneaky feeling that's what you might need at some point in the future.

Chapter 25

Quickfire Software

In This Chapter...

Organize appointments, reminders, and contacts

Manage your accounts and do your banking online

Extract files from compressed archives and create your own

Use uninstall utilities to banish deleted software effectively

Quickfire Software

Over the last few chapters we've looked at some of the most common types of software found on the average computer. But in the PC world, as elsewhere, if there's a market for it, there's a product to meet that market – the list of software categories is almost endless. So, moving into quickfire mode, here's a brief rundown of some of the other tricks your PC can do if you feed it the right software!

Personal organizers

The software personal organizer is the computerized version of those portable leather binders that contain diaries, addresses, notes, and so on. The big differences are that the software version is usually cheaper (no leather involved!) and isn't as easy to lose. In geek-speak, the software organizer is known as a PIM, short for Personal Information Manager. One of the best (and coincidentally the cheapest) is Starfish Software's Sidekick, closely followed by Lotus

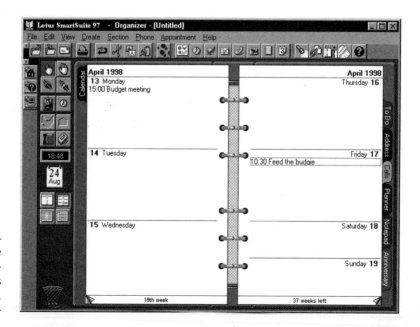

Separate tabbed book-sections in Lotus Organizer.

Organizer (included in the SmartSuite office package), which follows the FiloFax metaphor right down to animated page-turning.

The features you'll find in these programs include an appointments diary, address and phone book, To Do lists with priority planning, year-planners, and automatic phone dialling. You can also set a reminder alarm to sound at a preset interval before appointments, and print out your appointments in organizer-sized pages to carry around in your leather-bound version.

Microsoft produces Outlook, which it inexplicably calls a DIM (for Desktop Information Manager). Leaving aside the obvious 'dim outlook' references, the program itself is a powerful combination of contact manager, appointments calendar and reminder system, task manager, and email/fax utility. Outlook is available as a stand-alone program, but it also comes bundled with all editions of Microsoft Office and integrates well with other Office applications to help you organize your projects and files.

Accounts software

For simple accounting, such as adding up lists of income and expenditure, a spreadsheet program will do just fine. But if you have monthly and quarterly standing orders, income paid directly into your bank account, loans and other complications, it's easy to lose track of your finances between one statement and the next. Accounts packages allow you to enter all these details once and will then keep the totals balanced for you automatically – your only job is to remember to enter everything necessary at the start.

The two biggest players in accounts software are Intuit's Quicken and Microsoft Money. Both are cheap, and can track a variety of bank, building society, and credit-card accounts, as well as loans and investments. Of the two, Quicken is the winner for its ability to handle VAT, but if you don't need to bother about VAT you'll find Microsoft Money easier to set up and use. For professional accounting, one of the most popular programs is Sage Instant Accounting.

One major advantage of Microsoft Money is online banking. If you have a modem and your bank provides this service, you can simply dial-in at any time of the day or night and pay bills, check your balance, download a statement, and transfer funds from one account to another.

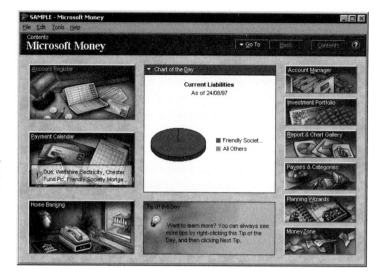

Account
management
and online
banking with
Microsoft
Money.

File compression utilities

Once in a while you'll come across files with the extension .zip, particularly if you download files from the Internet or BBSs (bulletin board services). These are known as archives, and they contain one or more files compressed to take up less space (and thus download faster). There are actually several other types of archive, which are less frequently encountered, with the extensions .lzh, .arj, .tar and .arc, but each works in a similar way.

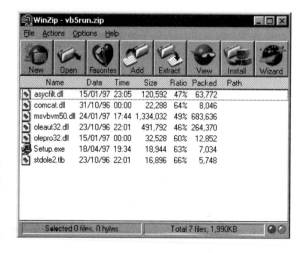

WinZip
displaying the
contents of an
archive.

In order to decompress (extract) the files from an archive, or create new archives, you need a program capable of working with these files, and the undoubted leader in this field is the shareware utility WinZip from Nico Mak Computing (shown in the screenshot above). WinZip can create and open many different types of archives and integrates itself neatly with Windows for single-click archive extraction.

Memory doublers

As we've established, RAM is a vital part of your computer and you'll want quite a lot of it to run modern operating systems and applications at a decent speed. But RAM costs money and seems to be needed in increasingly large quantities. So enterprising software companies have started to produce so-called 'memory-doubling' software which, in theory at least, makes your computer work as if you had twice as much RAM installed.

The results of using RAM-doubling programs vary according to the situation, but there have been some amusing stories about a few outright failures: not only could they not provide you with any extra memory, they were *using* memory themselves while they were running – a net result of less memory! True, these programs were pretty cheap, but if something doesn't work it's expensive at any price! This isn't to imply that all RAM-doubling software is a washout; some will certainly be more effective than this. But why take the chance? If more RAM is what you need, buy more RAM – at least you know it works!

Uninstall utilities

Although most of the software you install has its own uninstall program or routine in case you change your mind, the results of an uninstall are not always perfect. Some files may be left behind even if no other program uses them, folders and shortcuts may not be removed, and orphaned entries in the Windows Registry that slow down your system may remain.

Programs such as Quarterdeck's CleanSweep do a much better job by watching your system during software installations and noting every change that takes place. If you later decide to uninstall a program, just click the Uninstall Wizard button. You can view logs of all the files and settings to be removed, and the program will backup all removed files in case you change your mind a second time and want to put the program back again.

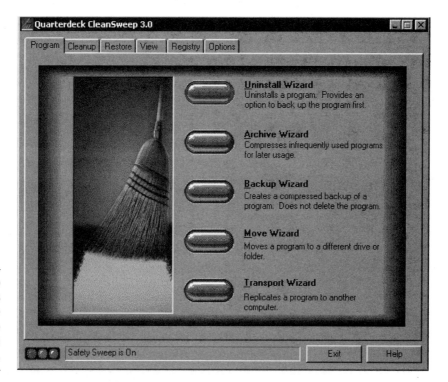

CleanSweep
monitors
software
installations to
make thorough
removal easy.

All the removals carried out by CleanSweep and similar programs are *intelligent*: files required by another program on your system will be left intact, along with any documents you created yourself and saved into the program's folder.

Shareware

The shareware concept is a way of selling software, rather than a type of program. Because the cost of packaging, advertising and distributing programs is so high, many software programmers and companies allow their creations to be distributed on disks found on computer magazine covers, on bulletin board services, or the Internet.

The benefit for the consumer is that you get the opportunity to try out the software before you pay for it. A secondary benefit is that the software is usually a lot cheaper than a similar commercial product would be, but the understanding is that you *should* pay for it if you choose to continue using it beyond the specified trial-period – this is known as *registering* the software. In return for registering you'll normally receive the latest version plus a manual, and be entitled to free upgrades as they become available. Here's a few variations on the shareware theme:

Postcard ware – Instead of actually paying for the software you send the author a picture-postcard of your town. The author still retains full copyright.

Freeware – Once again the author retains copyright, but this time it doesn't even cost you a postcard to continue use!

Nag-ware – Every time you use the software, a dialog appears that will only vanish if you click on it. It may appear every few minutes, forcing you to either give up or register.

Time-limited – This is a common method employed by larger companies eager to generate sales of more expensive applications. You have full use of the program for a period of around 30 days, after which time it will cease to run.

Save-disabled – The software has no nag-screens or time-limitations, but you won't be able to save or print any of the documents you create.

Beta versions – As new software is developed it goes through various phases. Beta versions are early but working versions of products given away free for anyone to use at their own risk. The benefit for the user is that of having the very latest software; in return, you're expected to report any bugs or problems you experience with the software in some detail to help the company identify and eradicate them. This is known as beta-testing.

Part Four

Surfing the Internet

In This Part...

Meet the Internet

Making the Connection

Exploring the World Wide Web

Exchanging Messages by Email

Newsgroups – The Human Encyclopaedia

Grabbing the Goodies with FTP

Chat & Talk without Moving your Lips

Finding Stuff on the Internet

Safety on the Internet

Building your own Web Site

Chapter 26

Meet the Internet

In This Chapter...

Find out what the Internet *really* is

Discover some of the great things you can do on the Net

Meet the six most popular areas of the Internet

What do you need, and what does it cost?

Meet the Internet

Before you can really get excited at the prospect of 'getting on the Internet', it helps to have some idea of what it really is, what you can use it for, and (I hate to say it) how it works. So let's kick off by looking at how the Internet is organized, and at some of the ways you can use it. I'm also going to introduce most of the technical-sounding stuff you'll need to know in this chapter – it's all quite painless, and this appetizer should leave you hungry for the main course.

What is the Internet?

The technical explanation is that the Internet is a giant, worldwide computer network made up of lots of smaller computer networks. As with any network, these computers are connected to one another so that they can share information. Unlike most networks, though, the vastness of the Internet means that this information has to be passed around using modems and telephone lines rather than an office full of cables.

But all that's just hardware, and it's probably not making your mouth water. Instead, let's zoom in on that word 'information' – the key to the *real* Internet. The types of information these computers can share covers a huge (and expanding) range – pictures, sounds, text, video, applications, music, and much more – making the Internet a true multimedia experience. Anyone can connect their computer to the Internet and gain instant access to millions of files, browse around, or search for some specific item, and grab as much as they want while they're there.

People power

The other aspect of the real Internet is people. All the information you'll find is put there by real people, often simply because they want to share their knowledge, skills, interests, or creations with anyone who's interested. The people themselves may be companies keen to promote their products; organizations such as universities, charities and governments; or individual users like you and me.

Along with people, of course, comes communication, and the Internet is a great communications system. You can exchange messages (email) with other users, hold conversations or online meetings by typing messages back and forth or by actually sending your voice over the Internet using a microphone instead of a telephone, and take part in any of over 30,000 discussion groups on every subject under the sun.

The Internet can be immensely useful, or just plain fun. Here is a taste of some of the things you can do on it:

● Control robots and movie cameras on other continents while the live camera footage is beamed straight to your desktop.

● Book a skiing holiday online, and check the snow conditions in your chosen resort with up-to-the-minute pictures.

● Explore 3D 'virtual reality' worlds, and play games with people visiting the same world.

● Manage your bank account, transfer money, and pay bills at any time of the day or night, or do all your shopping in online supermarkets and stores.

● Download the latest versions and updates of your software long before they hit the shops, or be among the first to use brand new 'test editions' of major software titles (beta releases).

JARGON BUSTER

Download

The act of copying a file from one distant computer across a network of computers and telephone lines to your own hard disk. The opposite term is 'upload' – copying a file from your own disk to a remote computer.

The popular Internet services

What you've just read is a general taste of what's on offer on the Net, but all the things you want to do (or get, or see) will be scattered around the world on different computers. In other words, these computers offer the services you want to use. The Internet is made up of a bundle of different services, but here's a quick look at the six most popular:

- **Email** – Email is the oldest and most used of the Internet services with millions of messages whizzing around it every day. Most email messages are just ordinary text, but you can attach almost any type of computer file you want to send along with it (such as a spreadsheet or a small program), and encrypt the message so that no-one except the intended recipient will be able to read it.

- **The World Wide Web** – This service, often known simply as the Web, has had so much publicity and acclaim that you might think it *is* the Internet. In fact it's the Net's new baby, which was born in 1992. It's a very lively, gurgling baby though, packed with pictures, text, video, music, and information about every subject under the sun. All the pages on the Web are linked together, so that a page you're viewing from a computer in Bristol might lead you to a page in Tokyo, Brisbane, or Oslo with a single mouse-click. Many individual users have their own pages on the Web, as do multinational companies, political parties, universities and colleges, football teams, local councils, and so on.

- **Newsgroups** – A newsgroup is a discussion group that focuses on one particular subject. The discussion itself takes place through a form of email, but the big difference is that these messages are posted for the whole group to read and respond to. You can join any group you like from a choice of more than 30,000 with subjects ranging from spina-bifida support to alien landings, and James Bond films to Turkish culture.

- **Chat** – This isn't chat as in 'yakety-yak' – more 'clickety-click'. You can hold conversations with one or more people by typing messages back and forth which instantly appear on the screens of everyone involved. Some recent chat programs allow 'whiteboarding' (drawing pictures and diagrams in collaboration), private online conferences, and control of programs running on someone else's computer.

- **Voice on the Net** – This *is* chat as in 'yakety-yak'. As long as you've got a soundcard in your computer, and a microphone plugged into it, you can talk to anyone in the world just as you do with the telephone (provided they're online and have a soundcard and microphone too). So why not use the telephone? Your Internet connection will be a local call, letting you hold these conversations for as little as 60p per hour. Compare that with the cost of a direct-dialled call to New York (roughly £12.60 per hour) and you've got a pretty good reason!

- **FTP** – The computers that make up the Internet hold a combined library of millions upon millions of files. The FTP system lets you look inside directories on some of these computers, and copy files straight to your hard disk just as if you were copying files around between your own directories.

Although other services exist, these are almost certainly the ones you'll be using most (and you may use nothing but email and the World Wide Web – the services are there if you want them, but you don't *have* to use them).

Understanding Internet addresses

So the Internet is big, the computers that form the Internet are counted in millions, and yet somehow all that information manages to get wherever it's supposed to go. But how does that tiny, helpless file find its way from deepest Ohio to your own computer all by itself? The answer is in much the same way that an ordinary letter manages to arrive at your house: it has an address attached to it. Every single computer on the Internet has a unique address, called its IP address, which consists of four numbers separated by dots, such as 194.72.6.226.

Domain names – the easier way

Of course, if you need to connect to one of these computers you'll need to know its address. But don't panic! You don't have to remember streams of meaningless numbers, there's an easy way. As well as this numerical IP address, each computer is given a much friendlier **domain name**. Going back to that IP address I mentioned just now, the domain name of that computer is the much more memorable **btinternet.com**. Best of all, most of the Internet programs you'll be using will store these addresses for you so that you can just recall them with a few mouse-clicks.

> If you're ever in that awkward situation where you have to say a domain name out loud, use the word 'dot' to replace the dot itself, such as 'bcc dot co dot uk' for **bbc.co.uk.**

Dissecting domain names

Apart from being a lot easier to remember than numbers, domain names can also tell you whose computer you're connected to, what type of organization it is, and where the computer is located. The 'who' part is usually easy: given an address like **www.channel4.com**, the computer almost certainly belongs to the Channel 4 television company. It's the bits that come after that (known as top-level domains) which can be interesting, so here's a few to look out for:

Domain	Used by
.co	A commercial company
.com	Until recently, a US company; now also used for companies outside the US
.ac	An academic establishment (college, university, etc.)
.edu	Another college or university domain
.gov	A government agency
.mil	A military establishment
.net	An Internet access provider
.org	An organisation (as opposed to a commercial company)

US domain names stop at this point (this is one way to identify them as US addresses). Most of the domain names in other countries have an extra dot and a country code tagged on to the end; for example, you'll see **.uk** for United Kingdom, **.se** for Sweden, **.fr** for France, **.jp** for Japan, and **.fi** for Finland.

What do you need?

To begin with, of course, you'll need a computer. Contrary to popular belief, it doesn't have to be a stunningly fast or powerful computer: you'll get more from the Net's multimedia aspects with a soundcard and 2Mb RAM on your graphics card, but don't feel you'll be missing out if you don't have either.

You'll also need a telephone line, with a socket fairly close to your computer so that you can plug your modem into it. For a pound or two you can buy an adapter to let you plug a phone and a modem into the same socket, and this is a worthwhile investment. If you find yourself spending a lot of time online, you might want to consider installing a second phone line just for Internet access so that people can still telephone you while you're surfing, but that's a decision for later.

> **TIP**
>
> If you have the Call Waiting service on your phone line, make sure you turn it off every time you go online (by dialling #43#) and back on again when you've finished (*43#). Otherwise an incoming call at the wrong moment could disconnect you and cancel anything you were doing.

Finally, you need a way to connect to a computer that's a part of the Internet. There are hundreds of companies in the UK which specialize in selling dial-up links to the Internet via their own computers, so the next step is to choose one of these companies and set up an account with it.

This leads to the main decision you have to make: do you want an account with an Internet access provider (often just called an IAP) or with an online service?

Online services & Internet access providers – what's the difference?

The most important thing that access providers and the major online services have in common is that both let you connect to the Internet. It's the way they do it and what else they have to offer that makes them different, along with their methods of deciding how much you should pay. To round off this chapter, and help you decide which path to follow, let's take a look at the two options and the pros and cons of each.

Online services

You may have heard of the 'big three' online services, America Online (AOL), CompuServe (CSi), and the Microsoft Network (MSN). In fact, if you buy computer magazines you're probably snowed under with floppy disks and CD-ROMs inviting you to sign up to one or other of these. One of the main plus-points of online services is the speed and ease with which you can sign up: just this one disk and a credit- or debit-card number are all you need.

But it's important not to confuse online services with the Internet itself. An online service is rather like an exclusive club: once you subscribe you'll have access to a range of members-only areas such as discussion forums, chat rooms, and file libraries. Although you can 'escape' to the Internet from here, non-members can't get in. You won't find much in the members-only areas that you can't find on the Internet itself, but online services do have the combined benefits of ease of use, online help if you get lost, and a friendly all-in-one program from which you can reach everything you need. Although the Internet certainly isn't the chamber of horrors that some newspapers would have you believe, there's little control over what gets published there; online services carefully filter and control their members-only content, making them the preferred choice for getting the whole family online.

Online services probably sound pretty good so far – you get the Internet, and a bit more. So what counts against them? Mainly the price. The major online services charge a low monthly subscription fee of around £6 which includes five free hours online. This is ideal for a light user, but five hours per month can pass in a flash if you plan to surf the World Wide Web or download files. Once your free hours are used up you'll be paying extra for subsequent hours, so the online service could be an expensive option. Most services offer alternative pricing plans though, so try to gauge how much time you're likely to spend online as you use your free first month, and change to a different plan if necessary before the second month begins.

Finally, online services tend to offer Internet access as an 'extra' – when you step out on to the Net itself you might find that the information doesn't travel as quickly as it does on a direct Internet connection.

Internet access providers

An Internet access provider gives you direct access to the Internet, plain and simple. When you dial in to your access provider's computer, you'll see a message on the screen that tells you you're connected. Instead of clicking buttons to access areas of the Internet as you would with an online service, you'll start your email program or web software yourself and do whatever you wanted to do.

The IAP account has several valuable points in its favour. First, you'll only pay a single monthly charge of around £12 (plus your telephone bill, of course), with no restrictions or charges for the time you spend online. Second, you'll have far greater flexibility in your choice of software. Most access providers will give you a bundle of programs when you sign up, but you don't have to use them – try some of the programs mentioned in this book until you find the ones you're happy with.

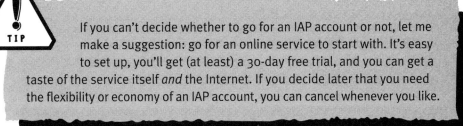

If you can't decide whether to go for an IAP account or not, let me make a suggestion: go for an online service to start with. It's easy to set up, you'll get (at least) a 30-day free trial, and you can get a taste of the service itself *and* the Internet. If you decide later that you need the flexibility or economy of an IAP account, you can cancel whenever you like.

IAPs have their negative side too, of course. Until quite recently, as soon as you'd signed up your IAP would be vanishing into the distance, clutching your money and giggling insanely at the mess it had left you in. My first account took 14 hours of slaving over a hot keyboard before I finally managed to connect. However, with growing competition among companies eager to part you from your cash, most now send out preconfigured software (all the complicated settings are made for you) so that you can just install it and connect. Many also provide free telephone support in case you get stuck. Sadly, some IAPs still haven't caught on, so you'll have to ask a few searching questions before committing yourself.

Phone calls & connections

Whether you've chosen to hook up with an IAP or an online service, you'll have to dial in to that company's computer every time you want to go online. This means that if you connect for 20 minutes you'll pay for a 20-minute phone call (although it's your modem using the line, not your phone). So how much are these phone calls going to cost?

The good news is that you should always be able to connect through a local phone number. At the time of writing, British Telecom's local call rate (per minute) is 4p peak, 1.7p cheap, and lp at weekends. Add your access number to your 'Friends & Family' list and you'll save at least 10 per cent. And if your phone bill is high enough to qualify for the PremierLine scheme you'll be able to knock off another 15 per cent. Prices change, of course, and different phone companies' charges will vary, so make sure you check these details before relying on them!

Chapter 27

Making the Connection

In This Chapter...

How to pick the best IAP for your needs

The six essential questions to ask an IAP before subscribing

Choosing and signing up with an online service

Reaching the Internet from your online service software

Making the Connection

Now that you've made the all-important decisions, this is where things start to happen – after following the instructions in this chapter you'll be online and ready to start exploring the Internet. Right now you're just two steps away from connecting: you need to choose and subscribe to an access provider or online service, and install the software it supplies.

Choosing an access provider

Okay, it's decision time again! There are countless IAPs in the UK, and the number is increasing all the time. You'll find a list of several dozen UK access providers in the Directory at the back of this book, and the first step is to whittle this lot down to a shortlist of half-a-dozen or so, using these tips as a guide:

- **Are they local?** You need to know the location of the computer you're dialling into, which is sometimes called a 'node' or a PoP (Point of Presence) – it's the crucial factor in determining whether you should consider an IAP. You *must* be able to dial in using a local phone number! Many IAPs have nodes all over the UK, so you can probably include them on your list. Others might be smaller companies with, perhaps, a single computer in Blackpool. This could be ideal if you live in the Blackpool area, but if you're in Torquay, forget it.

- **Did someone recommend them?** If a particular IAP can offer you local access *and* you've heard positive things about them (in terms of reliability of connection, good telephone support, etc.), it's definitely worth adding them to the shortlist.

The next step is to get on the phone. Any company that takes itself seriously will be happy to answer your questions, so pick a promising candidate from your shortlist and give them a ring. If you can't get straight answers to the following questions, either press the point harder or cross the company off the list (and don't let them blind you with jargon either!).

Asking questions – six of the best

First, check any details from the list at the back of this book, and any that were given to you by another subscriber, to make sure they're accurate and up to date. Then work your way down this list:

1. **What is your monthly subscription fee?** A common price is about £12 including VAT. If this IAP charges more it's worth asking what else it provides that other companies don't. Many companies offer reductions if you pay annually.

2. **Do you charge extra for the time I spend online?** The correct answer to this is 'No'. If the company gets this one wrong, go no further!

3. **What is your fastest modem connection speed?** If you have a 56Kbps modem (see page 52) you don't want to connect at a slower speed. Many companies have upgraded their systems to handle 56Kbps modems, but there are still a few around that haven't.

4. **Will you give me a PPP connection?** The two options are PPP or SLIP. You *don't* want a SLIP connection, but a few companies still use them. A PPP connection is faster, and it's easier to set up (especially in Windows 95 and later).

5. **When is telephone support available?** You'll almost certainly need telephone support at some point, so make sure it'll be available when you're most likely to be using the Internet (for example, during evenings and weekends).

6. **Do you provide preconfigured connection software for my computer?** Many companies will ask you questions about your computer and operating system, and then send you software that's ready to install with all the tricky stuff taken care of. (The software may be on CD-ROM, so be sure to check this if you don't have a CD-ROM drive!) Find out if the connection will be easy to set up on your computer, and whether the technical support phone line will be able to talk you through the process if you get stuck.

When you've found the access provider of your dreams, you're almost ready to subscribe. But first...

Choosing your username

When you start a subscription with an access provider, you'll be identified by your choice of username (some companies refer to it as a user ID, logon name, or member name). You'll need to quote this when you call the support line with a question, and when you log on to the provider's computer to surf the Internet. More importantly, it forms the unique part of your email address. If you were to start an account with **mycompany.co.uk**, your email address would be *username*@**mycompany.co.uk** and this is the address you'd give out to friends and colleagues so that they could send you email. As an example, my username is **rob.young** and my IAP is **btinternet.com**, so my email address is **rob.young@btinternet.com**.

> **TIP**
>
> You don't have to use your own name, you can use just about anything you want. It'll be easier for you (and other people) to remember if it doesn't contain numbers, but there's nothing to stop you having a username like **jellyfish** or **zapdoodle**, as long as your IAP doesn't already have a zapdoodle on its subscriber list.

The rules on usernames vary a little between providers. In general, they can't contain spaces (in common with any Internet address), but dots, dashes, and underscores are usually okay. Most importantly, it must be a username that hasn't already been scooped by another subscriber to your chosen access provider, so it's worth putting a bit of thought into a second and third choice in case your first is unavailable.

And now... subscribe!

It's time to get back on the phone to your chosen provider to subscribe. An account will be set up for you, but exactly what happens next will depend on the individual access provider:

- You may receive a disk in the post that's preconfigured for your computer, operating system, and account. If so, follow the instructions that accompany it and it ought to be as easy to install as any other program.

- You may receive a disk of software and some documentation that tells you how to install it and how to configure your computer. Make sure that you read the documentation before you start.

Your provider should have included instructions telling you how to install the software, so this should be a pretty painless step. All the same, keep that support-line number handy, just in case! You should also receive a wonderfully technical-looking list of IP addresses, domain names, and so on, to accompany the software package. Even if your software is preconfigured for quick and easy installation, make sure you hang on to this list for reference – you'll need to enter some of these settings into other software you use in the future.

Choosing an online service

This should be an easy choice to make – not only is the list of online services fairly short, but most offer a free 30-day trial, so you've got nothing to lose by picking one at random. All the same, it's better to make an informed choice if you can so let's take a look at the four most popular UK online services, CompuServe, America Online, The Microsoft Network and Virgin Net.

CompuServe

CompuServe (CSi) has more than a thousand different 'forums' covering just about every conceivable subject, including finance, news, TV listings, articles from popular magazines, travel information, film and music previews, along with interactive chat rooms. Many retail companies have their own forums offering advice and product support, and business users will probably find more to interest them on CompuServe than the other online services. The program used to move around this lot is smart and fairly formal, although not quite as easy to get to grips with as America Online, and it's also unaccountably slow in use. UK-specific content is sparse for a company with so many UK users, but CompuServe is trying to improve things in this area. Parents can download a program called Cyber Patrol to restrict kids' access to areas of CompuServe itself or the Internet, and limit the time they can spend online.

Even if you haven't opted for an online service account, there are many good programs available that you can use with an Internet access provider account to restrict access to different areas of the Net, or to particular types of information. You'll learn about those programs in Chapter 34.

America Online

In comparison with CompuServe, America Online (AOL) has a very sunny, friendly, and informal feel to it, making it a good choice for children and inexperienced computer-users. The content provided is very similar to that of CompuServe, but business content, although growing, is still far from comprehensive. However, you will find plenty of UK content, and parental controls are very good, although there's currently no way to restrict how long your kids stay online. One major bonus is that AOL allows an account-holder to have up to five different member-names (AOL calls them screen names), which means that you can have five email addresses: for families or small businesses, this allows everyone to receive their own personal email. More importantly perhaps for families, it also means that you can prevent your children from accessing certain areas of the service without restricting your own use.

The Microsoft Network

The Microsoft Network (or MSN) has a very stylish and modern appearance, contrasting massively with CompuServe's formality and AOL's friendliness. It also requires Windows 95 or 98, and a reasonably fast computer. MSN is 'cool', and unashamedly American, and this follows through to its content which is geared more towards entertainment than information. The service is primarily split into four main areas – OnStage, Essentials, Communicate, and Find. The first of these splits into 'channels', with each aimed at users with particular types of interest. Parental controls do exist, but they don't match those of CompuServe or AOL –

you'll have to grab Junior by the ear and drag him away. Also in contrast with CompuServe and AOL, MSN is an Internet-based service: when you decide to explore the rest of the Net's offerings you should find that the information travels much more speedily than the other services can manage.

Virgin Net

Virgin is the foremost UK-only online service, and is positioning itself halfway between IAPs and the 'usual' online services. Although a range of online content is included (chiefly information and entertainment rather than business), Virgin's aim is to provide the easiest possible access to the Internet, which includes a 24-hour telephone support line. Like MSN, Virgin Net is an Internet-based service, so you'll notice little difference in speed when you move from the members-only areas to the Net itself. Being a UK-only company, its content is UK-specific, with news, sport, chat rooms, and ready-sorted links to places of interest on the Internet.

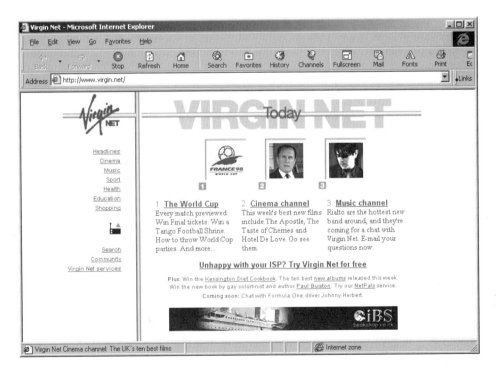

Virgin Net's simple Internet-based service.

How do you sign up?

The first job is to get your hands on the free connection software. These disks are regularly glued to the covers of computer magazines so you might have dozens of them already. If you have, make sure you pick the most recent. If you haven't, either take a trip to your newsagent or phone the services and ask them to send you the correct software for your computer and operating system. You'll find their contact details in the Directory at the back of this book.

That was the tricky part! Somewhere on the disk you'll be told how to start the program that signs you up, and the whole process will advance in simple steps. The exact routine will vary from one service to another, so I can't tell you exactly what to expect, but here are a few tips to bear in mind:

● Somewhere on the disk packaging you'll find a reference number (perhaps on a small label, or perhaps on the disk itself). Don't lose it – you'll have to enter this to start the sign-up procedure.

● Make sure you've got your credit card or debit card handy. Although you won't be charged for the first 30 days' access, you'll have to enter the card number and its expiry date when you sign up.

● You may be asked to choose a dial-in phone number from a list covering the whole country. If so, make sure you choose a local number. (In some cases the software will work out the best dial-in point for you, based on your own phone number, or it may use a local-rate 0345 number.)

● After you've entered all the necessary personal details, the program will dial up the service's computer and set up your subscription automatically. Within a minute or two you'll receive a username and password. These are your entry-ticket, so write them down and keep them safe.

> **!** **TIP**
>
> Keep your password private. Never include it in an email message, don't type it in front of anyone, and make sure you change it at least once a month (you'll find instructions for this online). If possible, use a combination of letters and numbers at least five characters in length. And don't even consider using the word 'password' as your password!

How do you use an online service?

When you dial into your online service and log on using your username and password (which should happen automatically), you won't actually be on the Internet. However, by clicking a few buttons you can enter the service's own chat rooms or join in with its activities and forums, and you'll find plenty of assistance if you get lost, both in help files and online support areas.

The main AOL desktop lets you click on a button to access the Internet or to use one of its own private services.

Access to the Internet itself will be marked as one of the areas you can visit, and you'll probably see a big friendly button marked 'Internet' that will take you there. Once you've clicked that 'Internet' button, you're surfing the same Internet as everyone else. In most cases, any extra software needed for Internet access was installed when you signed up, but you might be told that you need to download it yourself. If so, another button will probably appear and all the spadework will be done for you while you sit back and wait.

Chapter 28

Exploring the World Wide Web

In This Chapter...

Discover the amazing World Wide Web

Learn to use your Web browser and start surfing

Keep track of where you've been and where you're going

Find out what else your multi-talented browser can do

Exploring the World Wide Web

The World Wide Web is the jewel in the Internet's crown, and the whole reason for the 'Internet explosion'. A large part of the Web's popularity lies in its simplicity: you don't have to be a networking genius or a computer whiz to use it, you just point with the mouse and click. In this chapter you'll learn the basics of finding your way around this powerful system.

Understanding the Web

The 'pages' you find on the Web contain a scattering of words that are underlined and highlighted in a different colour from the text around them. Just move your mouse-pointer on to one of these words or phrases (you'll see it change into a hand with a pointing finger as you do so) and click. Hey presto, another page opens. The entire 'web' of pages is being 'spun' by millions of people at the rate of several million new pages per day, and every page includes these point-and-click links to many other pages.

Web page

A 'page' is a single document that can be any length, like a document in a word processor. Pages can contain text, graphics, sound and video-clips, together with clever effects and controls made possible by new programming languages such as Java and ActiveX.

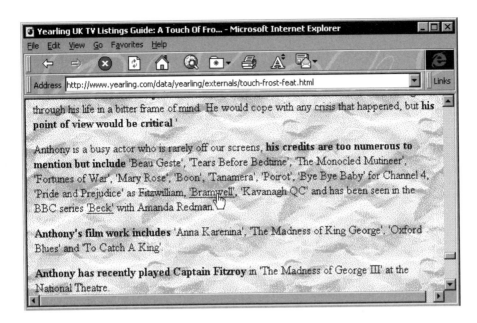

To jump
between pages,
move the
pointer over the
coloured
hypertext and
click to open the
related
document.

This system of clickable text is called **hypertext**, and you've probably seen it used in Windows help-files and multi311311media encyclopaedias as a great way to make cross-references. The Web takes the system a few stages further:

- The hypertext links aren't restricted to opening a document stored on the same computer: you might see a page from the other side of the world.

- A hypertext link doesn't have to be a word or phrase: it might be a picture that you click on, or it might be a part of a larger picture, with different parts linking to different pages.

- The link doesn't necessarily open a new web page: it might play a video or a sound, download a compressed archive (.zip file) or an application, display a picture, run a program... the list goes on.

The Web is made up of millions of files placed on computers called web servers, so no-one actually owns the Web itself. The Web servers are owned by many different companies, which rent space (or give it away for free!) to anyone who wants to put their own pages on the Web. The pages are created using an easy-to-use, text-based language called HTML (HyperText Markup Language) which you'll learn about in Chapter 35.

Once the newly created pages are placed on the web server, anyone who knows their address can look at them. This partly explains why the Web became such an overnight success: a simple page can be written in minutes, so a web site can be as up-to-date as its creator wants it to be. Many pages are updated daily, and some might even change every few minutes.

Web site

Web site is a loose term that refers to the pages belonging to an individual or company. A site might be just a single page that your Auntie Ethel wrote to share a nice fruitcake recipe, or it might be hundreds of pages belonging to a supermarket chain.

What do you need?

To view pages from the World Wide Web you'll need a program called a browser. In fact, this single program will be the most powerful weapon in your Internet arsenal, and not just because you'll be spending so much time on the Web – you can use this program to handle many of your other Internet-related tasks as well. Although there are many different browsers available, the most capable is Microsoft's Internet Explorer.

If you're connected through one of the online services you'll usually be able to use Internet Explorer. Both MSN and CompuServe provide Explorer by default (although you can switch to something different if you want to); America Online and Virgin Net will let you use any browser that takes your fancy.

If you're using Windows 98, Internet Explorer is already installed on your computer and you should see its icon on your desktop. (If you can't see this icon, double-click the icon labelled **Connect to the Internet** instead, and answer the questions using the information you were given by your service provider.) A copy of Internet Explorer is also included with Windows 95, but it won't necessarily be installed on your system. You can install it yourself from the **Windows Setup** tab of Control Panel's Add/Remove Programs applet, but you may prefer to install the more recent version included on the CD-ROM accompanying this book.

Start browsing

When you open Internet Explorer, the first thing you'll see is your **Home Page**. Unlike a word processor or a paint program, the browser must always display a document, and until you tell it which document you want to look at it will display the document set as its Home Page. By default, Explorer is set to display the first page of Microsoft's Internet site.

On Internet Explorer's toolbar you'll see a button with the word 'Home' beneath it. Wherever your Web-wanderings lead you, you can just click the **Home** button to return to your Home Page any time you want to.

Anatomy of a web page

Now it's time to get acquainted with the basic workings of the browser and with the Web itself. If you look at the Home Page you should see several hypertext links (underlined, coloured text). Move your mouse pointer on to any link that looks interesting and click. When you do this, your browser sends a message to the server storing the page you want. If everything goes according to plan, the server will respond by sending back the requested page so that your browser can display it.

Spend a little time following links to see where they lead. Don't limit yourself to clicking textual links alone, though – many of the pictures and graphics you see on a page will lead somewhere too. Take a look at the page shown in the following screenshot from *Time Out* magazine's site (**http://www.timeout.co.uk**) for a few clues to the type of thing you'll find on a web page.

- **Plain text** – Ordinary readable text. Click it all you like – nothing will happen!

- **Hypertext link** – A text link to another page. Hypertext links will almost always be underlined, but their text colour will vary from site to site.

- **Image** – A picture or graphic that enhances a web site. Like most pictures, it paints a thousand words, but it won't lead anywhere if you click it.

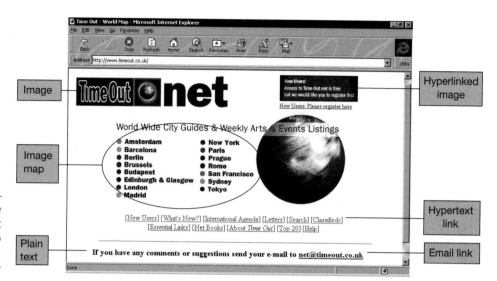

Some of the elements that make up a web page.

- **Hyperlinked image** – Clicking this image will open a new page. In most cases a hyperlinked image will look no different to an ordinary image, but it may have a box around it that's the same colour as any hypertext links on the page.

- **Image map** – An image split up into small chunks, with each chunk leading to a different page. In this case, every city name is linked to its own page listing forthcoming events in that city.

- **Email link** – Click on this link and your email program will open so that you can send a message to the web page's author. The author's address will be automatically inserted into the message for you.

The tricky thing can be to tell an ordinary image from an image that links somewhere. The solution is always to watch your mouse-pointer: when you move the pointer on to any link (image or text), it will turn into a hand shape with a pointing finger. In a well-constructed image map, the different areas of the picture itself should make it clear where each link will lead.

Charting your course on the Web

By now, you should be cheerfully clicking links of all descriptions and skipping from page to page with casual abandon. The problem is, you can only move forwards. If you find yourself heading down a blind alley, how can you retrace your steps and head off in a different direction? This is where the browser itself comes to your rescue, so let's spend some time getting acquainted with its toolbars and menus.

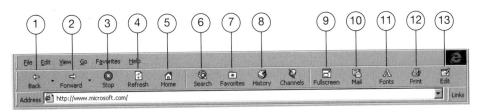

Internet Explorer's button bar and address bar.

1. **Back** – Clicking this button will take you back to the last page you looked at. If you keep clicking, you can step all the way back to the first page you viewed this session.

2. **Forward** – After using the Back button to take another look at a previously-viewed page, the Forward button lets you return to pages you'd viewed later. This button will be greyed-out if you haven't used the Back button yet.

3. **Stop** – Stops the download of a page from the web server. This can be useful if a page is taking a long time to appear and you're tired of waiting, or if you clicked a link accidentally and want to stay where you are.

4. **Refresh** – Clicking this tells your browser to start downloading the same page again. See 'Sometimes things go wrong...' later in this chapter for reasons why you might need to Refresh.

5. **Home** – Opens your Home Page, mentioned earlier in this chapter.

6. **Search** – Opens a small frame at the left of the browser window from which you can choose a web search site and search for pages by subject or keyword. You'll learn about searching for information on the Internet in Chapter 33.

7. **Favorites** – Displays the contents of your Favorites list (see below).

8. **History** – Opens a list of sites you've visited recently, letting you revisit one with a single click (see 'Retracing your steps with History' later in this chapter).

9. **Fullscreen** – Expands Internet Explorer's window to fill the screen, covering the Windows Taskbar and everything else, and leaving just a tiny toolbar visible.

10. **Mail** – Opens a menu from which you can run your email or newsreader software, or opens a blank form to send an email message.

11. **Font** – Clicking repeatedly enlarges or reduces the size of text on the page. You can do this in a more controlled way by selecting **View | Fonts**.

12. **Print** – Prints the current page. You can choose your printer and change printing options from the File menu.

13. **Links** – If you double-click on this word, a new button bar will slide across revealing links to Microsoft's own web site and some useful jumping-off points for your web travels. To hide the Links bar again, double-click the word 'Address' to its left.

One useful extra tool is a facility to search the page you're viewing for a particular word or phrase. Open the **Edit** menu, choose **Find (on this page)...** (or press **Ctrl+F**), and type the word you're looking for.

Many happy returns – using Favorites

One of the most powerful Explorer tools is the **Favorites** system (known as Bookmarks or Hotlists in other browsers). Any time you arrive at a page you think might be useful in the future, you can add its address to your list of Favorites and return to it by opening the menu and clicking the relevant shortcut. To add the current page to the list, click the **Favorites** toolbar button and click **Add to Favorites**. A small dialog will appear giving a suggested title (you can replace this with any title you like to help you recognise it in future). To place the shortcut directly on the menu, click **OK**.

You can also organise your shortcuts into submenus to make them easier to find. Click the **Create in...** button and **New Folder**, then type a name for the folder. Click the folder into which you want to save the new shortcut and click the **OK** button to confirm. (If it ends up in the wrong place, don't worry! Select **Organize Favorites** from the Favorites menu and you'll be able to move, rename and delete folders and shortcuts, and create new folders.)

When you want to reopen a page that you added to your **Favorites** list, either select Favorites from the menu bar and click the name of the site on the menu, or click the Favorites toolbar button to open a clickable list in a small frame in the left of the browser's window (shown in the screenshot opposite).

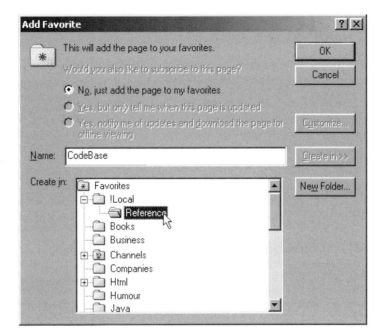

Add a new shortcut to a **Favorites** submenu by clicking the submenu's folder followed by the OK button.

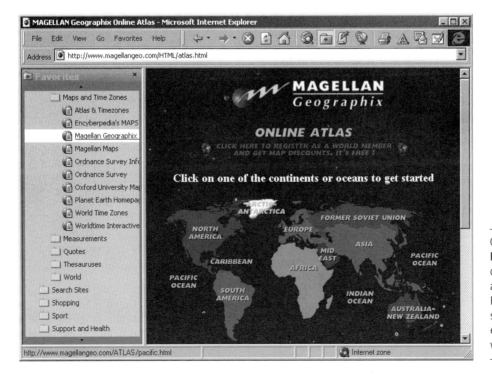

Click the **Favorites** button on the toolbar and your Favorites list stays within easy reach while you surf.

Retracing your steps with History

The History list provides a handy way of finding an elusive site that you visited recently but didn't add to your Favorites list. Internet Explorer maintains this list automatically, and you can open it by clicking the **History** button on the toolbar. The sites are sorted by week and day, with links to the various pages you visited on each site placed into folders. You can revisit a site by finding the week and day you last viewed it, clicking the folder for that site and clicking the page you want to see again. You can choose how long Explorer should store details of visited pages by clicking your way to **View | Internet Options | General**.

The address bar & URLs

Every page on the World Wide Web has its own unique **URL**. URL stands for Uniform Resource Locator, but it's just a convoluted way of saying 'address'.

You'll also notice URLs at work as you move from page to page in Explorer, provided you can see the toolbar (if you can't, go to **View | Toolbars | Address Bar** to switch it on). Every time you open a new page, its URL appears in the address bar below the buttons. You can also type an URL into the address bar yourself – just click once on the address bar to highlight the address currently shown, type the URL of the page you want to open, and press Enter. For example, if you want to look at today's peak-time TV listings, type: **http://www.link-it.com/tv** into the address bar. In a similar way, if you find the URL of a site you'd like to visit in an email message or word-processor document,

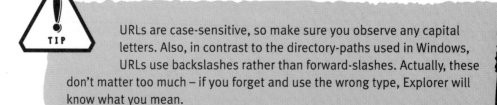

TIP URLs are case-sensitive, so make sure you observe any capital letters. Also, in contrast to the directory-paths used in Windows, URLs use backslashes rather than forward-slashes. Actually, these don't matter too much – if you forget and use the wrong type, Explorer will know what you mean.

copy it to the clipboard using **Ctrl+C**, click on the address bar, and paste in the URL by pressing **Ctrl+V**.

Understanding URLs

You'll come into contact with a lot of URLs on your travels around the Internet, so it's worth knowing what they mean. As a specimen to examine, let's take the URL for the Radio 1 web site at the BBC and break it up into its component pieces. The URL is: **http://www.bbc.co.uk/radio1/index.html**

http://	This is one of the Internet's many protocols, and it stands for HyperText Transfer Protocol. It's the system used to send web pages around the Internet, so all web page URLs have the **http://** prefix.
www.bbc.co.uk	This is the name of the computer on which the required file is stored (often referred to as the host computer). Computers that store web pages are called web servers and their names usually begin **www**.
radio1	This is the directory path to the page you want to open. Just as on your own computer, the path may consist of several directories separated by back-slashes.
index.html	This is the name of the file you want. The **.html** (or **.htm**) extension indicates that it's a web page, but your browser can handle any number of different file types.

Sometimes things go wrong...

Things don't always go smoothly when you're trying to open a web page. To begin with, the server might not be running and you'll eventually see a message telling you that the operation 'timed out' – in other words, your browser has waited a minute or so for a response from the server and doesn't think anything is going to happen. If the server *is* running it might be busy. In this case, you might get a similar result, or you might get a part of the page and then everything seems to stop dead. You may be able to get things moving by clicking the **Refresh** button on the browser's toolbar, forcing your browser to request the document again, but be prepared to give up, visit a different web site, and try this one again later.

And then there's the Mysterious Vanishing Page syndrome. Although all web pages contain links, sometimes the pages those links refer to no longer exist and you'll see an error message instead. The reason is simple: on the perpetually changing landscape of the World Wide Web, pages (and even entire sites) move elsewhere, are renamed, or just disappear. In fact, the average lifespan of a site is a mere 90 days! Anyone putting links to these sites in his or her own pages has no way of knowing when this happens other than by regularly clicking through all the links to check them. The endless arrivals and departures are a fact of Web life, but also a part of it's magic.

- *So how does anyone find what they're looking for on the Web? Turn to Chapter 33 to find out.*

Saving files from the Web

There are two groups of files you can grab from the World Wide Web – those that are a part of the web page itself (such as an image), and those that aren't. The second group is huge, covering applications, sound files, videos, spreadsheets, ZIP files, and a whole lot more. Although the methods of saving *any* file are straightforward enough, that second group is going to lead us into a few complications, so let's begin with the first.

Saving page elements

Saving the web page's text – To save the text from the entire page, open the **File** menu and choose **Save File As...**. Select **Text File** from the **Save as type** list and choose a name and location for the file. Alternatively, if you only need a portion of the text on the page, you can highlight it using the mouse, copy it to the clipboard by pressing **Ctrl+C** and then paste it into another application.

Saving the web page's source – The *source* of a web page is the text you see in your browser plus all the weird codes added by the page's author that make the page display properly. These codes belong to a language called HTML (HyperText

Markup Language) which you'll learn about in Chapter 35. To save the HTML source document, follow the same routine as above, but choose **HTML** from the **Save as type** list. (If you just want to have a peep at the source, right-click the web page's background and choose **View Source** from the context menu.)

Saving images from the page – To save an image, right-click it and choose **Save Picture As**. You can also save the background, a small image file that the browser tiles to fill the entire viewing area. You can right-click the background and choose **Save Background As...** to save the image file to the directory of your choice. You can also copy images or the background to the clipboard with a right-click, so that they are ready to paste into another application.

Saving other types of file

Although most of the links you find on web pages will open another page, some will be links to files that you can download (don't worry – it should be obvious, and if it isn't, just hit the Cancel button as soon as you get the chance!). As I mentioned earlier, this is where things get a bit more complicated. Come what may, the file must be downloaded to your own computer before you can do anything with it, but how you choose to handle the download will depend upon what you want to do with the file itself. The browser may be multi-talented, but it can't display every type of file that exists!

However, what it can do is to launch an **external viewer** to display the file. An external viewer is just a slightly technical way of saying 'another program on your computer'. Two vital elements are required for your browser to be able to do this:

● You must have a program on your hard disk that can open the type of file you're about to download.

● The browser needs to know which program to use for a particular type of file, and where to find it on your hard disk.

After you click the link, Internet Explorer will start to download the file it refers to and then show the dialog in the next screenshot. It wants to know what to do with the file when it's finished downloading: do you want to save the file and carry on surfing, or open it immediately using an external viewer?

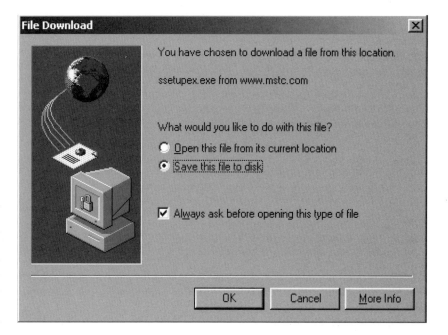

Explorer wants
to know whether
it should open
this file after
downloading, or
save it to your
hard disk.

Save this file to disk – If you choose this option, Explorer will present a Save As dialog so that you can choose a directory to save the file into, followed by a smaller dialog that will keep you posted on the progress of the download and how much longer it should take. While the file is downloading you can wait, or continue surfing the Web, and there's a handy Cancel button you can use if you change your mind halfway through, or the download seems to be taking too long. The **Save this file to disk** option is the best (and safest) option to use.

Open this file from its current location. For a file that you want to view or play straight away, you can select the **Open** option. If Explorer hasn't previously been told how to handle files of this type it will then prompt you to choose the program you want to use to view or display the file once it's been downloaded, so click the **Browse** button in the next dialog to locate and double-click a suitable program on your hard disk, and then click **OK**. Explorer will download the file and then launch that program to display the file. There's also a checkbox labelled **Always ask before opening this type of file**. If you remove the checkmark from this box, Explorer will use the option you select this time whenever you download the same type of file in future. So if you choose to **Open this file from its current location**, and select a program to use, that same program will automatically be used on all future occasions.

You can view and edit the settings for different types of file by opening **My Computer** and selecting **View | Folder Options | File Types**. Click a file type in the list, and click the **Edit** button. If the box beside **Confirm open after download** isn't checked, this type of file will always be opened - you can check this box if you'd like the chance to save this type of file in future or use a different program to open it. To find out which program will open this type of file, click on either **Play** or **Open** in the **Actions** box, then click the **Edit...** button.

Always run a virus-checker before running any program you've downloaded. Although people get a bit *too* hysterical about it, there's a small risk that a program might contain a virus. It only takes a few seconds and might just save a lot of hassle later.

Chapter 29

Exchanging Messages by Email

In This Chapter...

What's so great about email anyway?

Choose and set up your email software

Send and receive your first email message

Take the mystery out of sending files by email

Learn the secret language of the Internet –
emoticons and acronyms

Exchanging Messages by Email

Email is the old man of the Internet, and one of the reasons the network was constructed in the first place. It's one of the easiest areas of Net life to use, and one of the most used – for many people, sending and receiving email is their only reason for going online. By the end of this chapter you'll be able to send email messages and computer files to millions of people all over the world (well, perhaps not *all* of them!) in less time than you can stick a stamp on an envelope.

Why use email?

First, it's incredibly cheap. A single first-class stamp costs 26p at present, and will get a letter to a single, local (in global terms) address. But for a local phone call costing 5p you can deliver dozens of email messages to all corners of the world. Secondly, it's amazingly fast – in some cases your email might be received within seconds of you sending it. (It isn't always quite as fast as that, however: on occasions, when the network conspires against you, it might take several hours.) Thirdly, it's easy to keep copies of the email you send and receive, and to sort and locate individual messages quickly.

JARGON
BUSTER

Snail mail

This is a popular term for ordinary mail sent through the land-based postal service, the speed of which is closer to that of a certain mollusc than email.

There's a possible fourth reason for using email, but it should be regarded with some caution. If you agonize for hours over ordinary letter-writing, email should make life easier for you. An inherent feature of email is its informality: spelling, grammar, and punctuation are tossed to the wind in favour of speed and brevity.

Everybody's first question...

Whenever the subject of email arises among Internet beginners, the same question will undoubtedly be asked within the first minute. So that you can concentrate on the rest of this chapter, I'll put your mind at ease by answering it straight away. The question is: 'What happens if email arrives for me and I'm not online to receive it?'

Email arrives at your access provider's computer (its mail server) and waits for you to collect it. In fact, it will wait there a long time if it has to: most mail servers will delete messages that remain uncollected for several months, but if you take a week's holiday you can collect the week's email when you return.

JARGON BUSTER

Newbie

You're a newbie! It's okay, I'm not being abusive – it just means that you're new to the Internet. You wouldn't be proud to describe yourself as a newbie, but you might want to do so when appealing for help in a newsgroup, for example, to keep responses as simple as possible.

Understanding email addresses

There are two easy ways to spot an Internet 'newbie': the first is that their messages begin 'Dear...' and end 'Yours sincerely', and the second is that they tell you their 'email number'. Don't fall into either trap! I'll tell you how to avoid the first pitfall later in the chapter; in the second case, you definitely have an email *address*!

Email addresses consist of three elements: a username, an '@' sign, and a domain name. Your username will usually be the name in which your account was set up, and the name that you log on with when you connect. The domain name is the address of your IAP or online service. For example, my username is **rob.young**, and my access provider's address is **btinternet.com**, so my email address is **rob.young@btinternet.com**.

If you have to say your email address out loud, replace the dots with the word 'dot' and the @ sign with the word 'at'. My email address is pronounced 'rob dot young at btinternet dot com'.

Email addresses & online services

The email address of someone using an online service is structured in a similar way, although CompuServe calls the username a 'User ID', and AOL calls it a 'screen name'. If you have an account with an IAP and you want to send email to an AOL member, for example, use the address *ScreenName@aol.com*. To send to a member of MSN, use *username@msn.com*, and for CompuServe members use *UserID@compuserve.com*.

Members of online services can also send email out on to the Internet to someone with an IAP account. In fact, members of AOL and MSN can use the email address without making any changes to it; however, CompuServe members will have to insert the word 'Internet:' (including the colon) before the address. To send me a message, for example, a CompuServe member would use the address **internet:rob.young@ btinternet.com**. The word 'internet' isn't case-sensitive, and it doesn't matter if you leave a space after the colon.

If you're a member of an online service, and you want to email another member of the *same* service, all you need to enter is the username (or User ID, or screen name) of the person you want to email. There's no need to add the address of the service.

What do you need?

If you have an account with an online service such as CompuServe or AOL, you don't need anything more – the software you use to connect to and navigate the service has built-in email capability. If you have an IAP account, you'll need an email client (geek-speak for 'a program that works with email'). There are many of these to choose between, and your IAP may have provided one when you signed up. There are three major factors to consider when choosing an email program:

- It's compatible with the protocols used by your email account (I'll explain that in a moment).

- It will let you work offline.

- It will let you organize incoming and outgoing messages into separate 'folders'.

JARGON BUSTER

Offline

Software that lets you work offline allows you to read and write your messages without being connected to your IAP or online service, therefore clocking up charges. You only need to go online to send your messages and receive any new email. The earliest email had to be written online, which is why speed mattered more than spelling.

Oh dear, more of those protocols again – this isn't too tough, though. There are two protocols used to move email around: SMTP (Simple Mail Transport Protocol) and POP3 (Post Office Protocol, which is currently at its third version). SMTP is the protocol used to *send* email messages to the server, and POP3 is (usually) the protocol used by the server to *deliver* messages to you. You need to know if you have a POP3 email account, and your IAP should have made this quite clear. There are several dull, technical reasons why a POP3 account is better than an SMTP-only account, but the reason you care about right now is that you'll have a far wider range of email software available to choose from.

If you do have a POP3 account, the most popular email clients on the Internet are:

- **Outlook Express** – This all-in-one Microsoft package gives you both email and newsgroup programs which integrate themselves with Internet Explorer very neatly. If you have Windows 98 (or you've installed a recent copy of Internet Explorer such as the one on the CD-ROM accompanying this book) you should have Outlook Express installed already. You can also find Outlook Express as a separate package at **http://www.microsoft.com/ie/download**.

- **Pegasus Mail** – An excellent free program that you can download from **http://www.let.rug.nl/pegasus/ftp.html**.

- **Eudora Light** – This is 'postcard ware' (it's basically free, but the author would like a picture-postcard of your home town as payment). You can download it from **http://www.eudora.com**.

If you don't have a POP3 account:

- **Tetrix Reader Plug** is simple and neat, doubling as a newsreader program. Type **ftp://sunsite.cnlab-switch.ch/mirror/winsite/win3/winsock/ trpll0.zip** into your browser's address bar and press **Enter** to start the download.

If you use the Netscape Navigator browser, you may have an email program already. Navigator is part of an integrated suite of programs named Netscape Communicator, and this suite includes Netscape's own email program. You can find Communicator on Netscape's site at **http://www.netscape.com** but, just as with Internet Explorer, if you prefer to use an unrelated email program the choice is entirely yours.

Setting up your email program

Before you can start to send and receive email, your software needs to know a bit about you and your email account. This simply involves filling in the blanks on a setup page using some of the information given to you by your access provider. The first time you start the program it should prompt you to enter this information, but it's worth knowing where to find it in case you ever need to change it in the future.

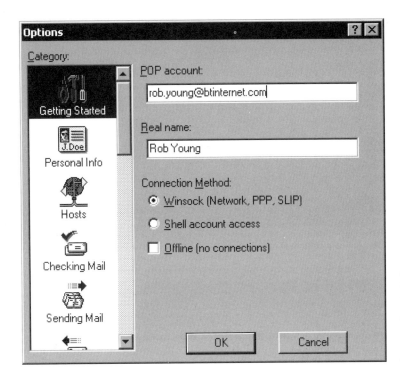

Entering
personal email
account details
into Eudora
Light.

- In **Eudora**, go to **Tools | Options**. Click the icons in the left pane to open the various option pages. The settings you're concerned with at this point are scattered over the first five pages. On the **Sending Mail** page, remove the check-mark from the **Immediate Send** box.

- In **Pegasus**, click **Tools | Options**. Click on **General Settings** and **Network Configuration** in turn to fill in the details.

- In **Outlook Express**, choose **Tools | Accounts** and click the **Mail** tab.

In the first two programs especially, you'll find a bewildering array of checkboxes and options – ignore them! Just fill in personal details about your email address, POP3 account name and password, SMTP and POP3 mail server addresses, and so on. We'll look at some of the other options later in this chapter. For now, though, they're set at sensible defaults, so leave them this way until you're sure you want to change something.

Sending an email message

You probably feel an overwhelming temptation to email everyone you know and tell them you've 'joined the club', but hold that thought for a moment. Start by sending a message to yourself instead – that way you can check that everything's working, and learn what to do when you receive a message as well. Fire up your email program or your online service's software and click the button that opens a message window. In Eudora and Pegasus, the button shows a pen and paper; in Outlook Express, click the Compose Message button.

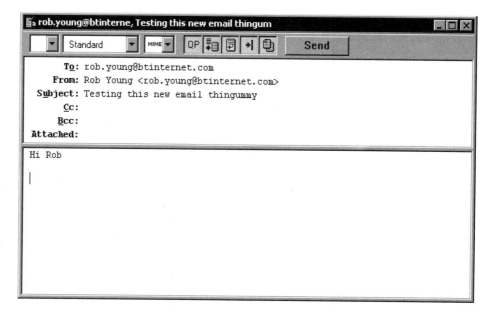

Eudora Light's mail message window.

Although all email programs look a little different, the important features are the same:

To: Type the email address of the person to whom you want to send the message.

CC: Carbon copy. If you want to send the message to several people, type one address in the **To:** field and the rest in the **CC:** field. Using this method, all recipients will know who else received a copy of the message.

BCC: Blind Carbon Copy. If you want to send the same message to several people and you don't want any of them to know who else is getting a copy, place their addresses in this field instead of the CC: field.

Subject: Enter a short description of your message. In some email programs you can send a message with a blank subject line, but avoid doing this. Although most people will open any email they receive (even if the subject is blank), this entry really comes into its own when the recipient is looking for this message again in six months time.

Attached: Lists the names of any computer files you want to send to the recipient along with the message. You'll learn about attaching files later in this chapter.

Below these fields is the area in which you type the message itself. Because you're going to send this message to yourself, type your own email address into the **To:** field, and anything you like in the **Subject:** field (just to get into the habit!), and then write yourself a welcoming message.

Now you need to send the message. Once again, the programs differ here, but look for a button marked **Send**. Some programs will send email immediately, and try to log on to your service to do so; others add mail to a 'queue' of messages to be sent all together when you're ready to do so. You may even have two Send buttons with a choice of **Send Now** or **Send Later**. Pegasus and Outlook Express score highly for ease of use in this department: messages you write are automatically 'queued', and you can click a single button that will send all mail in the queue and retrieve any incoming mail in a single operation. If you have to make a choice on an Options page about how the program should send mail, always choose to queue/send later.

If you're not sure how your program handles all this, just take a deep breath and click the Send button. (You'll have to go online first, but your email program may start your connection automatically when you click Send.) If the message really *is* being sent, something on the screen should tell you so. If nothing seems to be happening, look for a button or menu option that says something like **Send Mail Now** or **Send Queued Mail**.

> **TIP**
>
> If your program sends and receives mail in a single operation, the email you're posting to yourself may come back to you instantly. On the other hand, it may not. Email messages usually take a few minutes to get to where they're going, and can take hours or even days in the very worst cases.

You've got new mail!

You really feel you've arrived on the Internet when you receive your first message, but how do you know there are messages waiting for you? You don't, unfortunately – your email program has to go and look. With an online service account, you'll see an onscreen indication that new mail is waiting after you log on, and you can retrieve it by clicking the obvious button. With an IAP account, if you're using one of the email programs mentioned earlier you'll have a button labelled something like **Check for new mail**, or you might have the more useful combined **Send & Receive All Mail** button.

When you log on to CompuServe a message at the bottom of the screen informs you of new messages. Click the envelope button to retrieve them.

Most email programs use an Inbox/Outbox system: email waiting to be sent is placed in the Outbox, and new mail will arrive in the Inbox. When new mail arrives, all you'll see is a single entry giving the subject line of the message and the name of the sender (although some programs give a wealth of information including dates and times of sending and receiving the message, its size, and the number of attached files). To read the message, double-click this entry.

At this point, you can decide what to do with the message. You can delete it if you want to, and until you do it will remain visible in the program's Inbox or main folder. You should also be able to print it on to paper. Good email programs allow you to create named folders to store and organize your messages more efficiently (for example, you might want to create a Business and a Personal folder), and you can move or copy messages from the Inbox to any of these folders. In addition, you might be able to save a message as a separate file on to your hard disk or a floppy disk.

Replying & forwarding

One of the things you're most likely to do with an incoming message is send a reply, and this is even easier than sending a brand new message. With the message open (or highlighted in your Inbox) click on the program's **Reply** button. A new message window will open with the sender's email address already inserted and the entire message copied. Copying the original message this way is known as 'quoting', and it's standard practice in email, so that the recipient can see what it is you're replying to. The program should insert a greater-than sign (>) at the beginning of each line, and you can delete all or any of the original message that you don't need to include in the reply.

The Reply button also inserts the word **Re:** at the beginning of the subject line, indicating to the recipient that it's a response to an earlier message. Although you can change the subject line of a reply, it's often best not to – many email programs have search and sort facilities that can group messages according to subject (among other things), making it easy to track an earlier email 'conversation' you've long since forgotten about.

You can also send a copy of a received message to someone else, and you'll probably have a **Forward** button on the toolbar that does the job. Enter the recipient's email address and any extra message you want to add, then click the **Send** button. Just as in new messages, you can include **CC:** or **BCC:** addresses when replying or forwarding. Forwarded messages usually have **Fwd:** at the start of the subject line.

Getting attached – sending files via email

Ordinary email messages are plain text (7-bit ASCII) files, and have a size limit of 64Kb. While 64Kb is an awful lot of text, it's a pretty small measure in terms of other types of computer file you might want to send with a message. And most other types of file are binary (8-bit) files, so you'd expect your email program just to shrug its shoulders and walk away. Until recently it would do just that, and many people still delight in telling you that attaching binary files to email messages is a job for the brave or the foolish.

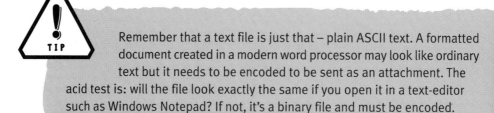

Remember that a text file is just that – plain ASCII text. A formatted document created in a modern word processor may look like ordinary text but it needs to be encoded to be sent as an attachment. The acid test is: will the file look exactly the same if you open it in a text-editor such as Windows Notepad? If not, it's a binary file and must be encoded.

However, most modern email programs are much more capable: you choose the file or files you want to attach, your emailer converts them to ASCII ready to be sent, and the recipient's emailer converts them back again at the other end. In most cases, it really should be as simple as that. The only blot on the landscape is that there are several methods used to do it, and both sender and recipient must be using the same method.

- **UUencode** — The original (rather messy) conversion system for PCs. The file is converted into ASCII and, if necessary, broken up into chunks to get around the email size restriction. It looks like pure gobbledegook until converted back by a **UUdecoder**.

- **MIME** — A modern successor to UUencoding, which is now also used on the Web for transferring files. It can identify the type of file you're sending and act appropriately, and the whole system works completely unaided at both ends.

- **BinHex** — A conversion system mostly used on Macintosh computers, similar to UUencoding.

> **TIP**
>
> If your email program handles MIME, use that in preference to other formats. Only use a different system if your recipient doesn't have a MIME-compatible email program (and refuses to do the sensible thing!)

If you know that your software and that of your recipient both use the same system, attaching files is simple: look for a toolbar button with a paperclip symbol and click it (in Outlook Express and Pegasus you'll find the button in the New Message window itself). You can then browse your computer's directories to find and double-click any files you want to attach; the software will handle the rest.

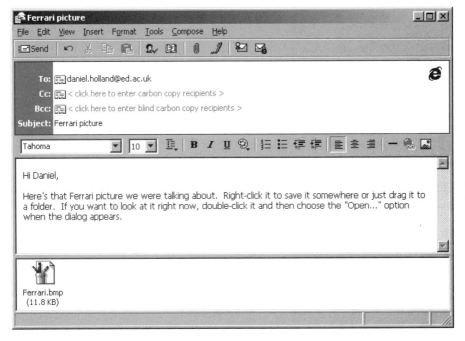

Attachments in Outlook Express appear as file icons. Right-click the icon to open or save the attached file, or drag it to your desktop.

Receiving attachments in incoming email should be just as simple and transparent, especially if your email program recognizes both MIME'd and UUencoded attachments, as many do. Eudora, for example, will decode attachments and put them in a directory called Attach; Outlook Express will show an attached file as an icon at the end of the message.

What else should you know about email?

Like most simple tools, email software has grown to offer a lot more than the basic requirements of writing, sending, receiving, and reading. Once you feel comfortable using the program you've chosen, spend a little time reading the manual or Help files to see what else it offers. (Remember that you can keep sending yourself test-messages to find out if or how an option works.) Here's a selection of options and issues worth knowing about.

Address books

An address book is simply a list of names and email addresses. Instead of typing the recipient's address into a new message (risking mistakes and non-delivery), you can click the **Address Book** button and double-click the name of the intended recipient to have the address inserted for you. You may be able to add new addresses to the book by clicking on a message you've received and selecting an **Add to address book** option. Many programs will allow you to create multiple address books, or to group addresses into categories, for speedy access to the one you want.

> **TIP**
>
> Believe it or not, the only truly reliable way to find someone's email address is to ask them, but there are search facilities on the World Wide Web that can find people rather than places, and you'll learn where to find these and how to use them in Chapter 33.

A similar option is the address group (known by different names in different software). You can send the same message to all the addresses listed in a group by simply double-clicking the group's name. This is an option worth investigating if you need to send an identical memo or newsletter to all the members of a team or club.

Signatures

An email 'signature' is a personal touch to round off an email message. You'll find a Signature option on one of your program's menus that provides a blank space for you to enter whatever text you choose, and this will be added automatically to the end of all the messages you write.

A signature commonly gives your name, and might also include the URL of your web site if you have one, your job description and company if you're sending business mail, and (very often) a quotation or witticism. Try to resist getting carried away with this, though – eight lines is an absolute maximum for a signature.

Emoticons & acronyms

Emoticons, otherwise known as 'smilies', are little expressive faces made from standard keyboard characters used to convey feelings or to prevent a comment being misunderstood in email messages, newsgroup postings, and textchat. As an example, you might put <g> (meaning 'grin') at the end of a line to say to the reader 'Don't take that too seriously, I'm just kidding'. Here's a little bundle of the more useful or amusing emoticons. (If you haven't come across emoticons before, turn the page sideways.)

:-)	Happy	:-#)	Has a moustache
:-(	Sad	:-)>	Has a beard
:-))	Very happy	(-)	Needs a haircut
:-((	Very sad	(:-)	Bald
;-)	Wink	:-)X	Wears a bow-tie
>:-)	Evil grin	8-)	Wears glasses
:-D	Laughing	:^)	Has a broken nose/nose put out of joint
:'-)	Crying	:-w	Speaks with forked tongue
:-O	Surprised	:-?	Smokes a pipe
:-&	Tongue-tied	:-Q	Smokes cigarettes
:-|	Unamused	*-)	Drunk or stoned
:-||	Angry	<:-)	Idiot
X-)	Cross-eyed	=:-)	Punk rocker

Acronyms came about as a result of Internet users initially having to compose their email while online and clocking up charges. Although messages are now mostly composed offline, these acronyms have become a part of accepted email style, and have been given new life by the emergence of online text-chat which you'll learn about in Chapter 32.

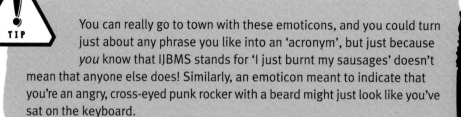

TIP

You can really go to town with these emoticons, and you could turn just about any phrase you like into an 'acronym', but just because *you* know that IJBMS stands for 'I just burnt my sausages' doesn't mean that anyone else does! Similarly, an emoticon meant to indicate that you're an angry, cross-eyed punk rocker with a beard might just look like you've sat on the keyboard.

In fact, most of these aren't actually acronyms at all, but fall under the banner of TLAs (Three Letter Acronyms). Er, no, they don't all consist of three letters either!

AFAIK	As far as I know	KISS	Keep it simple, stupid
BCNU	Be seeing you	L8R	Later (or see you later)
BST	But seriously though	LOL	Laughs out loud
BTW	By the way	OAO	Over and out
FAQ	Frequently asked question(s)	OIC	Oh I see
FWIW	For what it's worth	OTOH	On the other hand
FYI	For your information	OTT	Over the top
GAL	Get a life	PITA	Pain in the a~!#
IMO	In my opinion	ROFL	Rolls on the floor laughing
IMHO	In my humble opinion	RTFM	Read the f*%£?!# manual
IMNSHO	In my not-so-humble opinion	TIA	Thanks in advance
IOW	In other words	TNX	Thanks

Another common need in email and newsgroup messages is to emphasize particular words or phrases, since the usual methods (bold or italic text, or underlining) aren't available. This is done by surrounding the text with asterisks (*never*) or underscores (_never_).

Undelivered email

If an email message can't be delivered it will be 'bounced' straight back to you, along with an automatically generated message telling you what went wrong. If the address you typed doesn't exist, or you made a mistake, the message should come back within seconds or minutes. In some cases, a message might be returned to you after several days, which usually indicates that the problem lies in delivering the message at the other end. If this happens, just send the message again. If the problem persists, try altering the address so that it looks like this:

[**SMTP:***username@domain*]

(including the square brackets), or send a message addressed to **postmaster@***domain* (using the domain of the person you were trying to contact), asking if there's a problem with email delivery and quoting the email address you were trying to send to.

Other email bits & pieces

Filtering — Modern email programs offer filtering options (sometimes known as 'Rules') that let you decide how to handle certain types of incoming email; for example, you might choose to have all messages from a particular person moved to a special folder as soon as they arrive.

Formatting — Many email programs allow you to add formatting to your email as if it were a word-processor document, choosing fonts, colours, layout styles, and even themed background pictures, creating a result that looks a lot like a web page and is sent in the same format. The problem is that your recipient must be using an email program that can understand all this formatting or he'll just receive a plain message with all the formatting codes placed in a meaningless attached file. More and more email programs do understand these formats now, however, so the problem crops up a lot less often. It's best not to add background images though – some people receive dozens of messages every day and don't want to wait 10 times as long for one of yours to download!

Delete on receipt — As soon as you collect your email it should be deleted from your access provider's mail server. The reason for this is that your provider won't give you unlimited space for email on the server: when your mailbox is full, mail will be bounced back to the sender. Your email software may give you an option to delete retrieved messages, but it will usually be switched on by default. (Of course, this means that you can only retrieve a message *once*, so think carefully before deleting a message from your own system!)

Writing style — Don't start with 'Dear...' and end with 'Yours sincerely'. You might send a message that starts 'Hi Rob', or 'Hello Rob' if you really want some sort of salutation, or you might just start 'Rob,'. But its perfectly acceptable, and not considered rude, just to get straight into the message. Similarly, although you might sign off with 'Regards' or 'Best wishes', there's no need to put anything at all but your name. (You might find it a hard habit to break – I know I do – just don't think people rude when *they* do it!)

> **TIP**
>
> Remember that email isn't supposed to look like a letter. You don't need to put the date or the recipient's postal address at the top, or use any letter-writing formalities. On some occasions you might want to include your own postal address and phone number, but only do this when the recipient *needs* to know them.

Email netiquette

The term 'netiquette' is an abbreviation of 'Internet etiquette' – a set of unwritten rules about behaviour on the Internet. In simple terms, they boil down to 'Don't waste Internet resources' and 'Don't be rude', but here are a few specific pointers to keep in mind when dealing with email:

- Reply promptly. Because email is quick and easy, it's generally expected that a reply will arrive within a day or two, even if it's just to confirm receipt. Try to keep unanswered messages in your Inbox and move answered messages elsewhere so that you can see at a glance what's waiting to be dealt with.

- DON'T SHOUT! LEAVING THE CAPS LOCK KEY SWITCHED ON IS REGARDED AS 'SHOUTING', AND CAN PROMPT SOME ANGRY RESPONSES. IT DOESN'T LOOK AT ALL FRIENDLY, DOES IT?

- Don't forward someone's private email without their permission.

- Don't put anything in an email message that you wouldn't mind seeing on the nine o'clock news! Anyone can forward your email to a national newspaper, your boss, your parents, and so on, so there may be times when a phone call is preferable.

Chapter 30

Newsgroups – The Human Encyclopaedia

In This Chapter...

What are newsgroups all about?

Choose a newsreader and download a list of available newsgroups

Start reading (and writing) the news

Send and receive binary files with news articles

Mailing lists – have your news delivered by email

Newsgroups – The Human Encyclopaedia

News, as we generally think of it, is a collection of topical events, political embarrassments, latest gossip, and so on. All of that, and more, can be found on the Internet, but it's not what the Net calls 'news'. The newsgroups we're talking about here are more formally known as Usenet discussion groups; there are over 35,000 of them (and counting!) covering everything from accommodation to zebrafish.

Newsgroup discussions take place using email messages (known as 'articles' or 'postings'), but instead of addressing articles to an individual's email address they're addressed to a particular group. Anyone choosing to access this group can read the messages, post replies, start new topics of conversation, or ask questions relating to the subject covered by the group.

How does it work?

Your access provider has a computer called a news server that holds articles from thousands of newsgroups that form part of the Usenet system. This collection of articles will be regularly updated (perhaps daily, or perhaps as often as every few minutes) to include the latest postings to the groups. Using a program called a **newsreader**, you can read articles in as many of these groups as you want to, and post your own articles in much the same way that you compose and send email messages. Messages that you post will be added to the server's listings almost immediately, and will gradually trickle out to news servers around the world (the speed with which this happens depends on how often all the other servers update themselves).

Although there are currently more than 35,000 groups, you won't find *every* group available from your access provider. Storage space on any computer is a limited commodity so providers have to compromise. In addition, many providers are now taking a moral stance against groups involving pornography and software piracy (among others) and these are unlikely to be available. But if you really needed access to a group concerned with grape-growing in Argentina (and one existed), most reasonable providers will subscribe to it if you ask nicely.

Newsgroup names

Newsgroup names look a lot like the domain names we met in earlier chapters – words separated by dots. Reading the names from left to right, they begin with a top-level category name and gradually become more specific. Let's start with a few of these top-level names:

comp	Computer related groups such as **comp.windows.news**
rec	Recreational/sports groups like **rec.arts.books.tolkien**
sci	Science-related groups such as **sci.bio.paleontology**
misc	Just about anything – items for sale, education, investments, you name it…
soc	Social issues groups such as **soc.genealogy.nordic**
talk	Discussions about controversial topics such as **talk.atheism** or **talk.politics.guns**
uk	UK-only groups covering a wide range of subjects including politics, small ads, sport.

> **TIP**
>
> Some newsgroups are moderated, which means the creator of the group (or someone else appointed to run it) reads all the messages and decides which to post. The aim is to keep the topics of discussion on course, but they often tend to weed out deliberately argumentative or abusive messages too.

One of the largest collections of groups comes under a completely different top-level heading, **alt**. The alt groups are not an official part of the Usenet service, but are still available from almost all service providers. Because almost anyone can set up a group in the alt hierarchy they're sometimes regarded as anarchic or 'naughty', but in truth, their sole difference is that their creators chose to bypass all the red-tape involved in the Usenet process. Here's a taste of the breadth of coverage you'll find in the alt hierarchy:

alt.culture.kuwait	alt.education.disabled
alt.fan.david-bowie	alt.games.dominoes
alt.ketchup	alt.paranormal.crop-circles
alt.windows95	alt.support.spina-bifida

What do you need?

You need two things: a program called a newsreader and a little bit of patience. We'll come to the second of those in a moment; first let's sort out the newsreader. These come in two flavours: first, there's the online newsreader – you don't want one of those, as reading and posting articles all takes place while you're connected and clocking up charges; second is the offline newsreader, which is definitely the type you want, but offline readers also vary. Some offline readers automatically download all the unread articles in your chosen group so that you can read them and compose replies offline; the problem is that in a popular group you may have to wait for several hundred articles to download, many of which you won't be interested in. The second (and by far the best) type of offline reader just downloads the headers of the articles (the subject-line, date, author, and size). You can select the articles you want to read, based on this information, and then reconnect to have them downloaded.

If you need a good offline newsreader, here are my recommendations:

Outlook Express. As mentioned in the previous chapter, this integrates neatly with Microsoft's Internet Explorer browser, and gives you an email client too. If you have Windows 98, you should have Outlook Express already installed. Windows 95 users can install Internet Explorer from the CD-ROM in the back of this book which will set up Outlook Express at the same time.

Agent or **Free Agent** – A popular newsreader available in two versions – one is free, the other you'll have to pay for (guess which is which!). Point your browser at **http://www.forteinc.com** to download Free Agent or a trial version of Agent.

TIFNY. A stylish, colourful and oddly-named newsreader that packs a lot of handy information into a small space. You can download a trial copy from **http:// www.tifny2.com**.

Having got your hands on one of these, the setting up is fairly simple. The program should prompt you for the information it needs the first time you run it, which will include your name, email address, and the domain name of your news server (usually **news.*accessprovider.co.uk***). You'll probably see other options and settings, but don't change anything just yet.

Now switch on your patience circuits! Before you can go much further, your newsreader has to connect to the server and download a list of the newsgroups you can access. How long this takes will depend upon the number of groups available, the speed of your modem, and whether you strike lucky and get a good connection. It might take two or three minutes, but it could take 15 or more.

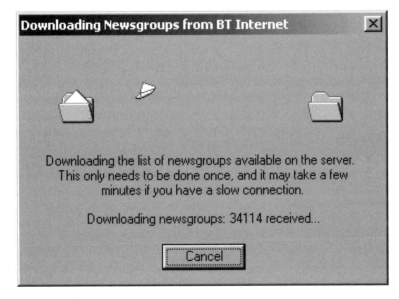

While your newsreader downloads a list of groups, you'll have to sit tight and count to ten – lots of times.

That was the bad news. The good news is that you'll only need to download the group list once, as long as you don't decide later that you want to use a different newsreader. In future, when your newsreader connects to the server to download new articles, it will automatically fetch the names of any new groups that have been created and add them to the list.

You can also access the newsgroups from online services. In AOL, use the keyword **newsgroups**; in CompuServe, use the Go word **usenet**. When you look at the list of groups your online service provides, many may be missing (such as the entire 'alt' hierarchy). You can often access these, but you need to 'switch on' access to them yourself; for example, AOL has an Expert Add function for this. Check the Help files for details, or contact the service's support line.

Subscribing to newsgroups

Before you can start reading and posting articles, you need to subscribe to the groups that interest you. ('Subscribing' is the term for letting your newsreader know which groups to download headers from – there are no subscription fees!) Although you can scroll your way through the thousands of groups in the list, it's easier to search for a word you'd expect to find in the group's name. In Outlook Express, click the button with the newspaper symbol on the toolbar (or press **Ctrl+W**), and type a keyword into the box above the list; in Agent, click the toolbar button with the torch symbol and type a word into the dialog box. To subscribe to a newsgroup in Outlook Express, click its name, and click the **Subscribe** button. When you've subscribed to all the groups you want, click **OK**. In Agent, right-click a newsgroup's name and click **Subscribe**.

> **TIP**
>
> If you want to subscribe to a group that your access provider doesn't (and won't) subscribe to, you may be able to access it through one of the public-access news servers instead. Visit **http://www.jammed. com/~newszbot** for a list of public servers. There are no lists of the groups covered by each server; you'll have to configure your newsreader to connect to it, download a list of groups, and see if the group you want is there.

● *If you need to find out whether a newsgroup exists on a particular topic, or you want to search the newsgroups for information, turn to 'Searching the newsgroups' in Chapter 33 to find out how to do it.*

Reading the news

When you've chosen the groups to which you want to subscribe, you're ready to download the headers from one of the groups. In Outlook Express, click the name you chose to describe your news server in the Outlook Bar on the left, and then double-click the name of one of your subscribed newsgroups in the upper window. The program will connect to your news server and download the headers from articles in the selected group (shown in the next screenshot). By default, Outlook Express will download 300 headers at a time (as long as there are that many articles in the group!), but you can change this figure by going to the **Tools** menu, selecting **Options** and changing the figure shown on the **Read** tab.

In Agent, click on **Group** | **Show** | **Subscribed Groups** (or click the large button marked **All Groups** until it says **Subscribed Groups**). You'll see the list of newsgroups you subscribed to, and you can double-click one to download its headers. Agent will present a dialog asking if you want to collect *all* the headers, or just a sample of 50. Some popular newsgroups have several thousand articles, so it's best to start with a sample just to get a flavour of the group first. Change the figure if you want to, and then click the button marked **Sample Message Headers**.

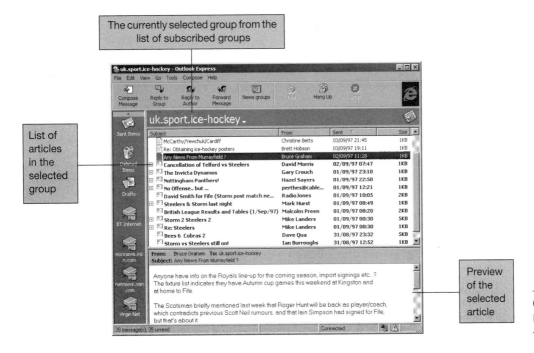

The currently selected group from the list of subscribed groups

List of articles in the selected group

Preview of the selected article

Outlook Express News.

To download and read an article immediately in the preview window, click the header once in Outlook Express, or double-click it in Agent. (If you prefer not to use the preview window in Outlook Express, you can double-click a header to open an article in a message window.)

Usually you'll want to download articles to read offline, and Outlook Express makes this easy: just tell it which articles you want. If you want to grab every article in the group, click **Tools | Download All**. If you just want selected articles, either right-click each article separately and choose **Mark Message for Download**, or hold the Ctrl key while clicking all the required articles and then right-click on any of them and choose **Mark Message for Download**. Beside the headers for messages you've marked you'll see a blue arrow indicator so that you can tell what you've chosen at a glance. You can now select another group to download headers for, and mark those in the same way. When you've finished marking the articles you want in all groups, open the **Tools** menu and click the appropriate **Download** button.

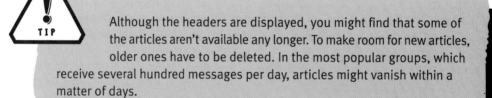

TIP   Although the headers are displayed, you might find that some of the articles aren't available any longer. To make room for new articles, older ones have to be deleted. In the most popular groups, which receive several hundred messages per day, articles might vanish within a matter of days.

Agent (and most other newsreaders) use similar methods. To mark a message for download in Agent, highlight it and press **M**, or right-click it and choose **Mark for Retrieval**. Once you've marked all the articles you want to download, click the toolbar button with the blue arrow and thunderbolt symbol and Agent will fetch them for you and mark them with a little 'page' icon.

Threads – following a conversation

Although a newsgroup is dedicated to one subject, there may be dozens (or hundreds) of different conversations going on. Fortunately all newsgroup articles have a subject-line just like email messages, so all messages with the same subject-line will be part of the same conversation, or in newsgroup parlance, the same 'thread'. Most newsreaders let you choose how you want to sort the list of articles (for example by date or sender), but the best way to view them is by thread so that articles from one conversation are listed together. The contents of each thread will be sorted by date, making it easy to track the course of a conversation.

Status	Subject
⊕	[+1] **Billy Joel autog'd photo FS** (Nathan Dresler)
	8 **Joelster** (Phu Luong)
⊕	[+2] **Re: After the Flood** (AJ Tru Blu)
⊕	[+1] **Wheres Billy?** (DMWMJ)
	3 **OMA** (Walter Hubner)
	6 **Belgium Rhythm 'n' Blues Festival** (Bob Ver Meylen)
⊖	9 **Childrens Album** [BrCr1]
	9 CHERYL1DRJ
	6 CrimeDawg3
	3 **for piano-bar music lovers**............. (CIRAKLIZER)
	218 **My Billy Joel Site!!** (Scott Crumpler)

Click the '+' icon to reveal the rest of the thread, or the '–' icon to hide it.

So how do threads work? When you post a brand new message to a newsgroup, you're starting a new thread. If someone posts a reply, their newsreader will insert the word **Re:** in the subject-line (just as in email replies). Your newsreader gathers together the original message and all replies (including replies to replies) and sorts them by date. The original message will have a little '+' icon beside it indicating that it's the beginning of a thread, and you can click this to reveal the other articles in the thread.

It's worth bearing in mind that some threads go on and on for months and may eventually have nothing to do with the article that started it all, despite the subject line. All it takes is for someone to raise a slightly different point in a reply, and someone else to pick up on it in *their* reply, for the entire thread to veer onto a whole new course.

Marking messages

In most newsreaders, as soon as you open an article to read it, the article will be marked as **Read**. (In Outlook Express the read articles turn from bold type to normal; in Agent they turn from red to black.) You can also mark a message as Read even if you haven't read it, or mark an entire thread as Read (perhaps you read the first couple of articles and decided everyone was talking rubbish). In modern newsreaders this just acts as a useful way to remember what you've read and what you haven't – you might just as easily delete messages you've read if you don't want to read them again.

Older newsreaders don't store the headers: they download them, display them, and then forget them again when you move to a different newsgroup or log off. All they know is which messages are marked as Read. Next time you open this newsgroup, the 'unread' headers will be downloaded, so it makes sense to mark as Read any headers that you're definitely not interested in so that they're not continually being downloaded. (You can even mark *every* message in the group as Read so that you'll only see any newer messages that appear.)

Posting articles to newsgroups

Newsgroup messages work just like email: the only difference is that the address you use is the name of a newsgroup, not an email address, and whereas you *send* an email *message*, you *post* a newsgroup *article*. Don't ask why, just accept it!

Although just reading articles can be very addictive, sooner or later you'll want to get involved. There are various ways to post articles, and they're common to just about every newsreader you'll come across. In the following list I'll take Microsoft's Outlook Express as an example, but if you're using something different you'll still have all the same options (although their precise names will vary).

- To reply to a message you're reading, click the **Reply to Group** button, or right-click the header and choose **Reply to Newsgroup**. (In many newsreaders, a reply is called a follow-up). A new message window will open with the name of the group already entered, and the same subject-line as the message you were reading. Type your message and click the **Post** button (or press **Alt+S**).

- To reply to the author of the article privately by email, click the **Reply to Author** button and follow the routine above. In this case the article won't be posted to the newsgroup.

- To reply to the newsgroup *and* send a copy of your reply to the author by email, go to **Compose│Reply to Newsgroup and Author**. Once again, the routine is the same as above.

Before posting an article to a 'proper' newsgroup where everyone can see it, you'll probably want to send a test message first as you did with your email program in the previous chapter. You can send a message to **alt.test**, but it's worth checking to see if your access provider has its own 'test' group. You might even get a reply from another newcomer. Allow at least a few minutes before checking the group to see if your message is listed.

- To create a new message (and start a new thread), click the **Compose Message** button (or press **Ctrl+N**). A new message window will open with the currently selected newsgroup shown. To send to a different newsgroup, or to more than one group, click the newspaper icon beside the name to add and remove groups from the list. Enter a title for the article on the **Subject** line, and then write your message. Click **Post** to send.

In keeping with email, any replies to newsgroup articles automatically 'quote' the original article. Make sure you delete any of the original article that doesn't need to be included. Remember that newsreaders list earlier messages in the thread in a well-organized fashion, so most people will have already read the message you're replying to.

When replying to an existing thread, *never* change the subject line! If just one character is different, newsreaders will regard it as the start of a new thread and won't group it with the other articles in the thread.

Attachments & newsgroup articles

At the risk of being boring let me just say again: newsgroup articles and email messages are so similar even their mother couldn't tell them apart. A case in point is that you can send and receive computer files as part of a newsgroup article just as you can with email. So I'm going to assume that you've read the section on attachments in the previous chapter.

In most newsreaders, attaching a binary file to an article is a simple case of clicking a button marked **Attach File** (often marked with a paperclip icon), browsing your directories for the file you want to send, and double-clicking it – your newsreader should do the rest.

Most modern newsreaders, including those mentioned earlier in this chapter, will also decode any attachments in an article you open, with no need for intervention on your part: these may be automatically saved to a directory on your computer, or you may have to click a button on the toolbar (as in Agent) to view them. Outlook Express displays attachments as an icon at the bottom of the window.

On occasion, an attached file might be split into several messages due to its size (known as a multi-part attachment) and the subject-lines for each message will include additions like **[1/3]**, **[2/3]** and **[3/3]** to number the parts of a three-part file. If you try to open any one of these, many newsreaders will realize that the file isn't complete and automatically download the other two as well and piece them together. In the remaining few programs, you'll have to select all three parts in advance.

Newsgroup netiquette & jargon

Newsgroups are pretty hot on netiquette, the 'rules' you should follow when using them, and Usenet has invented its own brand of weird language to go with some of these rules:

- It's good practice to 'lurk' a while when you visit a new group (especially if you're a newcomer to newsgroups generally). Lurking is reading newsgroup articles without posting any yourself. Get an idea of the tone of the group, the reactions of its participants to beginners' questions, and the types of topic they cover.

- Before diving in and asking a question in the group, read the FAQ. This stands for Frequently Asked Question(s), and it's an article that tells you more about the group, its topics, and other related groups. Many groups post a FAQ every few weeks, but if you don't see an article with 'FAQ' in its header, send a short message asking if someone could post it.

- Don't post 'test' articles to any newsgroup that doesn't have the word 'test' in its name.

- Don't post articles containing attachments to any newsgroup that doesn't have the word 'binaries' in its name. This is out of respect for people whose newsreaders give them no choice but to download *every* article, and who don't expect to spend five minutes downloading an attachment they don't want.

- Don't 'spam'! Spamming is a lovely term for sending the same article to dozens of different newsgroups, regardless of whether it's relevant. These messages are usually advertising mailshots, get-rich-quick schemes, and similar stuff that no-one finds remotely interesting. The risk is greater than just being ignored though, as you might get 'mail-bombed' – many people will take great delight in sending you thousands of email messages to teach you a lesson! So, why 'Spamming'? Monty Python fans might remember a sketch about a certain brand of tinned meat... try asking for a copy of the script in **alt.fan.monty-python**!

- When replying to an article requesting information, or an answer to a question, it's good practice also to send the author a copy by email, in case your newsgroup reply doesn't get noticed. By the same token, if someone asks for answers by email, post your answer to the group as well – it may be of interest to others.

- Don't rise to 'flame' bait! Some people delight in starting arguments, and deliberately post provocative articles. Personal attacks in newsgroups are known as 'flames', and on occasions these can get so out of hand that the whole group descends into a 'flame war', with little else going on but personal abuse.

Chapter 31

Grabbing the Goodies with FTP

In This Chapter...

It sounds horrible! What is FTP?

FTP-ing using your web browser

Setting up and using a 'real' FTP program

Getting into private and anonymous FTP sites

How to find the files you want

Grabbing the Goodies with FTP

Imagine you've been left alone in a room full of computers with huge hard disks. You can root around as much as you like, grab any files you want, and take them home with you. If that sounds like a little slice of happiness, you'll like FTP – that's what it's for. FTP stands for File Transfer Protocol, and it works a lot like Windows Explorer or File Manager – you can open directories by clicking them, browse around, and click on any file to copy it to somewhere else. There's just one difference: rather than copying a file from one directory to another, or to a floppy disk, FTP copies the file to another *computer* – your own.

What is FTP?

We've already looked at links to files on the World Wide Web in Chapter 28. What you didn't realize is that you were already using FTP just by clicking these links and letting the file download. Some of the files are stored on a web server, others are stored on an FTP server, but you don't need to know what type of server it is: you click the link, the file is sent, end of story. However, if you're interested, move your mouse pointer on to the link and look at your browser's status bar to see where the link points. If the address starts with **ftp://** you'll know it's an FTP site. It might be worth knowing, as you'll learn in a moment.

One thing to remember is that FTP sites differ from web sites; for example, a site might be closed, or it might be too busy to let you in. Some FTP sites put a limit on the number of people that can visit at once, and others don't allow anonymous logins during business hours, so try again later. It's good netiquette to avoid accessing FTP sites during their local business hours (some knowledge of time zones is helpful here!), and you'll usually get a much faster service too. Of course, if you can't get on to the site at all, you might just have typed the address wrongly.

Using your browser for FTP

FTP addresses look a lot like web addresses: they begin with the name of the computer, and continue with the directory path to the file you want. To use your browser to visit an FTP site, you'll usually need to prefix the whole thing with **ftp://** (the only exception is when the *name* of the computer starts with 'ftp', but you can still use the prefix in these cases if you prefer to). To get acquainted with FTP using the browser, let's visit an FTP site. Start up your browser, type the following address into the address bar, and press **Enter**.

ftp://sunsite.doc.ic.ac.uk

Once you're connected to the site, you'll see a dull grey background with a plain black welcoming message. (This is how the whole World Wide Web looked until a couple of years ago!) Scroll downwards in the window and a list of blue hypertext links will come into view. In true Web style, the blue text is clickable and will lead somewhere else. To the left of each hypertext entry you'll see either **Directory** or a set of figures. The word Directory indicates that this is a link to another directory (like clicking a folder icon in Windows); the figures show that the entry links to a file and give its size. Further to the left you'll see the date and time that the file was

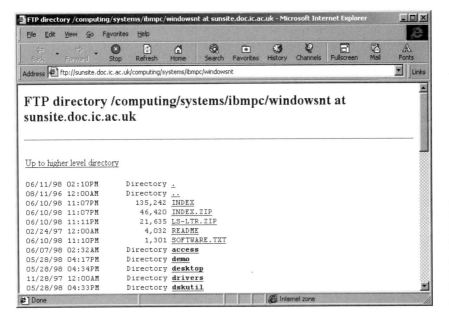

One-click browsing through an FTP site using Internet Explorer.

placed on the computer. On some FTP sites, you might see friendly icons next to the hypertext links – a folder icon for a directory, and a page icon for a file.

To get to the directory shown in the screenshot above, click on the directory entry **computing**. Explorer will display the contents of the computing directory and you can then click on the **systems** directory, followed by **ibmpc**, and then **windowsnt**. From here, you could click on another directory to open it, or click on one of the files to start downloading it. To go back to the **ibmpc** directory you just left, click the text at the top of the list that reads **Up to higher level directory**, or click the second entry in the list that consists just of two dots.

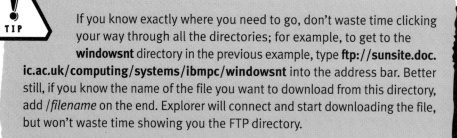

If you know exactly where you need to go, don't waste time clicking your way through all the directories; for example, to get to the **windowsnt** directory in the previous example, type **ftp://sunsite.doc. ic.ac.uk/computing/systems/ibmpc/windowsnt** into the address bar. Better still, if you know the name of the file you want to download from this directory, add /*filename* on the end. Explorer will connect and start downloading the file, but won't waste time showing you the FTP directory.

Keep a look out for files called Index. These will tell you something about the site you're visiting, and give a list of all the files on the site or in the current directory (depending on the individual site – some give more detail than others). As you can see in the screenshot, there are two Index files. One is a text file that you could read in any word processor or in your browser's window; the other is a compressed version of the same file (indicated by its **.zip** extension and much smaller size) and needs a program like WinZip to decompress it (covered in Chapter 25). It's well worth grabbing Index files to read offline: they usually include a brief description of each file to supplement the rather cryptic filenames you see listed on the screen.

Private sites & anonymous sites

To gain access to any FTP site you have to log in, just as you do when you connect to your IAP or online service. Some of these sites are private, and you'll need a username and password to get access. For example, a company might allow you access to its site in order to upload information or files rather than sending them by email. If you create your own web site and upload the files by FTP, you'll have a username and password to prevent anyone else having access to your directory and tampering with your web pages.

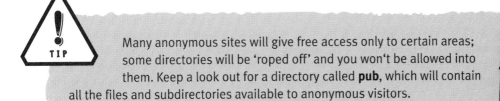

Many anonymous sites will give free access only to certain areas; some directories will be 'roped off' and you won't be allowed into them. Keep a look out for a directory called **pub**, which will contain all the files and subdirectories available to anonymous visitors.

Many other sites are accessible to the public, and anyone can log on and delve in. These are known as anonymous sites, because the system doesn't need to find out who you are before letting you in. To access these sites, you'll log in with the username **anonymous** and give your email address as the password. If you're using your browser, this is handled automatically and you won't be prompted to enter anything, and if you're using an FTP program, as you'll learn in a moment, you just click a box labelled **Anonymous** to have the details entered for you.

Using a 'real' FTP program

So if the browser can cope with FTP, why would you want to use anything different? Quite simply, a 'real' FTP program is custom-built for the job. With a few minutes' practice, it's actually easier and friendlier to use, and it can usually connect to an FTP site faster than your browser can, speeding up the transfer of files that you download. It also gives you more information about the progress of downloads from FTP sites than your browser does. Finally, it will let you upload files as well as download them which, at the moment, browsers can't do.

First you'll need to grab a copy of an FTP program, and three of the best are listed below. For the rest of this chapter I'm going to assume you're using FTP Explorer, but don't worry if you're not: all three programs have very similar features.

- **FTP Explorer**. A neat program for Windows 95 and later, which you can find at **http://www.ftpx.com**.

- **CuteFTP**. No more cuddly than the others, but every bit as good. If you choose to use this program for longer than 30 days, head for **http:// www.cuteftp.com** to register it.

- **WS_FTP Professional**. One of the most popular programs, despite the dull name. You can find and download an evaluation copy from **http:// www.ipswitch.com**.

Setting up FTP Explorer couldn't be easier: when you first start it up, you'll be asked to enter your email address, and that's it. A dialog will appear to ask if you'd like some 'sample profiles' to be created, and it's worth clicking the **Yes** button: this puts a list of useful FTP sites just a couple of clicks away, and you'll see this list in the next window that opens, the **Connect** dialog.

If there's a particular site you want to visit and you know you'll only want to visit it once, you can cancel this dialog, and use the Quick Connect option instead. Click the toolbar button with the lightning flash, type the URL of the site and click **OK**, and FTP Explorer will try to connect you.

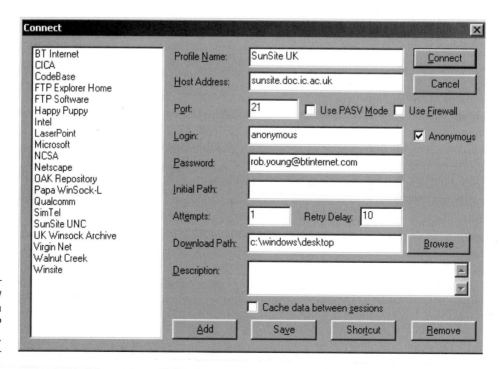

Creating a new connection profile in FTP Explorer.

The more practical way of working is to create a new 'profile' for the site. This can be saved so that you can use it again in the future (rather like Internet Explorer's **Favorites** menu). As an example, let's set up a profile for the SunSite FTP site we visited earlier using the browser. In the **Connect** dialog, click the **Add** button and follow these steps:

1. In the **Profile Name** box, type any name that will help you recognise the connection to this FTP site in future, such as **SunSite UK**.

2. Type the address of the computer you want to connect to in the **Host Name/ Address box** – in this case **sunsite.doc.ic.ac.uk**.

3. If you're visiting a private site, type your logon name in the **Login** box and your password in the **Password** box. SunSite, like most of the sites you'll visit, is a public anonymous site, so click the checkbox marked **Anonymous**. This will fill in those two boxes for you automatically.

4. In the **Initial Path** box, you can type the path to the directory you want to see after connecting, such as **/computing/systems/ibmpc** (not forgetting that first forward slash!). If you leave this blank, you'll arrive at the root directory of the SunSite computer.

5. In the box marked **Download Path**, you can type the path to a directory on your own computer that you want any files to be downloaded into. This directory will be selected for downloads every time you connect to this site.

6. Click **Save** to add this new profile to the list on the left. In future you can click the **Connect** button on the toolbar to see this dialog again, choose 'SunSite UK' from the list and click Connect to visit it. For now, as the dialog is already in front of you, click Connect and FTP Explorer will dial up (if necessary) and try to connect to the site.

TIP

The major online services will let you transfer files by FTP too. In America Online, use the keyword **ftp**; in CompuServe, use the Go word **ftp**. In either program you can click on the big **Internet** button on the main desktop and choose FTP from the next menu.

If the connection is made successfully, you'll see the window shown in the next screenshot. Exploring the contents of the FTP computer is as easy as exploring your own hard disk: use the tree structure in the left pane to select directories and open directories, and view their contents in the right pane. Select the file(s) you want to download and click the Download button on the toolbar to copy it to the directory you entered into the **Download Path** box. A small dialog will keep you posted on the transfer progress. You can also drag and drop files from FTP Explorer's main window to your desktop or elsewhere to download them. If you find an Index or text file that you'd like to read immediately rather than store, right-click it and choose the **Quick View** option.

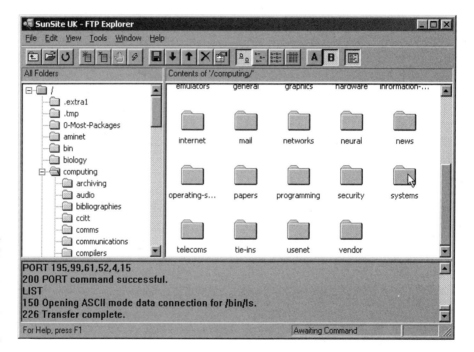

Browsing directories on the remote computer with FTP Explorer's familiar layout.

Uploading files is just as easy as downloading them. You can click the Upload button on the toolbar and choose one or more files from a standard file dialog, or simply drag them from one of your own directories and drop them into FTP Explorer's main window. You can also drag folders into this window and the folder will be uploaded along with its contents. To create a new directory on the server, right-click on a blank area in the main window, choose **New** and **Folder**, and type a name. You can then just double-click this new folder to open it and start copying files into it.

Finding the stuff you want

The big trick with FTP is to actually locate what you're looking for. There may be dozens of directories, all containing more directories, and the structure may not always be as intuitive as the way you structure your own hard disk. Let's look at several things you might want to do, and come up with some solutions.

- If you know the name and location of the file you want, type it into your browser's address bar, or type the path into FTP Explorer's **Initial Path** box, and look for the file when the directory's contents are shown.

- If you know the location of the file you want, but not its name, visit that directory and either **View** or download one of the Index files, which should give a short description of each file in that directory.

- If you don't know the location of the file (or the one you were given is wrong), but you know its name, you could see if it's listed in an Index file, or use your browser to visit FTP Search at **http://ftpsearch.ntnu.no/ftpsearch**. Type the name of the file into the **Search for** box and click the **Search** button. (If FTP Search doesn't do the trick, a similar search at **http://www.snoopie.com** might yield different results.)

- If you're just searching for 'stuff' generally, it's fun just browsing through directories until you find something interesting. Directory names tend to become more specific as you dig deeper; for example, if you're looking for email programs, start in the **pub** directory, and from there you might find a **computing** directory, which will lead you to **software**, then **internet**, then **email**. If the pub directory has an Index or Readme file, grab that first – it may contain a listing of all its subdirectories and an explanation of what each contains.

Chapter 32

Chat & Talk without Moving your Lips

In This Chapter...

Chat, Talk, and Voice on the Net – what's it all about?

Using online services' chat rooms

Take part in IRC chat sessions on the Internet

Spice up your chat sessions with cartoon characters

Cut your phone bill using Talk and Voice on the Net

Chat & Talk without Moving your Lips

In Internet-speak, 'chatting' and 'talking' are two different things, but what they have in common is their immediacy: you can hold conversations with people from all over the world at a speed almost comparable with talking on the phone. In most cases, you won't know who these people are, and you may never 'meet' them again.

Reactions to this area of cyberspace vary considerably. Many people find it exciting or addictive, to the point of spending hours every day 'chatting'. Many more find it inane, frustrating, or offensive. Quite simply, these services bring Internet users into the closest possible contact with each other, and are used by many to meet members of the opposite sex – however unsatisfying you might imagine cybersex to be, it's very real, and all potential 'chatters' should be aware of its existence before taking part. That being said, chatting and talking can also be sociable and fun, practical and informative – to a large extent, the choice is yours.

What are chatting & talking?

Chatting means holding live conversations with others by typing on your keyboard. You type a line or two of text into a small window and press Enter, and the text is visible almost instantly to everyone else taking part. They can then respond by typing their own messages, and you'll see their responses on *your* screen almost instantly. Chatting usually takes place in a 'chat room', which may contain just two or three people, or as many as 50.

Talk is a little different. Although the method of sending messages to and fro is the same, 'talk' usually takes place between just two people, and in a more structured way. Using a talk program, you'd usually enter the email address of the person you want to talk to, and if that person is online (and willing to talk to you!) the conversation begins. To cloud the issue a bit, chat programs also allow two people to enter a private room and 'talk', and many talk programs will allow more people to join in with your conversation if you permit them to enter.

So the boundary between chat and talk is a little smudged. Making things even more complicated is the recent arrival of Voice on the Net (VON), where people can *really* talk to each other using microphones. Most talk programs support VON, and it's slowly being added to chat as well. Actually, this isn't all as confusing as it sounds; let's look at these three methods of communication one at a time to see how each works.

Chat & the online services

One of the major reasons for the early popularity of online services was their built-in, easy-to-use chat systems. The major online services put a lot of effort into improving their chat facilities, and also now offer parental controls that can bar access from certain chat areas. As a measure of how seriously they regard these facilities, online services regularly enlist celebrity guest speakers to host chat sessions and answer questions. The simplicity of these chat areas makes them a good introduction to the workings of chat, even if you have an IAP account, so we'll look at the online services' offerings first.

Both AOL and CompuServe have a large button on their desktops marked **Chat** that will take you to the chat rooms, or you can use the Go or Key word, 'chat'. In CompuServe this will lead to a short menu from which you can choose the General or the Adult chat forum. Click the forum of your choice and you can use the buttons on the left to switch between chat, file, and message areas. The list of chat rooms shows how many people are in each room, and the Who's Here tab behind it gives a list of CompuServe members currently chatting and the rooms they're in. To enter a chat room, click its name and then choose **Participate** or **Observe** (depending on how adventurous you're feeling!).

In AOL you'll see a menu allowing you to choose between UK and US chat. Choose either, and you'll be launched into a chat room called the New Members Lobby (although you can leave this if you choose to). You'll also see a list of chat rooms. To enter a room, double-click its name in the list. In both AOL and CompuServe you can leave a chat room by closing its window.

Once inside a chat room you can watch the conversations unfold in the upper portion of the window, or participate by typing text into the space at the bottom and pressing

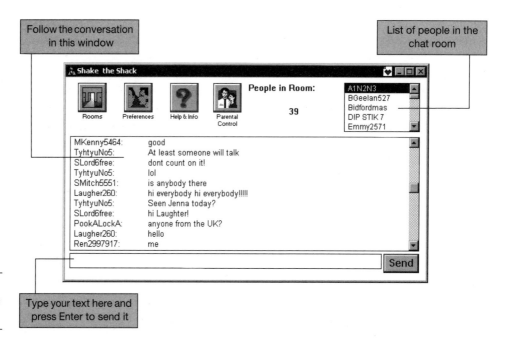

Follow the conversation
in this window

List of people in the
chat room

Chatting in
AOL's Shake the
Shack room.

Type your text here and
press Enter to send it

Enter. (Don't type your username before each line – the chat program displays that automatically.) AOL shows a list of the people in the room in the top right corner; in CompuServe, click on the **Who's Here** button for a similar list. Some members fill in a Member Profile giving details such as age, location, and interests, which sheds some light on the people you're chatting to. In AOL, double-click the name in the **People In Room** list and click the **Get Info** button; in CompuServe, click **Who's Here**, click on a name, then select **Member Profile**.

You can also invite someone to 'talk' privately. In AOL, double-click the name of the person you want to talk to in the **People In Room** list, click the **Message** button and type a short message (such as 'Do you want to talk?'). If the person accepts, a small window will open in which you can type messages back and forth. In CompuServe, click the **Private Chat** button.

Chatting on the Internet

The Internet has its own chat system called Internet Relay Chat, or IRC. Like all the other Internet services, you'll need to grab another piece of software to use it. One of the best, and the easiest to use, is mIRC from **http://www.mirc.co.uk**. The first time you run mIRC, you'll see a dialog into which you can enter the few details the program requires.

Enter your name and email address in the appropriate spaces, and choose a nickname (or 'handle') by which you'll be known in chat sessions. A nickname can be anything you choose: it might give an indication of your hobby or job, or a clue to your (adopted?) personality, or it might just be meaningless gibberish, but it can't be more than nine characters in length. Finally, choose a UK server from the list and click **OK**.

JARGON BUSTER

Channels

In the weird world of IRC, which bases its jargon heavily on CB radio, a channel is the term for a chat room.

Now you're ready to connect and start chatting. Make sure you're connected to your service provider first (mIRC won't start the connection for you), and then click the thunderbolt button at the extreme left of the toolbar. As soon as you're connected, you'll see a small dialog box listing a collection of channels that mIRC's author thought you might like to try. You could double-click one of these to enter a particular channel, but now is a good time to use one of the many IRC commands. Close the little list of channels, type **/list** in the box at the bottom of the main window, and then press **Enter**. A second window will open to display all the channels available on the server you chose (shown in the next screenshot). There could be several hundred channels, so this might take a few seconds. Beside each channel's name you'll see a figure indicating how many people are on that channel at the moment, and a brief description of the channel's current subject of discussion. Choose a channel, and double-click its list-entry to enter.

Some long-time IRC users can be a bit scathing towards newcomers, so it's best to choose a beginners' channel while you take your first faltering steps. Good channels to start with are **#beginners**, **#mirc** (for mIRC users), **#irchelp**, or **#ircnewbies**. You may see some more channel names that refer to help, beginners, or newbies – try to pick a channel that has at least half-a-dozen people in it already so that you won't feel too conspicuous!

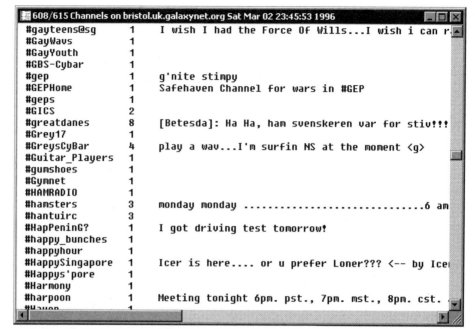

```
#gayteens@sg      1      I wish I had the Force Of Wills...I wish i can r
#GayWavs          1
#GayYouth         1
#GBS-Cybar        1
#gep              1      g'nite stimpy
#GEPHome          1      Safehaven Channel for wars in #GEP
#geps             1
#GICS             2
#greatdanes       8      [Betesda]: Ha Ha, ham svenskeren var for stiv!!!
#Grey17           1
#GreysCyBar       4      play a wav...I'm surfin NS at the moment <g>
#Guitar_Players   1
#gumshoes         1
#Gymnet           1
#HAMRADIO         1
#hamsters         3      monday monday ..........................6 am
#hantuirc         3
#HapPeninG?       1      I got driving test tomorrow!
#happy_bunches    1
#happyhour        1
#HappySingapore   1      Icer is here.... or u prefer Loner??? <-- by Ice
#Happys'pore      1
#Harmony          1
#harpoon          1      Meeting tonight 6pm. pst., 7pm. mst., 8pm. cst.
#Haven            1
```

The complete channel listing from GalaxyNet's Bristol server. Choose any channel from 615 possibles!

When a channel window opens, you'll see your nickname listed among the channel's other occupants on the right, with the conversation taking place on the left. As soon as you enter the channel, your arrival will be broadcast to everyone else (you'll see this happen when others arrive and leave), and you may receive an automated Welcome message, or someone might even say Hello. To join in with the chat, just start typing into the text box at the bottom and press **Enter** to send. If you want to leave a channel, type the command **/leave** and press **Enter**.

TIP

Whenever you arrive in a channel there's likely to be a conversation going on. If no-one brings you into the chat, it's a good idea to 'lurk' for a few moments to see what it's all about, but it's quite acceptable to type something like 'Hi everyone, how's it going?', and you'll usually get a friendly response from someone. If you don't, follow the conversation and try to interject with something useful.

IRC commands – chat like a pro

The IRC system has a huge number of commands that you can learn and put to good use if you're really keen, and mIRC includes a general IRC help-file explaining how they work. You certainly don't need to know all of them (and mIRC has toolbar buttons that replace a few), but once you feel comfortable with the system you can experiment with new ones. Here's a few of the most useful to get you started:

Type this	To do this
/help	Get general help on IRC.
/list	List all the channels available on the server you are connected to.
/list -min n	List all the channels with at least n people in them (replace *n* with a figure).
/join #channel	Enter a channel. Replace channel with the name of your chosen channel.
/leave #channel	Leave the specified channel (or the channel in the current window if no channel is specified).
/quit message	Finish your IRC session and display a message to the channel if you enter one (see below).
/away message	Tell other occupants you're temporarily away from your computer, giving a message.
/away	With no message, means that you're no longer away.
/whois nickname	Get information about the specified nickname in the main window.

So what are those *messages*? When you quit, you might want to explain why you're leaving by entering a command such as **/quit Got to go shopping. See you later!** Similarly, if you suddenly have to leave your keyboard, you might type **/away Call of nature. BRB**, to indicate that you'll be back in a minute if anyone tries to speak to you. (BRB is a common shorthand for 'Be right back' – turn back to Chapter 29 for a few more of these.) When you return, just type **/away** to turn off this message again.

You can also 'talk' privately to any of the participants in a channel. If you want to start a private talk with someone called Zebedee, type the command **/query Zebedee Can I talk to you in private?** (of course, the message you tag on the end is up to you). Zebedee will have the opportunity to accept or decline the talk: if he/she accepts, a separate private window will open in which the two of you can exchange messages. When you want to stop talking, close this window in the usual way.

TIP All commands begin with a forward slash. If you type the command without the slash it will be displayed to all the participants in your channels, and give everyone a good giggle at your expense.

Chatting can be comical!

Simple though it is, chatting can be very addictive. But it's still plain text, and in Internet-land that just won't do. The latest thing is graphical chat software in which you choose a cartoon character called an 'avatar' to represent yourself. These programs offer you a list of avatars to choose from, and some even let you create your own if you're handy with a graphics program.

The following screenshot shows one of the most popular graphical chat programs, Microsoft Chat (which also supports ordinary textual chat if those avatars get on your nerves!). If you have Windows 98, you already have Microsoft Chat though it may not be installed on your system. Grab your Windows CD-ROM, go to Control Panel's Add/Remove Programs applet and install it from the **Communications** heading of the **Windows Setup** tab. If you're using Windows 95, you can download Chat for free from **http://www.microsoft.com/ie/chat**.

Microsoft has set up its own chat rooms for Microsoft Chat, but you can also connect to the usual IRC channels, and Chat will assign other occupants an avatar so that you can still take part using avatars rather than plain text. If you do connect to an IRC channel, though, go to Chat's **View | Options | Settings** page and check the box beside **Don't send graphics information**, or the rest of the channel will see some very strange stuff alongside your typed text!

Finally on the subject of chat, never give out personal details other than your name, age, sex, and email address. After chatting with someone for a while, it's easy to forget that you really know nothing about them but what they've told you (and that may not be true!).

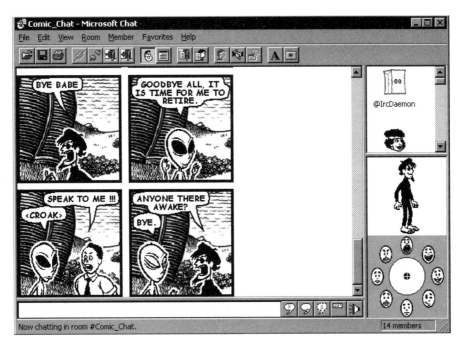

Microsoft's visual Chat program lets you choose an avatar, and select different emotions to match your text.

Voice on the Net – talk really *is* cheap!

The sort of chat we've looked at so far is 'unplanned' – you arrive in a channel or chat room and chat to whoever happens to be there. If you get on well enough, you might invite someone else to have a private chat (or 'talk') in a separate window. But what if there's someone in particular you want to talk to? Until recently, your options were limited: you could agree to meet in a chat room at a certain time and take it from there, or you could pick up the phone. But the latest 'big thing' on the Internet is Voice On the Net (VON). VON is the Internet equivalent of a telephone: you start the program, choose an email address to 'dial', and start talking. But in this case, talking really is *talking*. You can hold live conversations with anyone in the world by speaking into a microphone, and hear their responses through your speakers or a headset.

So how does VON differ from an ordinary telephone conversation? First and foremost, the price – because you're dialling into your local access provider, you're only paying for a local phone call although you may be speaking to someone in Australia. But it's the extra goodies that VON programs offer that make them valuable. Depending on the program you use, you can send computer files back and

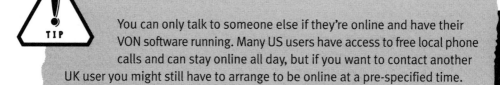

You can only talk to someone else if they're online and have their VON software running. Many US users have access to free local phone calls and can stay online all day, but if you want to contact another UK user you might still have to arrange to be online at a pre-specified time.

forth, hold conferences, use a whiteboard to draw sketches and diagrams, and you can even take control of programs on the other party's computer. Recent programs have even made the fabled 'video phone' a reality at last – admittedly the pictures are small, rather jerky (especially with a slow modem) and a bit blurred, but you can finally see and be seen while you talk! Of course, you'll need a digital video camera (a so-called 'webcam') and software, but these can be bought for under £100.

Sounds good, what's the catch?

The downside is that the other party must also be online to receive the 'call', so you'll both pay phone charges, but even added together these could amount to less than 10 per cent of an international call charge. In fact, there are already programs such as Net2Phone (from **http://www.net2phone.com**) that allow you to dial someone's phone number rather than email address, making it possible to make these cheap international calls to someone who doesn't even have an Internet account!

A second catch (at the moment) is that you must be using the same program as the person you want to talk to. If you talk to a lot of people, you might need several different programs that do the same job just because they all use different programs. Fortunately, some of these programs are free, so it's probably easiest to pick a free one and then convince your friends to grab a copy themselves! Hopefully, the various software companies involved will soon get their acts together on this as they have with the other Internet services.

What do you need?

Unlike the other services you use on the Net, VON programs have some definite hardware requirements. To begin with, you'll need a soundcard. It doesn't need to be a flashy, expensive card since the quality of these voice calls isn't high, but look out for a full-duplex card (see Chapter 5). You need a reasonably fast Pentium computer too, with a bare minimum of 16Mb RAM, and you'll need a microphone and speakers plugged into your soundcard; the quality of these doesn't matter too much and any computer peripherals store can supply them very cheaply.

Next there's your Internet connection and modem to consider. You might just get by with a 14.4Kbps connection, but you'll get much better results from a 28.8Kbps or 33.6Kbps modem, and most access providers now support these speeds. Finally, of course, you need the software. There are many different programs to choose between, some of which are aimed more at business use than personal use, but here's a brief selection:

● **PowWow** – A very friendly, free program from Tribal Voice, which we'll look at in a moment. You can download this from **http://www.tribal.com**.

● **PowWow For Kids** – A version of PowWow for children of up to 13 years old, with excellent security features that filter out profanity and warn the child when they try to contact an adult or when an adult requests a chat with them. However, the child will need a personal email address rather than sharing yours. Visit **http://www.tribal.com/kids.htm** for details and download.

● **NetMeeting** – Microsoft's free VON program. This is aimed largely at business users, but (seemingly) is used more by personal talkaholics. NetMeeting supports video, voice, and multi-user conferences, and you can use programs on the other person's computer by remote control. This program is included with both Windows 98 and 95 and should be installed on your system already. If it isn't, you can install it yourself from Control Panel's Add/Remove Programs applet, or download it as a separate item from **http://www.microsoft.com/netmeeting**.

● **Web Phone** – A multi-talented, and very stylish, VON program based on a mobile phone design with features such as video, text-chat, and answerphone, as well as four separate voice lines. You'll need to 'activate' the evaluation copy (an unusual way of saying 'pay for') to unlock some of its smartest features by visiting **http://www.itelco.com**. Although inexpensive, Web Phone is targeted more at the business user than NetMeeting or (particularly) PowWow.

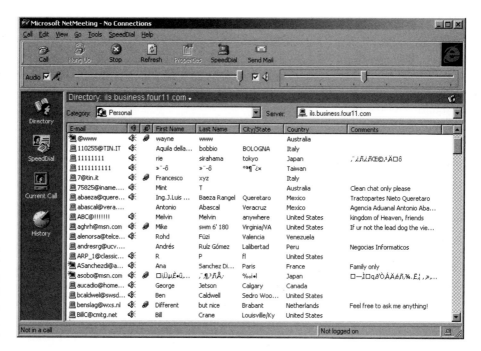

Select a server
and category in
NetMeeting and
double-click an
entry to talk.

- **Internet Phone** – A true VON program in that it has no 'text talk' or whiteboard facilities, so it will be no good to you without soundcard, microphone, and speakers. Until you pay for your copy, your talk time will be limited. You can find an evaluation copy by pointing your browser at **http://www.vocaltec.com**.

Start talking

As usual, most VON programs have similar features, although their names and toolbar buttons vary. The most popular VON programs are the free ones, so let's take a look at Tribal Voice's PowWow as a representative example.

When you first run PowWow you'll be prompted to enter your name, email address, and a choice of password. The program will then dial up and register these in the main PowWow database and you're ready to start. Click the **Connect** button on the left of the toolbar and type in the email address of the PowWow user you want to contact. To save their details to the Address Book for future use, fill in their name or nickname and click **Add**. Make sure you're connected to your IAP and click the **Connect** button. If the other person is online and running PowWow (and willing to speak to you, of course!), the main window will split into two and you'll see their reply. Just as in any chat program, you simply type your side of the conversation and press **Enter**.

The tricky thing is knowing who's online and able to chat. In some programs there's no way of knowing – you have to send a request to the person you want to speak to and see if you get a response. In other programs, such as NetMeeting and Internet Phone, as soon as you connect you'll see a list of users currently online; take your courage in both hands and double-click one!

To speak to someone by using your microphone, click the **Voice** button. Although PowWow lets you text-chat with up to seven people, you'll only be able to have a voice conversation with one at a time. Here's a brief rundown of features you'll find in PowWow (and most other VON programs):

● Transfer files by clicking the **Send File** button and choosing a file to send. You can continue to talk while the file is being transferred.

● Set up an Answering Machine message that will be sent to anyone trying to contact you when you're unavailable. Some programs (such as Web Phone) can also record messages left by anyone trying to contact you.

● Send a picture of yourself to the other user by entering its location in PowWow's setup page. Most programs can send images to be displayed on the other user's screen without interrupting the conversation.

● Click the **Whiteboard** button to collaborate in drawing pictures using a similar set of tools to those found in Windows Paint.

● Host a conference of up to 50 people taking part in text-chat.

● If you have your own web site, you can add a PowWow link to your page to tell visitors that you're online and available to chat. This is a slightly unusual feature, but Internet Phone users have a similar option. Visitors to the page can click the link to start their own software and invite you to talk.

● Stuck for someone to call? Click the **White Pages** button in PowWow and your web browser will open the main Tribal Voice page. Click a button to see a list of users currently online, then click one of the names to request a chat.

- Punctuate your chat with WAV audio files by clicking the **Sound** button. PowWow comes with its own set of sound files such as 'Applause', 'Hi', 'Cool', and 'Bye', and lets you choose between a male or female voice. Provided the same sound file is on the other person's system too, you'll both hear it.

Chapter 33

Finding Stuff on the Internet

In This Chapter...

Finding web sites using search engines and directories

Power-searching with Internet Explorer

Locate people, companies, and services using white pages and Yellow Pages

Track down newsgroups of interest, and useful articles

Check out the best (and worst!) that the Web has to offer

Finding Stuff on the Internet

Now that your connection is humming along sweetly, your software is installed, and you know how to use it, you're ready to start surfing the Internet. Almost immediately you'll hit a predicament: how on earth can you find what you're looking for? As you've probably guessed, the Internet is one jump ahead of you on that score, and there's no shortage of tools to point you towards web sites, email addresses, businesses, and people. Choosing the best tool to use will depend largely on the type of information you want to find, but don't panic – these search tools are ridiculously easy to use, and you'll probably use several of them regularly. Once again, all you need is your trusty browser.

Finding a search site

Anything you can find on the World Wide Web you can find a link to at one of the Web's search sites. Although finding a search site on the Web is easy (especially as I'm about to tell you where the most popular ones are!), picking the one that's going to give the best results is never an exact science. Essentially, there are two types of sites available: search engines and directories.

- **Search engines** are indexes of World Wide Web sites, usually built automatically by a program called a spider, a robot, a worm, or something equally appetizing (the AltaVista search engine uses a program it endearingly calls Scooter). These programs scour the Web constantly, and return with information about a page's location, title, and contents, which is then added to an index. To search for certain information, just type in keywords and the search engine will display a list of sites containing those words.

- **Directories** are hand-built lists of pages sorted into categories. Although you can search directories using a keyword search, it's often as easy to click on a category, and then click your way through the ever-more-specific sub-categories until you find the subject you're interested in.

Search engines have the benefit of being about as up-to-date in their indexes as it's possible to be, as a result of their automation. The downside is that if you search for 'pancake recipe' using a search engine, the resulting list of pages won't all necessarily contain recipes for pancakes – some might just be pages in which the words 'pancake' and 'recipe' coincidentally both happen to appear. However, the robot programs used by the search engines all vary in the ways they gather their information, so it's quite likely that you'll get results using one engine that you didn't get using another.

Directories don't have this problem because they list the subject of a page rather than the words it contains, but you won't always find the newest sites this way – sites tend to be listed in directories only when their authors submit them for inclusion.

Here's a short list of popular search engines and directories to get you started. When you arrive at one of these, it's worth adding it to Internet Explorer's Favorites menu so that you can return whenever you need to without a lot of typing.

Search site	URL
All In One	http://home.microsoft.com/access/allinone.asp
AltaVista	http://www.altavista.digital.com
Dogpile	http://www.dogpile.com
Excite	http://www.excite.com
HotBot	http://www.hotbot.com
Infoseek	http://www.infoseek.com
Lycos UK	http://www.lycos.co.uk
UK Plus	http://www.ukplus.co.uk
Yahoo! UK & Ireland	http://www.yahoo.co.uk

Using a search engine

For this example I'll pick Excite, but most search engines work in exactly the same way, and look much the same too. Indeed, directories such as Yahoo! and Infoseek can be used in the following way if you like the simplicity of keyword searches.

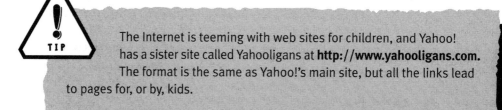

The Internet is teeming with web sites for children, and Yahoo! has a sister site called Yahooligans at **http://www.yahooligans.com.** The format is the same as Yahoo!'s main site, but all the links lead to pages for, or by, kids.

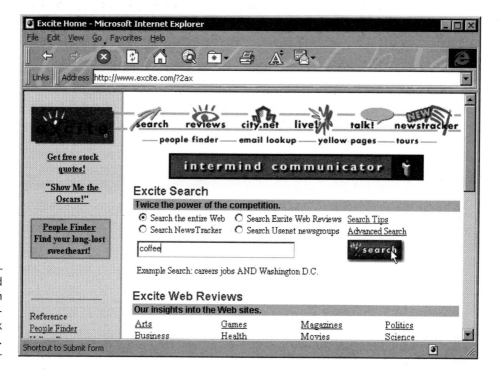

Type a keyword into the search engine's text-box and click Search.

When you arrive at Excite you'll see a page like the one shown above. For the simplest sort of search, type a single word into the text-box, and click on **Search**. If you want to search for something that can't be encapsulated in a single word it's worth reading the instructions – you'll probably see a link on the page marked **Help** or **Search Tips**, or something similar – but there are a few tricks you can use that most search engines will understand (and those that don't will generally just ignore them).

- If you enter several keywords, type them in descending order of importance; for example, if you wanted to find pictures of dolphins, type 'dolphin pictures'. The list will then present good links to dolphin sites before the rather more general links to sites just containing pictures.

- Use capital letters only if you expect to *find* capital letters. Searching for 'PARIS' may find very little, but searching for 'Paris' should find a lot. If you don't mind whether the word is found capitalized or not, use lowercase only ('paris').

- To find a particular phrase, enclose it in "quote marks". For example, a search for "hot dog" would find only pages containing this phrase and ignore pages that just contained one word or the other.

- Prefix a word with a '+' sign if it must be included, and with a '−' sign if it must be excluded; for example, if you're an economist searching for banking information, you might enter 'bank −river' to ensure that you didn't find documents about river banks. Similarly, you could enter '+printer inkjet −laser' if you wanted to find pages about printers, preferably including inkjet printers, but definitely not mentioning laser printers.

After entering the text you want to search for and clicking the **Search** button, your browser will send the information off to the engine, and within a few seconds you should see a new page like the one shown in the next screenshot listing the sites that matched your search criteria. I used the keyword 'coffee', and Excite found 272,017 different pages. It's worth remembering that when some search engines say they've found pages *about* coffee, what they've really found is pages that contain the word 'coffee' somewhere within the page's text. Many of these pages may be about something entirely different.

Of course, you won't find all 272,017 pages listed here. Instead, you'll see links to the 10 most relevant pages, with a few words quoted from the beginning of each. At the bottom of the page, you'll find a button that will lead you to the next 10 on the list, and so on. In true Web style, these are all hypertext links – click the link to open any page that sounds promising. If the page fails to live up to that promise, use your browser's **Back** button to return to the search results and try a different one.

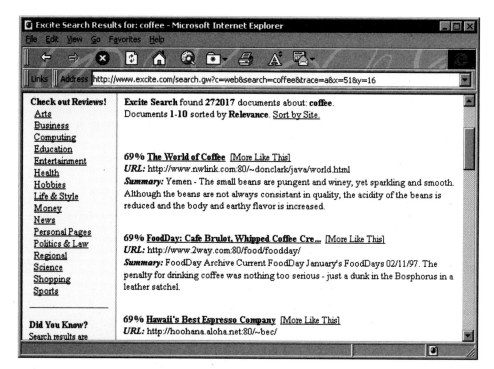

Hyperlinked
search results
with brief
descriptions and
relevancy
scores.

Most search engines give the pages a score for relevancy, and these are worth keeping an eye on. In many cases, a page scoring below about 70 per cent is unlikely to give much information. If you can't find what you want using one search engine, always try another – because they use different methods, the results can vary dramatically.

Searching the Web directories

Top of the league of web directories is Yahoo!, which now has a 'UK & Ireland' site at **http://www.yahoo.co.uk**. When you first arrive at the Yahoo! site you'll see a search-engine style text-box into which you can type keywords if you prefer to search that way. However, you'll also see a collection of hypertext links below that, and these are the key to the directory system. Starting from a choice of broad categories on this page, you can dig more deeply into the system to find links to more specific information.

To take an example, click on the **Computers and Internet** link. On the next page, you'll see the list of sub-categories, which includes **Graphics**, **Hardware**, **Multimedia**, **Training**, and many more Computer- or Internet-related subjects. Click on the **Multimedia** link, and you'll see another list of multimedia-related categories, shown in the following screenshot. Below this list of categories, you'll see another list: these are links to multimedia-related *sites* rather than more Yahoo! categories. To find out more about multimedia generally, you might click one of these to visit that site; to find out more about a specific area of multimedia such as sound, video, or virtual reality, you'd click that category in the upper list.

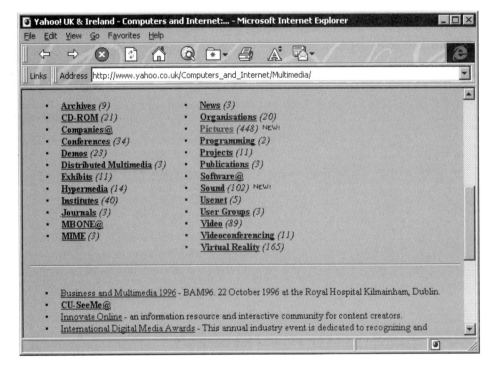

Choose a more specific Yahoo! category from the upper list, or a direct link to a web site from the lower.

The layout is pretty easy to follow when you've browsed around for a few minutes, but Yahoo! has simplified it further by using bold and plain text to help you identify where you're going. Bold text means that this is a link to another Yahoo! category; plain text indicates that it's a link to a page elsewhere on the Web that contains the sort of information you've been searching for. Beside most of the bold category-links, you'll also see a number in brackets, such as **Pictures (448)** – this number tells you how many links you'll find in that category.

Easy web searching with Internet Explorer

To reach a search site quickly in Internet Explorer, click the **Search** button on the toolbar (a globe icon with a magnifying glass). A frame will appear at the left of Explorer's window, similar to the Favorites and History list panels, displaying a mini version of a search engine. Explorer picks a search engine for you itself, but you can choose a different one from the **Select provider** list. Type in your query, click the obvious button and the results will appear in the same frame with the usual **Next 10** button at the bottom.

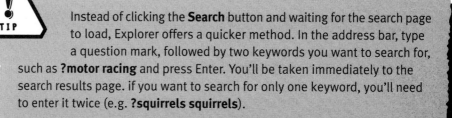

Instead of clicking the **Search** button and waiting for the search page to load, Explorer offers a quicker method. In the address bar, type a question mark, followed by two keywords you want to search for, such as **?motor racing** and press Enter. You'll be taken immediately to the search results page. if you want to search for only one keyword, you'll need to enter it twice (e.g. **?squirrels squirrels**).

The great benefit of this method of searching is that you can click any entry in the list to open it in the main part of the window without losing track of the search results. For a brief description of each site found, hold your mouse-pointer over the link for a moment as shown in the screenshot below (or, in the case of Excite, click the tiny button beside a link to show or hide its description).

Finding people on the Internet

Finding people on the Internet is a bit of a black art – after all, there are in excess of 40 million users, and few would bother to 'register' their details even if there were an established directory. In addition, of course, if you move your access account to a different online service or IAP, your email address will change too. So it's all a bit hit and miss, but let's look at a few possibilities.

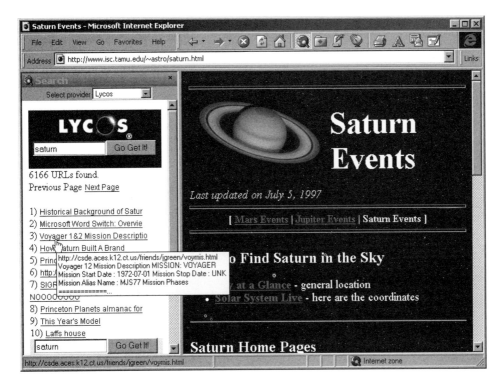

Internet Explorer's search panel keeps your results visible as you work your way through the most promising links.

Flick through the white pages

In the UK, the term Yellow Pages is synonymous with finding businesses. White pages is a type of directory listing people (what we usually just call a phone book), and the Internet has a few 'white pages' directories that may turn up trumps. Some of these rely on people actually submitting their details voluntarily; others take the more crafty approach of searching the newsgroups and adding the email addresses of anyone posting an article. Searching white pages is just like using any other search engine, usually requiring you to enter the user's first and last names and click on a Search button:

- **Bigfoot** at **http://bigfoot.co.uk** – Don't be fooled by the URL; the search engine itself is in the USA, but this is the directory most likely to find the email address of a UK Internet user.

- **Four11** at **http://www.fourll.com** – The biggest and most popular 'people locator' in the USA, which searches the Internet for email addresses *and* accepts individual submissions. Details found here may include a user's hobbies, postal address, and phone number, but most entries are from the USA.

- **Infospace** at **http://www.infospace.com/info/people.htm** – Another US service, again unlikely to produce an email address for anyone living outside the USA.

Back to the search engines

Some of the popular search engines mentioned earlier in this chapter have 'people-finder' options too. Lycos has a **People Find** button which leads to its own email search pages. Excite has buttons marked **People Finder** (for addresses and phone numbers), and **Email Lookup** (for email addresses). In Infoseek, click the arrow-button on the drop-down list-box and choose **Email Addresses**, then type someone's name into the text-box.

To find out about links to more white pages, try heading off to **http://www.yahoo.com/Reference/White_Pages**. You could also try The Directory Of Directories at **http://www.procd.com/hl/direct.htm**, which might help you track someone down if you know something about their hobbies, interests, or occupation.

Yellow Pages – searching for businesses

Just as there are white pages on the Net, there are Yellow Pages – the difference is that businesses want to be found, to the extent that they'll pay to be listed, so these searches will almost always yield results. Two of the most useful for finding UK businesses are Yell (the Yellow Pages we all know and love, in its online incarnation), and Scoot.

Yell, at **http://www.yell.co.uk**, is an ideal place to begin a search for a UK company. Click one of the icons on the left to look for a company's web site by category or in an alphabetical list. There's also a search engine dedicated to finding

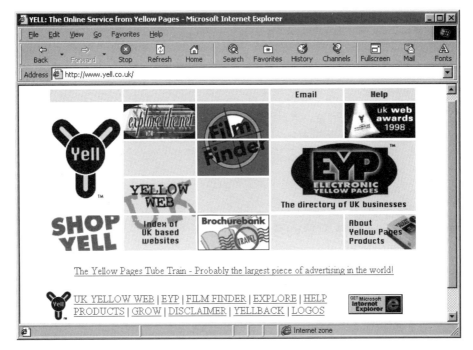

The (very) Yellow Pages online – the ideal place to find the web sites and contact details of UK companies, and to take your pick of the flicks.

UK web sites of all types. The EYP link on the right takes you to an automated search of the Electronic Yellow Pages: enter a company's location, and either a Business Type or Company Name, to start the search. The results mirror those you'd expect to find in the paper version. As an unusual bonus, click the centre icon to find out what films are showing at almost any cinema in the country.

The Scoot site, at **http://www.freepages.co.uk**, is dedicated to finding companies' addresses and phone numbers, and works in a slightly different way from Yell. Begin by entering a town or city in which the company is based. On the next page, confirm that the county listed is correct. Finally, on the third page, choose a category of business to search for from the drop-down list box. The search will return a list of all the businesses of that type in your chosen area. This is a great way to search if, for example, you need a plumber and you're currently too damp to care *which* plumber it is.

If you haven't found the company yet, it's either a US company or it doesn't want to be found! To search for US companies, head off to Excite at **http://www.excite.com** and click the **Yellow Pages** button. Enter a company name and category description, together with location details if known, and click the search button. If the category you chose doesn't match an Excite category, you'll be given a list of similar categories to choose from. You can also try **http://www.companiesonline.com**, which is a new addition to the Lycos search engine family. If you're looking for financial or performance-related information about a company, visit Infoseek and select **Company Profiles** from the drop-down list to search through almost 50,000 US companies. Finally, of course, there's the good old workhorse – Yahoo! Visit **http://www.yahoo.co.uk/Business _and_Economy/Companies** and you'll be presented with a list of more than 100 categories. The sites you'll find in Yahoo's categories cover the UK and Ireland as well as the USA and elsewhere.

Searching the newsgroups

There's more value to searching Usenet newsgroups than there appears at first; for example, with so many thousands of groups to choose from, a quick search for the keywords that sum up your favourite topic might help you determine the most suitable newsgroup to subscribe to. Or perhaps you need an answer to a technical question quickly – it's almost certainly been answered in a newsgroup article.

One of the best sites that you can use for newsgroup searches is Deja News at **http://www.dejanews.com**, which looks just like any other search engine you've come across in this chapter, except that there's a choice of two text-boxes for keywords. If you're looking for a newsgroup, enter a keyword into the lower of the two text-boxes to find groups that discuss the subject you want. If you're looking for individual articles, use the upper text-box. The search results list 20 articles at a time (with the usual button at the end of the page to fetch the next 20), and include authors' details and the names of the newsgroups in which the articles were found. Click on one of the articles to read it and you'll find a handy button-bar added to

TIP

If you search Deja News for newsgroups, you can click any newsgroup you find on the results list to read its articles. But, although it's possible, it's not the easiest way to navigate a newsgroup – you'll find it simpler to run your newsreader program and read the articles from the chosen group with that instead.

the page that lets you view the topic's thread, read the next or the previous article, and post replies to the newsgroup or to the article's author by email.

The great value of Deja News is that articles are available here long after they were first posted to Usenet. The only possible fly in the ointment is that the group you want may not be covered. If it isn't, head for Infoseek's search engine and choose Usenet from the drop-down list.

Surf's up! Now, where shall I go?

All dressed up and nowhere to surf? The sheer unpredictability of the World Wide Web will almost certainly tempt you at times, even if there's nothing in particular you need to do or find. For those moments when you've just got to surf, here's a brief list of sites that give you somewhere worth surfing *to*:

● **Cool Site Of The Day** – A single cool site every day, and every day the entire universe goes to visit the lucky recipient of the title. You'll also find **The Still Cool Archive, The Cool-O-Meter**, and **Cool Site Of The Year**. Bucketloads of cool, and you'll find it all at **http://cool.infi.net**.

● **Weekly Hot 100** – Links sorted into 26 categories such as Jobs, Finance, Jokes, Autos, ShowBiz, and Travel. The sites are sorted by how many visits they receive, although there's a fair sprinkling of 'dead' links (links to sites that no longer exist). Head for **http://www.100hot.com**.

● **PC Magazine's Top 100 Web Sites** – Top sites chosen by the magazine's editors, and sorted into five categories: Commerce, Computing, Entertainment, News, and Reference. For this one, go to **http://www.zdnet.com/~pcmag/special/web100**.

● **Top 50 UK Web Sites** – A simple list of sites numbered 1 to 50 according to how many visitors (or 'hits') each site has had in the last week. You'll find a huge variety of stuff at these sites, which must all be good, mustn't they? Skip off to **http://www.top50.co.uk**.

● **Jacob Richman's Hot Sites** – 28 categories of useful links sniffed out and sorted by Jacob himself, including Humour, Education, Law, and Music. Find this at **http://www.jr.co.il/hotsites/hotsites.htm**.

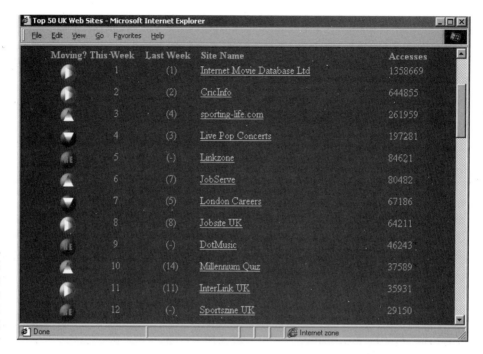

Moving?	This Week	Last Week	Site Name	Accesses
	1	(1)	Internet Movie Database Ltd	1358669
	2	(2)	CricInfo	644855
	3	(4)	sporting-life.com	261959
	4	(3)	Live Pop Concerts	197281
	5	(-)	Linkzone	84621
	6	(7)	JobServe	80482
	7	(5)	London Careers	67186
	8	(8)	Jobsite UK	64211
	9	(-)	DotMusic	46243
	10	(14)	Millennium Quiz	37589
	11	(11)	InterLink UK	35931
	12	(-)	Sportszine UK	29150

The top 50 UK web sites, as chosen weekly by several million people!

The World Wide Web is an art form, and like any form of art, some people can do it and some people can't. Depending on your viewpoint, bad art can be far more entertaining than good art: there are countless web sites out there which, far from being 'cool', have been caught with their trousers round their ankles. If you've overdosed on cool, try these as an antidote:

- **The Worst Of The Web** – Click on the large image to take a trip through the current 'worst sites', with comments from your three cartoon hosts. Alternatively, follow the links below the image to see previous award-winners in this category. Visit **http://www.worstoftheweb.com** for this 'bland bombshell'.

- **Mirsky's Worst Of The Web**. A famous site, sadly now closed, but you can still visit Mirsky's past winners, take the Drunk Browsing Test, and surf through the Nicknames Page. You'll find Mirsky's at **http://mirsky.com/wow**.

- **The World Wide Web Hall Of Shame** – Links to some of the best 'dead flies' that litter the Web, replete with introductory comments, can be found at **http://www.rt66.com/smcinnis/hos**.

Chapter 34

Safety on the Internet

In This Chapter...

Keep your kids safe on the Internet

The truth about credit-card security on the Net

Are cookies really dangerous?

Email – privacy and encryption

Safety on the Internet

Safety, or the lack of it, is a much-hyped area of Internet life. According to many press articles, as soon as you go online you're going to be faced with a barrage of pornography, your credit-card number will be stolen, your personal email messages will be published far and wide, and your children will be at the mercy of paedophile rings.

Of course, articles like these make good news stories, and are much more interesting than 'Child surfs Internet, sees no pornography', for example. In this chapter, we'll sort out what the risks actually are, and how they can be minimized.

Will my kids be safe on the Internet?

The Internet has its fair share of sex and smut, just as it has motoring, cookery, sports, films, and so on. I'm not going to pretend that your kids *can't* come into contact with explicit images and language, but there are two important points to note. First, you're no more likely to stumble upon pornography while looking for a sports site than you are to stumble upon film reviews or recipes – if you want to find that sort of content, you have to go looking for it. Secondly, most of the sexually explicit sites on the World Wide Web are private – to get inside you need a credit card. Nevertheless, there *are* dangers on the Net, and given unrestricted freedom, your kids may come into contact with unsuitable material.

But what sort of material? On the Web, the front pages of those private sites are accessible to all, and some contain images and language designed to titillate, and to part you from your cash. The Web's search engines are another risk – enter the wrong keywords (or the *right* keywords, depending on your viewpoint) and you'll be presented with direct links to explicit sites accompanied by colourful descriptions. Quite apart from the sexually explicit sites, there are pages on the Net containing views or language that you wouldn't want your kids to read.

However, these are not good reasons to deny children access to the Internet. Quite simply, the Internet is a fact of life that isn't going to go away, and will feature more strongly in our children's lives than it does in ours. More and more schools are recognizing this, and promoting use of the Internet in homework and class projects. The wealth of web sites created by and for children is a great indicator of their active participation in the growth of the Net. Rather than depriving children of this incredible resource, agree a few ground rules at the outset: when they can surf, why they should never give out their address, school name or telephone number, what sort of sites they can visit, and what to do if they receive messages that make them uncomfortable. For some excellent practical advice on this subject, I recommend that all parents visit Yahooligans at **http://www.yahooligans.com/docs/safety**.

If you're ever concerned about the web sites your children might be visiting, remember that you can open Internet Explorer's History panel (or the History subdirectory of your Windows directory) to see a list of all recently-accessed pages sorted chronologically by week and day. Similarly, if you go to **View | Internet Options** and click the **Settings** button followed by the **View Files** button you can also sort all recently-visited sites by time of day by clicking the **Last Accessed** header bar.

Finally, there are two Internet services that are definitely *not* suitable places for children to visit unsupervised: newsgroups and IRC chat channels. Many access providers refuse to carry certain newsgroups, such as the alt.sex and alt.binaries.pictures hierarchies, but articles in some quite innocent newsgroups may contain views or language you wouldn't want your kids to read. The same goes for IRC. As I mentioned in Chapter 32, many chat channels are sexual in nature, and often in name too, but the type of people trying to make contact with children through IRC won't limit themselves to those channels. I'd simply suggest that if you have kids in the house, you don't have an IRC program installed on your computer.

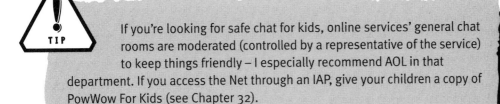

TIP

If you're looking for safe chat for kids, online services' general chat rooms are moderated (controlled by a representative of the service) to keep things friendly – I especially recommend AOL in that department. If you access the Net through an IAP, give your children a copy of PowWow For Kids (see Chapter 32).

Get a little extra help

If all this seems a bit too much to handle on your own, don't worry! There are many software programs around that can take over some of the supervision for you. To balance maximum access with maximum security, you need a program that can identify the actual content about to be viewed, rather than the name of the page or site. There are many such programs available, but here's a shortlist of the most respected:

- **Net Nanny** from **http://www.netnanny.com**.

- **CYBERsitter** from **http://www.solidoak.com/cysitter.htm**.

- **SurfWatch** from **http://www.surfwatch.com**.

- **Cyber Patrol** from **http://www.cyberpatrol.com**.

Some of these programs, such as Net Nanny, are especially powerful in that they don't work solely with Internet programs – they can bar access to documents viewed using any program on your computer. When you start your computer, Net Nanny runs invisibly in the background and watches for particular words or phrases. If they appear, Net Nanny instantly replaces them with X's, and threatens to shut down the program in 30 seconds unless you enter a valid password. The words in question may appear in email messages, web pages, or chat rooms, they may be in files on floppy disks or CD-ROMs, or they may form the name of a file. You can add words, phrases, applications, and web sites to Net Nanny's list, and download regularly updated lists of restricted sites. For added parental reassurance, Net Nanny also keeps a note of any attempts to access restricted sites, as do many other programs.

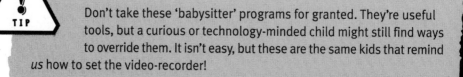

Don't take these 'babysitter' programs for granted. They're useful tools, but a curious or technology-minded child might still find ways to override them. It isn't easy, but these are the same kids that remind *us* how to set the video-recorder!

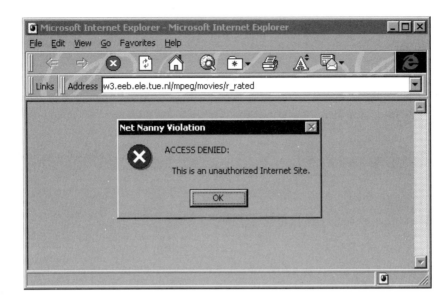

Net Nanny says
No.

Is it safe to use my credit card on the Internet?

Another popular myth about the Internet is that credit-card transactions are risky because your card number can be stolen. To put this in perspective, consider how you use your credit or debit card in the 'real world'. How many people get to see your card number during a normal week? How much time does your card spend out of your view when you use it? Do you always ask for the carbon paper after signing for a credit-card purchase? The truth is, card numbers are *easy* to steal. It takes a lot more effort and technical know-how to steal numbers on the Internet, and a single card number isn't valuable enough to warrant the exertion.

Making the computer-hacker's job more difficult in this department, modern browsers can now encrypt the data they send, and most of the web sites at which you can use your credit card run on secure servers that have their own built-in encryption. So when you visit one of these secure sites, enter your card number and click the button to send it, your number will appear as meaningless gibberish to anyone managing to hack into the system. In fact, credit-card companies actually regard online transactions as being the *safest* kind.

You can easily tell when you arrive at a secure site. In Internet Explorer, look for a little padlock symbol in the lower right corner of the browser. You'll also notice that the **http://** prefix in the address-bar becomes **https://**. More and more shopping sites are becoming secure, and those that aren't usually give alternative payment methods.

Cookies – are they safe to eat?

They sound cute and harmless, but what are they? Well, they're not particularly cute – cookies are small text files that are stored on your computer's hard disk when you visit certain web sites. To take a look at them, open your **Windows** directory, and then open the **Cookies** directory you find inside – you can double-click any of these cookies to read its contents in Notepad.

Cookies can serve several uses to the creator of a web site, and some can even benefit visitors like you and me. A cookie might contain a unique code that identifies you, saving the need to enter a name and password when you visit, and perhaps allowing you to access restricted areas of a site. They're also often used by online shopping sites as a sort of 'supermarket trolley' that keeps track of the purchases you select until you're ready to pay and leave. Sites that rely heavily on displaying banner advertisements for their income might track 'click-throughs', keeping a log of the path you follow through the site and the pages you decide to visit. Knowing a bit about your interests in this way helps enable the site to target you with the type of adverts most likely to grab your attention.

Not all cookies have practical uses. You may visit a personal site that asks you to enter your name which it then stores in a cookie. On future visits you'll see a message such as 'Hello Rob, you've visited this page four times' – it's pointless, but it's still harmless.

So, are they safe? Yes, they are. Cookies are often misunderstood – they can't be used to read any other data from your hard disk, to find out what software you've got installed, or to pass on personal information. When you visit a web site the page doesn't 'search' your hard disk for a cookie; instead, your browser sends the cookie containing the URL of the site as soon as you type in the address or click the link.

The wider question is whether you want anyone using your hard-disk as a type of mini-database in this way – it's a point of principle rather than safety. If you want to join the anti-cookie ranks, Internet Explorer can help. Click on **View | Internet Options | Advanced** and scroll down to the section headed **Cookies** near the bottom of the window. Here you can choose **Prompt before accepting cookies** to be given the choice of accepting or rejecting a cookie when a site tries to store one, or **Disable all cookie use** if you want to take a tougher stand against them. Be warned though – some sites just won't let you in if you won't eat the cookie! A more practical method is just to delete the entire contents of your Cookies directory as soon as you've finished surfing for the day.

How private is my email?

The words 'email' and 'private' don't go together well. I'm not saying that the world and his dog are going to read every message you send, but email *can* get you into trouble (and people have got into very deep water from using email where a phone call or a quiet chat would have been wiser). If you're concerned about who could read it, don't write it.

The most obvious problem is that your 'private' messages can be easily forwarded or redirected, or the recipient might simply fail to delete an incriminating message after reading it. But apart from existing on your computer and the recipient's computer, however briefly, the message also spends time on your access provider's mail server and that of the recipient's access provider. Will the message really be deleted from both? And what if the administrator of one of these systems decides to run a backup while your message is waiting to be delivered?

If you really must use email to exchange sensitive messages, you might want to consider using encryption to scramble them. Messages are encrypted and decrypted using two codes called 'keys' that you type into the encryption software. One is your private key, the other is a public key that you'd hand out to anyone who needed to use it, or perhaps post on the Internet. If someone wanted to send you an encrypted message, they'd use your freely available public key to encrypt it, and then send it off as usual. The message can only be decoded using your private key, and only you have access to that key. Likewise, if you wanted to send someone else a private message, you'd use his or her public key to encrypt it.

The most popular encryption program is called PGP (Pretty Good Privacy). Although unbreakable, it isn't easy to use and you might want an extra program that sits on top and puts a 'friendlier face' on it. Go to **http://www.yahoo.com/Computers_and_Internet/Security_ and_Encryption** to learn more about the system and the software available.

Chapter 35

Building your own Web Site

In This Chapter...

The Web page language – it's all tags

A simple Web page – title, heading, and paragraphs

Formatting text with bold and italic type

Inserting links to other pages and Web sites

Spicing up the page with colour and images

Building your own Web Site

Over the last few chapters you've learnt how to use just about every area of the Internet – the major services, the search engines, email, newsgroups, the whole shebang – but it's still *everyone else's* Internet you're using! Sooner or later, you'll want to grab a little corner of it and make it your own by building your own site on the Web. The mechanics of creating a web site are simple enough, and in this chapter I'll show you how to do it. Of course, whole books have been written on this subject so this isn't an exhaustive reference, but it should get you off to a flying start. There are many guides and tutorials on the Web itself, which can help you improve your skills, and you'll find two of the best at:

http://www.asiweb.com/htmlauth.htm
and
http://www.ncsa.uiuc.edu/General/Internet/WWW/HTMLPrimer.html.

HTML – the language of the Web

Pages on the World Wide Web are written in a language called HTML (HyperText Markup Language). So what's that all about? Well, we've met hypertext already – those underlined, clickable links that make the Web so easy to navigate. A markup language is a set of codes or signs added to plain text to indicate how it should be presented to the reader, noting bold or italic text, typefaces to be used, paragraph breaks, and so on. When you type any document into your word processor, it adds these codes for you, but tactfully hides them from view: if you wanted bold text, for example, it *shows* you bold text instead of those codes. In HTML, however, you have to type in the codes yourself along with the text, and your browser puts the whole lot together before displaying it.

These codes are known as 'tags', and they consist of ordinary text placed between less-than and greater-than signs. Lets take an example:

```
<B>Welcome to my homepage.</B> Glad you could make it!
```

The first tag, <B>, means 'turn on bold type'. Halfway through the line, the same tag is used again, but with a forward-slash inserted directly after the less-than sign: this means 'turn off bold type'. If you displayed a page containing this line in your browser, it would look like this:

Welcome to my homepage. Glad you could make it!

Of course, there's more to a web page than bold text, so clearly there must be many more of these tags. Don't let that worry you – you don't have to learn all of them! There's a small bundle that you'll use a lot, and you'll get to know these very quickly. The rest will begin to sink in once you've used them a few times.

Do I need special software?

Believe it or not, creating a web site is something you can do for free (once you've bought a computer and started paying for an Internet connection, that is). Because HTML is entirely text-based, you can write your pages in Windows' Notepad, and I'm going to assume that's what you're doing. But there are other options, so let's quickly run through them.

JARGON BUSTER

WYSIWYG

A delightful acronym (pronounced 'wizzywig') for 'What you see is what you get'. This is used to describe many different types of software that can show you on the screen exactly what something will look like when you print it on paper or view it in your web browser.

WYSIWYG editors

In theory, WYSIWYG editors are the perfect way of working: instead of looking at plain text with HTML tags dotted around it, you see your web page itself gradually taking shape, with images, colours and formatting displayed. There are a couple of drawbacks, though. First, WYSIWYG editors cost serious money compared to most other types of Internet software. Secondly, they probably won't help you avoid learning something about HTML. Once in a while the editor won't do what you want it to do, and you'll have to switch to its text-editing mode to juggle the tags yourself. My early experience with HTML was that it's far easier to learn the language itself than it is to learn how the WYSIWYG software works, but if you'd like to give the WYSIWYG method a shot, here are two of the most popular:

- **Microsoft FrontPage**
  You can find out more about this at **http://www.microsoft.com/frontpage**, but you'll have to take a trip into town to buy a copy.

- **Adobe PageMill**
  Visit **http://www.adobe.com/prodindex/pagemill/main.html** for details, downloads, and online payment.

Markup editors

Using a markup editor is rather like using Notepad – you see all the HTML codes on the page in front of you. But instead of having to type in tags yourself, a markup editor will insert them for you at the click of a button or the press of a hotkey, in the same way that you use your word processor. You might still choose to type in some of the simple tags yourself, such as the tag for bold text mentioned earlier, but for more complicated elements such as a table with a lot of cells, this automation is a great time and sanity saver.

Markup editors are also ideal for newcomers to HTML. If you don't know one tag from another, just click the appropriate buttons on the toolbar to insert them: once you've seen them appear on the page a few times, you'll soon start to remember what's what!

Here are three of the most popular and feature-packed markup editors. You'll need to register these if you want to use them beyond the trial period, but I wholeheartedly recommend picking one of them to start with:

- **HomeSite** from
  http//www.allaire.com/products/homesite

- **WebEdit PRO** from
  http://www.luckman.com

- **HTMLed** from
  http://www.ist.ca

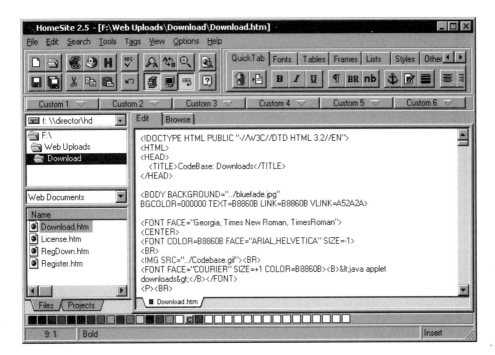

Colour-coding
and one-click
tag insertion in
HomeSite

Text converters

Some modern word-processors like Lotus WordPro and Microsoft Word have
begun to include features to turn your documents into web pages. At their simplest,
they'll let you create an ordinary word-processed document and then choose a
Save as HTML option from the **File** menu to convert it into a web page. The result
won't be as effective as other pages on the Web, but it's an ideal way to convert a
long document when the only other option is to add all the tags yourself!

You can also create web pages from scratch in these programs; for example,
Microsoft Word has its own Web Page Wizard that can set you up with a ready-to-
edit template. To start it up, go to **File** | **New...**, then click the **Web Pages** tab and

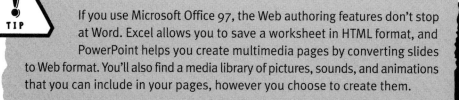

TIP If you use Microsoft Office 97, the Web authoring features don't stop at Word. Excel allows you to save a worksheet in HTML format, and PowerPoint helps you create multimedia pages by converting slides to Web format. You'll also find a media library of pictures, sounds, and animations that you can include in your pages, however you choose to create them.

double-click **Web Page Wizard**. You can add and delete elements on the page, and use the standard drawing and editing toolbars to slot in anything else you need.

Let's get started

There's a few bits and pieces that will appear in almost every HTML document you write, so let's start by making a template file you can use every time you want to create a new page. Start Notepad, and type the text below (without worrying about the exact number of spaces or carriage returns). Save this file using any name you like, but make sure you give it the extension **.htm** or **.html**. Every web page you write must be saved with one of these extensions – it doesn't matter which you choose, but you'll find life a lot easier if you stick to the same one each time!

```
<!DOCTYPE HTML PUBLIC "-//W3C//DTD HTML 3.2//EN">

<HTML>
<HEAD>
    <TITLE>Untitled</TITLE>
</HEAD>
<BODY>

</BODY>
</HTML>
```

None of those tags does anything exciting by itself, but it's worth knowing what they're all for. The first line is a piece of technical nonsense that tells a browser that the document is written in the latest version of the HTML language. The rest of the document is placed between the <HTML> and </HTML> tags, and falls into two separate chunks: the head (the section between <HEAD> and </HEAD>), and the body (between <BODY> and </BODY>). The document's head is pretty dull: all it contains is the title of the document, inserted between the <TITLE> and </TITLE> tags. There are other bits and pieces that can be slotted in here, but the title is the only element that *must* be included.

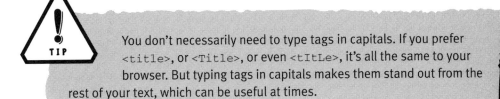

You don't necessarily need to type tags in capitals. If you prefer <title>, or <Title>, or even <tItLe>, it's all the same to your browser. But typing tags in capitals makes them stand out from the rest of your text, which can be useful at times.

The body section is the one that matters. Between these two tags you'll type all the text that should appear on your page, and put in the tags you need to display images, set colours, insert hyperlinks to other pages and sites, and anything else you want your page to contain.

Make a copy of the file (so that you keep this template unchanged for creating more web pages later) and open the copy in Notepad or your HTML editor.

Add a title & text

The first thing to do is to replace the word **Untitled** with a sensible title for the document, such as **Links To The Best Multimedia Sites** or **My EastEnders HomePage**. Pick something that describes what the page will be about, but keep it fairly short: the text between the <TITLE> and </TITLE> tags will appear in the title-bar at the very top of most browsers, and if your entry is too long to fit, it'll just get chopped off!

Now we'll add some text to the page. Either type the same as I've entered below, or replace my first and second paragraph entries with whole paragraphs if you prefer. When you've done that, save the file as **links.html**, but don't close Notepad yet.

```
<!DOCTYPE HTML PUBLIC "-//W3C//DTD HTML 3.2//EN">

<HTML>
<HEAD>
    <TITLE>Links To The Best Multimedia Sites</TITLE>
</HEAD>

<BODY>
<H1>Welcome To My Homepage!</H1>
Here's the first paragraph.
<P>And here's the second paragraph.

</BODY>
</HTML>
```

Now take a look at your masterpiece in your browser. There are several ways you can do this: find the file you just saved and double-click it, or open your browser and type the path to the file in the address bar, or choose **File** | **Open** and click on **Browse**. When your browser displays it, it should look just like the next screenshot.

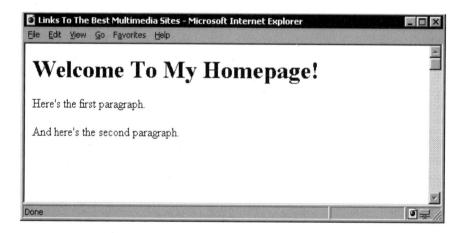

So what are those new tags all about? Let's take the <P> tag first. This tells your browser to present the following text as a new paragraph, which automatically inserts a blank line before it. And this raises an important point about HTML: you can't insert blank lines just by pressing Enter or Return. Although you can see blank lines in Notepad when you do that, your browser will just ignore them, which is why you need to start a new paragraph by entering `<P>`. (Notice that you don't have to put in a closing `</P>` at the end of a paragraph – the act of starting a new paragraph isn't an ongoing effect that has to be turned off again.)

Another tag, `<BR>`, will give you a 'line break'. In other words, the text that follows that tag will start at the beginning of the next line with no empty line inserted before it.

The other pair of tags that cropped up was `<H1>` and `</H1>`, which format a line of text as a heading. You can choose from six sizes: `<H1>` and `</H1>` are the largest, followed by `<H2>` and `</H2>` down to the smallest, `<H6>` and `</H6>`. In one nifty little manoeuvre, these tags change the size of the text you place between them *and* make it bold. They also automatically start a new paragraph for the heading (so you don't need to place a `<P>` tag at the start of the line), and start a new paragraph for whatever follows the heading. Try changing the size of the heading by altering those tags to see the different effects, re-saving the file, and clicking your browser's **Refresh** button to update it.

Be bold (or be italic...)

The tags for bold and italic text are easy to remember: `<B>` for bold, and `<I>` for italic. As both of these are ongoing effects, you'll have to enter closing tags (`</B>` or `</I>`) when you want the effect to stop. And, just as in your word processor, you can combine these tags, so if your document contained this:

This is `<I>italic</I>`. This is `<B>bold</B>`. This is `<B><I>bold & italic</I></B>`.

the result would look like this in your browser:

This is *italic*. This is **bold**. This is ***bold & italic***.

Lesser-used text-formatting tags that might prove useful are superscript (^{and}) and subscript (_{and}). You can also underline text using another memorable pair of tags, <U> and </U>, but use underline with care: most people surfing the Web expect underlined text to be a hyperlink, and might find your gratuitous use of these tags confusing.

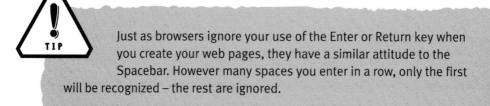

TIP Just as browsers ignore your use of the Enter or Return key when you create your web pages, they have a similar attitude to the Spacebar. However many spaces you enter in a row, only the first will be recognized – the rest are ignored.

Insert links to other sites

It's an unwritten rule of the Internet that a web site should contain links to other web sites. After all, the entire Web works by being interconnected, and if people surf their way to your site and have to retrace their steps before they can continue surfing, they'll steer clear in future! So let's put in another <P> tag to start a new paragraph, and add that sorely needed link as shown below:

```
<P>Visit Macromedia's snazzy <A
HREF="http://www.macromedia.com/shockzone">Shockzone</A>
Site
```

This is a more complicated tag, so let's look at it bit by bit. Although we call these 'links', in HTML they're known as 'anchors', and that's where the A comes from after the first < sign. An anchor usually begins with the <A HREF= tag. Following that comes the URL of the page you want to link to, always enclosed in double-quotes, and the > sign to finish the opening anchor tag.

Immediately after the opening anchor tag, type the text you want visitors to your page to click on. This might be a single word, a sentence, or even a whole paragraph, but don't forget to put *something* here, or there'll be nothing to click on to reach that site! Finally, type the closing anchor tag, </A>.

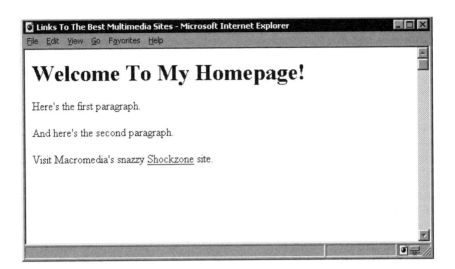

TIP You can position elements centrally on the page by placing them between <CENTER> and </CENTER> tags (note the US spelling, though!). This applies to headings, paragraphs of text, images, and almost anything else you might want to include.

Links to other pages on your own site

The link we just added used something called an 'absolute URL'. In fact, that's the only type of URL you've seen so far: an absolute URL gives the whole path to the page you want to open, including the http:// bit and the name of the computer. When you want to create links to other pages on your own site you can use a different, simpler method.

Create a new HTML document, and save it to the directory where the other is stored. Let's assume you've called it **morelinks.html**. Now, in your first document, you can create a link to this new page by typing this anchor:

```
<A HREF="morelinks.html">Here's a few more links.</A>
```

Yes, it's just a filename. This is called a 'relative URL'. It tells your browser to look for a file called **morelinks.html** and display it. The great thing about relative URLs is that you can test these on your own system to make sure they work: for absolute URLs, your PC would have to connect to your IAP to search for the page. Since the browser hasn't been told where else to look, it searches the directory containing the document it's displaying at that moment. As long as **morelinks.html** really is in that same directory, the browser will find it and open it.

You can make a browser look somewhere different for a file in a similar way. Open the directory containing these two documents, create a subdirectory called **pages**, and move the **morelinks.html** file into it. The link we just added now needs to be changed to the following:

```
<A HREF="pages/morelinks.html">Here's a few more links.</A>
```

The browser now looks in the current directory for another directory called **pages**, and looks inside that for **morelinks.html**.

Finally, let's open **morelinks.html** and create a link back to our original document (which we called **links.html**), so that you can click your way to and fro between the two. To do this, we need to tell the browser to look in the parent directory of **pages** to find this file: to move up one level in the directory tree, just type two dots:

```
<A HREF="../links.html">Here's my first links page.</A>
```

TIP
When you refer to a page or file in your document, the case is vital. If you type in a link to **Index.html** and the file is acutally called **index.html** or **Index.HTML**, the page won't be found. Most web authors save *all* their files with lower-case names to remove any uncertainty. Similarly, although you can use long filenames, they mustn't include any spaces.

So far, we've looked at linking to other web pages, but a hyperlink needn't necessarily point to a **.html** document. If you have a movie file, a text file, a sound file, or whatever, create the link in exactly the same way entering the location and name of this file between the double-quotes. If the file is particularly large, though, it's good practice to mention its size somewhere nearby so that people can choose whether or not to click that link.

Adding colour to the page

So far, in our example web page, everything looks a bit dull. The background is white, the text is black, the hyperlinks are blue – these are the default colours set up by Internet Explorer, and it's using them because we haven't told it to use anything different. All of this is easily changed, though, by typing our preferences into that opening <BODY> tag.

This brings us to a new area of HTML. A tag like <B> is self-contained – it simply turns on bold text, with no complications. Other tags need to contain a little more information about what you want to do. A good example is the <FONT> tag, which we'll look at more closely later in this chapter. By itself, it isn't saying anything useful: which font? what size? what colour? You provide this information by the addition of 'attributes' to the tag such as SIZE=3, FACE=Arial, and so on, so a complete font tag might be: <FONT SIZE=3 FACE=Arial>.

The <BODY> tag doesn't *have* to contain attributes, but browsers will use their own default settings for anything you haven't specified, and different browsers use different defaults. Most web authors like to keep as much control as possible over how their pages will be displayed, and make their own settings for the body attributes. There are six attributes you can use in the <BODY> tag:

This attribute...	... has this effect
BGCOLOR=	Sets the background colour of the web page
TEXT=	Sets the colour of text on the page
LINK=	Sets the colour of the clickable hyperlinks
VLINK=	Sets the colour of a link to a previously visited page
ALINK=	Sets the colour of a link between the time it's clicked and the new page opening
BACKGROUND=	Specifies an image to use as the page's 'wallpaper'

Without further ado, open the original **links.html** document you created earlier, and change the <BODY> tag so that it looks like this:

```
<BODY BGCOLOR=MAROON TEXT=WHITE LINK=YELLOW VLINK=OLIVE
ALINK=LIME>
```

Save the file, and take a look at it in your browser. Okay, the colour scheme may not be to your taste, but it's starting to resemble a 'real' web page! Try swapping colours around to find a scheme you prefer. There are 140 colours to choose from, so take a look at the Colour Chart on the CD-ROM.

The other attribute is BACKGROUND=, which places a GIF or JPEG image on the web page, and tiles it to fill the entire area. Let's assume you want to use an image file called **hoops.gif**, which is in the same directory as the current document. Inside the body tag, add: BACKGROUND="hoops.gif" (not forgetting the double-quotes). Your whole <BODY> tag might now look like this:

```
<BODY BACKGROUND="hoops.gif" BGCOLOR=MAROON TEXT=WHITE
LINK=YELLOW VLINK=OLIVE ALINK=LIME>
```

Set up your font options

At the moment, you're also stuck with a single font (probably Times New Roman). Once again, this is set up by your browser by default, and, of course, different browsers might use different default fonts. Fortunately, the <FONT> tag allows you to choose and change the font face, size, and colour whenever you need to. Here's an example of a <FONT> tag using all three attributes:

```
<FONT FACE="Verdana,Arial,Helvetica" SIZE=4
COLOR=RED>...</FONT>
```

Let's take these one at a time. The FACE attribute is the name of the font you want to use. Obviously this must be a font on your own system, but the same font needs to be on the system of anyone visiting your page too: if it isn't, their browser will revert to their default font. You can keep a bit of extra control by listing more than one font (separated by commas), as in the example above. If the first font isn't available, the browser will try the second, and so on.

> **TIP**
>
> Try to pick fonts that most visitors to your site will have on their systems so that they'll see the page as you intended. Most visitors to your site will have Arial and Times New Roman. Microsoft supplies a pack of fonts for the Web which many web authors now use; it includes Comic Sans MS, Verdana, Impact and Georgia. You can download any of these fonts that you don't already have from **http://www.microsoft.com/truetype/ fontpack/win.htm**.

Font sizes in HTML work differently than in your word processor. There are seven sizes numbered (unsurprisingly) from 1 to 7, where 1 is the smallest. The default size for text is 3, so if you want to make your text slightly larger, use SIZE=4. The SIZE attribute doesn't affect the headings we covered earlier, so if you've used one of these somewhere between your <FONT> and </FONT> tags, it will still be formatted as a heading.

The colour of the text has already been set in the <BODY> tag, but you might want to slip in an occasional <FONT COLOR=PURPLE>...</FONT> to change the colour of a certain word, paragraph, or heading. After the closing </FONT> tag, the colour will revert to that set in the <BODY> tag.

With the earlier changes to the <BODY> tag, and the addition of a couple of </FONT> tags, here's what the body of our document might look like now:

```
<BODY BGCOLOR=MAROON TEXT=WHITE LINK=YELLOW VLINK=OLIVE
ALINK=LIME>

<FONT FACE="Comic Sans MS" COLOR=YELLOW>
<H1>Welcome To My Homepage!</H1>
</FONT>

<FONT FACE="Arial">

Here's the first paragraph.
<P>And here's the second paragraph.
<P>Visit Macromedia's snazzy <A
HREF="http://www.macromedia.com/shockzone">Shockzone</A>
site.
</FONT>
</BODY>
</HTML>
```

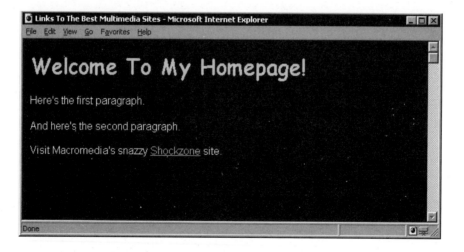

Horizontal rules (okay)

Horizontal rules are straight lines that divide a page into sections. For the simplest type of rule, the only tag you need is <HR>. This automatically puts a horizontal rule across the full width of the page, on a new line, and any text that follows it will form a new paragraph. Because the rule isn't something that needs to be turned off again, there's no closing tag.

If you want to, you can get clever with rules by adding some (or all!) of the following attributes:

Use this attribute...	...for this result
ALIGN=	Use LEFT or RIGHT to place the rule on the left or right of the page. If you leave this out, the rule will be centred.
SIZE=	Enter any number to set the height of the rule in pixels. The default setting is 2.
WIDTH=	Enter a number to specify the width of the line in pixels, or as a percentage of the page (such as WIDTH=70%).
NOSHADE	This removes the 3D effect from the rule. There's no equals sign, and nothing more to add.
COLOR=	Enter the name of a colour. The default setting depends upon the background colour. Only Internet Explorer supports this attribute – other browsers will ignore it.

It's worth playing with the <HR> tag and its attributes to see what unusual effects you can create. For example, the following piece of code places a square bullet in the centre of the page which makes a smart, 'minimalist' divider:

```
<HR SIZE=10 WIDTH=10 COLOR=LIME NOSHADE>
```

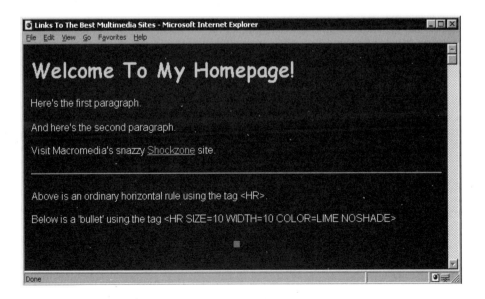

Add spice with an image

The horizontal rule is the simplest type of graphical content you can include on a page, but it's hardly exciting. To liven up a dull page, you can't go far wrong with a well-chosen image. Images on the Web are usually in either of two formats, GIF or JPEG, both of which are supported by almost any paint program.

Once you've chosen the image you want to use, the <IMG> tag will slot it on to the page. This tag works rather like the <FONT> tag – by itself it's meaningless, with all the information being supplied by adding attributes. Let's assume you want to insert an image called **splash.gif**, and the image file is in the same directory as your current HTML document:

```
<IMG SRC="splash.gif">
```

This is the <IMG> tag at its most basic: the SRC attribute (which is short for 'source') tells the browser where to find the image file you want to display, following exactly the same rules as those for relative URLs, which we looked at earlier. Unless you preceded this tag with <P> or <BR>, the image will be placed immediately after the last piece of text you entered. If you enclose the entire tag between <CENTER> and </CENTER> tags, the image will be placed below the previous line of text, centred on the page. You do get a little more choice than that about where the image should be, though, by adding the ALIGN attribute:

This attribute...	Does this...
ALIGN=TOP	Aligns the top of the image with the top of the text on the same line.
ALIGN=MIDDLE	Aligns the middle of the image with the text on that line.
ALIGN=BOTTOM	Aligns the bottom of the image with the bottom of the line of text.
ALIGN=LEFT	Places the image on a new line, and against the left margin.
ALIGN=RIGHT	Places the image on a new line, and against the right margin.

Using these attributes, then, you can place the image roughly where you want it on the page. What's still needed is a bit of fine tuning: after all, if you use ALIGN=MIDDLE, the image will butt right up against the text on the same line. The answer comes in the form of two more attributes that add some blank space around an image: HSPACE= inserts space either side of the image (horizontally), and VSPACE= adds space above and below it (vertically). Just enter a number in pixels after the equals sign. As usual with attributes, if you only need to use one of these, there's no need to include the other. So an image might be inserted with a tag that looks like this:

```
<IMG SRC="splash.gif" ALIGN=MIDDLE HSPACE=30 VSPACE=6>
```

Use an image as an anchor

Earlier in this chapter you learnt how to create hypertext links, or anchors, to a web page or file using the tag <A HREF="*URL*"> *clickable text*</A>. But the clickable section that appears on the page doesn't *have* to be text: you can use an image instead, or both image and text. For example, if you slot the whole image tag given above into the anchor tag, the image will appear exactly as it did before, but will now act as a clickable link:

```
<A HREF="morelinks.html"><IMG SRC="splash.gif"
ALIGN=MIDDLE HSPACE=30 VSPACE=6 WIDTH=84 HEIGHT=81
BORDER=0></A>Click this image to open my other links page.
```

If you want to make both the text *and* the image clickable, add some text before or after the <IMG> tag, as follows:

```
<A HREF="morelinks.html">Click this image to open my other
links page.<IMG SRC="splash.gif" ALIGN=MIDDLE HSPACE=30
VSPACE=6 WIDTH=84 HEIGHT=81 BORDER=0></A>
```

Here's what those two methods look like when displayed in your browser:

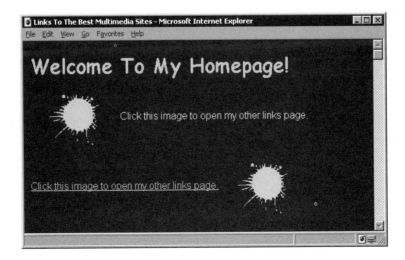

Directory

Directory

1: Choosing an Internet access provider

One of the most important aspects of choosing an IAP is to make sure you can connect by dialling a local phone number (known as a POP, or Point Of Presence). Most IAPs allow unlimited connection time in return for a monthly fee so your only ongoing expense is your telephone bill. However, this isn't the only important aspect. Here's a few other points to check:

Connection speed – Many IAPs now support 33.6Kbps modems on all their POPs and others are already shifting to the latest 56Kbps modems. If you've got a fast modem you don't want to dial in on a slower line.

How do you pay? – Most IAPs will need a credit-card number to take payment automatically each month.

Cancellation details – What are the terms for cancelling your subscription?

Software – Is software provided? Is it preconfigured or must you set it up yourself? Is it free or will you have to pay extra for it? (Some IAPs provide shareware software that you must register if you choose to use it.) Make sure the software will run on your version of Windows.

Which email protocol? – Is a POP3 account included in the price or do you have to pay extra for it? You'll have a much wider range of email software to choose from if you have a POP3 account.

Choose a username – When you take out a subscription you'll be asked what username you want to use. Choose two or three in advance so you're not caught on the hop if your first choice is unavailable.

SLIP or PPP – Make sure you're getting a PPP connection rather than a SLIP connection.

You might also want to ask whether the monthly rate includes space on the IAP's web server for you to publish your own pages, and if so, how many megabytes. It's also worth finding out what sort of technical support your IAP offers. It doesn't hurt to ask if you can have a month's free trial too!

2: UK Internet access providers

Use the list below to find an IAP with the services you're looking for and a local POP, then give it a ring and check some of the details mentioned above. All IAPs noted here offer the basic services of email, World Wide Web, FTP, Telnet, Gopher, IRC, and newsgroup access. Extra details are included under 'Notes'.

Bear in mind that this isn't an exhaustive list, and these details change regularly, so it doesn't hurt to ask if the details don't exactly match what you want. Most IAPs have special pricing packages for business users, as well as other connection options.

Company	Telephone	Email	WWW Site	POPs
Abel Internet	0131 445 5555	info@abel.net.uk	www.abel.net.uk	UK coverage
Notes: ISDN, 5Mb web space, unlimited email addresses				
AngliaNet	01473 211922	sales@anglianet.co.uk	www.anglianet.co.uk	Ipswich area
Notes: ISDN, 1Mb web space				
Atlas Internet	0171 312 0400	info@atlas.co.uk	www.atlas.co.uk	UK coverage
Notes ISDN				
Bournemouth Internet	01202 292900	sales@bournemouth-net.co.uk	www.bournemouth-net.co.uk	Bournemouth
Notes: ISDN, 5Mb web space				
BT Internet	0800 800001	support@btinternet.com	www.btinternet.com	UK coverage
Notes: ISDN, 5Mb web space, 5 email addresses				
Cable Internet	0500 541542	info@cableinet.co.uk	www.cableinet.co.uk	Almost full UK coverage
Notes: ISDN, 5Mb web space, 5 email addresses				
Cerbernet	0171 360 8000	sales@cerbernet.co.uk	www.cerbernet.co.uk	UK coverage
Notes: ISDN, 24-hour support				

Company	Telephone	Email	WWW Site	POPs
City NetGates	0117 907 4000	sales@netgates.co.uk	www.netgates.co.uk	UK coverage
Notes: ISDN, 3Mb web space, 5 email addresses				
CityScape	01223 566950	sales@cityscape.co.uk	www.cityscape.co.uk	UK coverage
Notes: ISDN, 6.5Mb web space, 24-hour support				
ClaraNET Ltd	0800 072 0723	sales@clara.net	www.clara.net	UK coverage
Notes: ISDN, 5Mb web space, unlimited email addresses, 24-hour support				
Cygnet Internet Services	0181 880 4650	info@cygnet.co.uk	www.cygnet.co.uk	London
Notes: ISDN, 5Mb web space, 5 email addresses				
Datanet International	01252 810081	info@data.net.uk	www.data.net.uk	UK coverage
Notes: ISDN, 1Mb web space, unlimited email addresses, 24-hour support				
Demon Internet	0181 371 1234	sales@demon.net	www.demon.net	UK coverage
Notes: ISDN, 5Mb web space, unlimited email addresses, 24-hour support				
Direct Connection	0800 072 0000	sales@dircon.net	www.dircon.net	UK coverage
Notes: ISDN, 5Mb web space, unlimited email addresses				
Direct Net @ccess	01232 201555	info@d-n-a.net	www.d-n-a.net	UK coverage
Notes: ISDN, 10Mb web space, 3 email addresses				
Dorset Internet	01202 659991	sales@lds.co.uk	www.lds.co.uk	UK coverage
Notes: ISDN, 5Mb web space, 2 email addresses, 24-hour support				
edNET	0131 466 7003	info@ednet.co.uk	www.ednet.co.uk	Edinburgh
Notes: ISDN, 1Mb web space				
Enterprise	01624 677666	sales@enterprise.net	www.enterprise.net	UK coverage
Notes: ISDN, 5Mb web space				
Force 9	0800 073 7800	sales@force9.net	www.force9.net	UK coverage
Notes: ISDN, 15Mb web space, unlimited email addresses				
Freeserve	0990 500049	info@freeserve.net	www.freeserve. net/default.htm	UK coverage
Notes: Free service with local-rate dial-up 5Mb web space. Free connection software from Dixons, PC World, Currys and The Link. 24-hour support available at premium rate.				
Frontier Internet Services	0171 536 9090	info@ftech.net	www.ftech.net	UK coverage
Notes: ISDN				
Gifford Internet	0117 939 7722	admin@gifford.co.uk	www.gifford.co.uk	Bristol
Notes: 2Mb web space, 3 email addresses				
Global Internet	0870 909 8043	info@globalnet.co.uk	www.globalnet.co.uk	UK coverage
Notes: ISDN, 3Mb web space, unlimited email addresses				

Company	Telephone	Email	WWW Site	POPs
GreenNet	0171 716 1941	support@gn.apc.org	www.gn.apc.org	UK coverage
Notes: N/A				
IBM Global Network	0800 973000	internet_europe@ie.ibm.com	www.ibm.net	UK coverage
Notes: ISDN, 24-hour support				
Internet Central	01270 611000	sales@netcentral.co.uk	www.netcentral.co.uk	UK coverage
Notes: ISDN, 2Mb web space, 5 email addresses				
IntoNet	0181 941 9195	hq@intonet.co.uk	www.intonet.co.uk	UK coverage
Notes: ISDN, 1Mb web space				
Ireland Online	00353 0855 1739	sales@iol.ie	www.iol.ie	Ireland
Notes: ISDN, 5Mb web space				
KENTnet Internet Services	01622 844801	sales@kentnet.co.uk	www.kentnet.co.uk	Ashford, Hastings, Heathfield, Maidstone, Rye, Staplehurst, Tunbridge Wells
Notes: 5Mb web space, 5 email addresses				
London Web Communications	0181 349 4500	contact@londonweb.net	www.londonweb.net	London
Notes: ISDN, 5Mb web space, 3 email addresses				
Mistral Internet	01273 747432	info@mistral.co.uk	www.mistral.co.uk	UK coverage
Notes: ISDN, 2Mb web space				
Mercia Internet	01827 69166	sales@mercia.net	www.mercia.net	UK coverage
Notes: ISDN, unlimited email addresses				
NetDirect Internet	0171 731 3311	info@netdirect.net.uk	www.netdirect.net.uk	UK coverage
Notes: ISDN, 25Mb web space, unlimited email addresses				
.netKonect	01420 542777	info@netkonect.net	www.netkonect.net	UK coverage
Notes: ISDN, 1Mb web space				
Nildram	0800 072 0400	sales@nildram.co.uk	www.nildram.co.uk	UK coverage
Notes: ISDN, 5Mb web space				
North West Net	0161 950 7777	info@nwnet.co.uk	www.nwnet.co.uk	Liverpool, Manchester, Stoke
Notes: ISDN, 5Mb web space, 11 email addresses				
Onyx Internet	0345 715715	sales@onyxnet.co.uk	www.onyxnet.co.uk	UK coverage
Notes: ISDN				
Paston Chase	01603 502061	info@paston.co.uk	www.paston.co.uk	UK coverage
Notes: ISDN, 5Mb web space				

Company	Telephone	Email	WWW Site	POPs
Power Internet	01908 605188	info@powernet.co.uk	www.powernet.co.uk	UK coverage
Notes: ISDN, 5Mb web space, 24-hour support				
Primex Information Services	01908 643597	info@alpha.primex.co.uk	www.primex.co.uk	UK coverage
Notes: ISDN, 5Mb web space				
Scotland Online	0800 027 2027	sales@sol.co.uk	www.scotland.net	UK coverage
Notes: ISDN, 10Mb web space, 24-hour support				
Talk-101	01925 245145	sales@talk-101.com	www.talk-101.com	UK coverage
Notes: ISDN, 2Mb web space				
Technocom	01753 714200	sales@technocom.co.uk	www.technocom.co.uk	UK coverage
Notes: ISDN, 3Mb web space, 3 email addresses				
The Internet In Nottingham	0115 956 2222	info@innotts.co.uk	www.innotts.co.uk	Nottingham
Notes: ISDN, 5Mb web space, 4 email addresses				
The Web Factory	0116 223 0070	sales@webleicester.co.uk	www.webleicester.co.uk	Leicester
Notes: ISDN				
Total Connectivity Providers	01703 393392	sales@tcp.co.uk	www.tcp.co.uk	UK coverage
Notes: ISDN, 5Mb web space				
Voss Net	01753 737800	staff@vossnet.co.uk	www.vossnet.co.uk	London, Slough
Notes: 2Mb web space				
Wave Rider Internet	0121 603 3888	info@waverider.co.uk	www.waverider.co.uk	UK coverage
Notes: ISDN, 5Mb web space, 5 email addresses				
Zetnet Services	01595 696667	info@zetnet.co.uk	www.zetnet.co.uk	UK coverage
Notes: ISDN, 10Mb web space, unlimited email addresses				
Zoo Internet	0181 961 7000	support@zoo.co.uk	www.zoo.co.uk	UK coverage
Notes: ISDN, 5Mb web space, 2 email addresses				

3: Choosing an online service

Online services offer full Internet access together with a range of other information sources which are not available to non-members. The software is free, fully integrated and usually easy to use: just double-click an icon to install it on your hard disk, then double-click another icon to run the sign-up program and enter your details. You'll then be connected to the service automatically so that your subscription can be logged and you'll receive a username or number (which will form part of your email address) and a private password. Follow the instructions to enter these into the main software program and you're done.

Choosing an online service is easier than choosing an IAP in several respects. First of all, the list is a lot shorter! More importantly, most online services offer a month's free trial membership – if you don't like it, just cancel before you've run up any charges and try a different one. All the same, there are still a few points worth checking:

- Find out *how* you cancel if you don't like it. It's always easy to sign up, but online services don't make much noise about the cancellation routine!

- Make sure your local POP matches or exceeds the speed of your modem.

- Have your credit card handy when you run the software that signs you up to the service. Although you won't pay for the first month, you won't be able to connect without it.

- Don't forget the username or password you're assigned when you run the connection software – write them clearly on a piece of paper straight away.

The following is a list of online services. If you don't have the software required to subscribe, phone up and ask for it. Many of these services have a variety of subscription schemes available and some offer free web space to their members.

Company	Telephone	Email	WWW site	POPs	Setup cost	Monthly cost	Hours per month	Cost per extra hour
America Online (AOL)	0800 279 1234	queryuk@aol.com	www.aol.com	UK coverage	Free	£5.95	3	£1.85
Notes: 10Mb web space, 5 email addresses								
CIX	0845 355 5050	sales@cix.co.uk	www.cix.co.uk	UK coverage	Free	£7.34	2.5	£2.40
Notes: ISDN, 5Mb web space, unlimited email addresses								
CompuServe (CSi)	0990 000 200	70006.101@ compuserve.com	world. compuserve.com	UK coverage	Free	£6.50	5	£1.95
Notes: ISDN, 5Mb web space								

Company	Telephone	Email	WWW site	POPs	Setup cost	Monthly cost	Hours per month	Cost per extra hour
Easynet	0171 681 4444	postbox@easynet.net	www.easynet.net	UK coverage	Free	£11.99	No limit	N/A
Notes: ISDN, 2Mb web space, 24-hour support								
Freedom2surf	0181 811 2111	sales@freedom2surf.net	www.freedom2surf.net	UK coverage	Free	£11.75	No limit	N/A
Notes: ISDN, 5Mb web space, 5 email addresses								
Hiway	01635 573300	info@inform.hiway.co.uk	www.hiway.co.uk	UK coverage	£17.63	£17.63	No limit	N/A
Notes: ISDN, 5 email addresses								
LineOne	0800 111210	enquiries@lineone.net	www.lineone.net	UK coverage	Free	£4.95	3	£2.35
Notes ISDN, 10Mb web space, 5 email addresses								
Microsoft Network (MSN)	0345 002000	ukweb@microsoft-contact.co.uk	www.msn.com	UK coverage	Free	£14.95	No limit	N/A
Notes: ISDN, 1Mb web space								
RedNet	01494 511640	marketing@red.net	www.red.net	UK coverage	£29.40	£17.60	No limit	N/A
Notes: ISDN, 10Mb web space, 10 email addresses								
Surflink	0800 243777	info@surflink.co.uk	www.surflink.co.uk	UK coverage	Free	£9.39	No limit	N/A
Notes: ISDN, 2Mb web space, 5 email addresses								
UK Online	01749 333333	sales@ukonline.co.uk	www.ukonline.co.uk	UK coverage	Free	£12.99	No limit	N/A
Notes: ISDN, 2Mb web space, 24-hour support								
UUNET Pipex Dial	0500 474739	sales@dial.pipex.com	www.uunet.pipex.com	UK coverage	£11.75	£14.98	No limit	N/A
Notes: ISDN, 2Mb web space, 5 email addresses								
Virgin Net	0500 558800	advice@virgin.net	www.virgin.net	UK coverage	Free	£11.99	No limit	N/A
Notes: ISDN, 10Mb web space, 24-hour support								
WEBplus	0345 932758	info@webplus.co.uk	www.webplus.co.uk	UK coverage	£25.00	£14.10	No limit	N/A
Notes: ISDN, 10Mb web space								

4: UK software companies

Some of the companies in the following list have been singled out earlier in the book as producers of high-quality and/or very popular software titles in particular areas of computing. In these cases, the products named are listed with the company's details for easy reference. This shouldn't be taken as an implication that these are the only products produced by that company, nor that they're the only *good* products produced by that company!

Company	Telephone	Products
Adobe Systems	0181 606 4000	Acrobat, Premiere, PhotoDeluxe, PhotoShop
Aldus	0131 451 6888	
Attica Cybernetics	01865 200892	
Autodesk	01483 303322	Autodesk Animator Studio
Avalon	01624 627227	
Borland	01734 320022	Paradox
Broderbund	01753 620909	Print Shop Deluxe, Living Books series
Brooklyn North Software Works	0500 284177	HTML Assistant Pro 2
Central Point International	01628 788580	
Claris	0181 756 0101	ClarisWorks, FileMaker Pro
Corel	01703 814142	CorelDRAW, Quattro Pro, PerfectWorks
Delrina	0181 207 7033	Fax and communications software
Digital Workshop	01295 258335	Illuminatus
Dorling Kindersley	0171 753 3488	Children's CD-ROM titles
Electronic Arts	01753 549442	Multimedia and children's titles
Gold Disk	01753 832383	Astound
Gremlin Games	0114 275 3423	
GSP	01480 496789	DesignWorks, PressWorks, MONEYmatters
Guildsoft	01752 895100	
IBM Software Enquiries	01329 242728	OS/2
Interplay	01235 821666	
Intuit	0181 990 5500	Quicken Deluxe, QuickBooks
Lotus Development	01784 455455	Lotus SmartSuite, Approach, WordPro, 1-2-3

Company	Telephone	Products
Macromedia	0181 358 5857	Authorware
Micrografx	0800 626009	
MicroProse	01454 329510	
Microsoft	01734 270001	Windows, Word, Excel, Office, Works
Mirage	01260 299909	
MoneyBox Software	01392 429424	
Ocean	0161 839 0999	
Pegasus Software	01536 495000	
Psygnosis	0151 282 3000	
Quark Systems	01483 454397	Quark Xpress
Quarterdeck UK	01245 494940	Cleansweep, QEMM
Sage	0191 255 3000	Instant Accounting
S&S International	01296 318700	Dr Solomon's Anti-Virus Toolkit
Serif	0800 924925	PagePlus, DrawPlus, PhotoPlus, Publishing Suite
Softkey	0181 789 2000	
SoftQuad	0181 236 1001	
Starfish Software	0181 875 4455	Sidekick, Dashboard
Symantec	01628 592222	Norton Tools, PC Desktop
TopLevel Computing	01453 753944	
Wang UK	0181 568 9200	

5: UK hardware companies

Company	Telephone	Products
AMD	01256 603121	Processors
Apricot Computers	0121 717 7171	PCs
Brother UK	0161 330 6531	Printers
Compaq	0181 332 3888	PCs, Notebook PCs
Conner	01294 315333	Hard drives
Creative Labs	01734 344322	Soundcards, Multimedia peripherals

Company	Telephone	Products
Cyrix	0800 137305	Processors
Diamond Multimedia	01753 501400	Display adapters, Multimedia peripherals
Epson UK	01442 227478	Printers
Fujitsu	0181 573 4444	Hard drives, Printers, Scanners
Hayes	01252 775533	Modems
Hercules	01635 861122	Display adapters
Hewlett-Packard	01344 369369	Printers
Hitachi	0181 849 2087	CD-ROM drives, Monitors
IBM	01345 500900	PCs, Notebook PCs
Iiyama	01438 745482	Monitors
Intel	01793 431144	Processors
Iomega	0800 898563	Archive and backup drives
IPC Corp UK	01282 618866	PCs, Notebook PCs, Peripherals
Jvc	0181 896 6000	CD-ROM drives
Kodak	01442 261122	Scanners, Digital cameras
Kyocera Electronics UK	01734 311500	Printers
Lexmark International	01628 488200	Printers
Logitech	01344 891313	Mice, Trackballs, Scanners
Matrox	01793 614002	Display adapters
Microsoft	01734 271000	Mice, Trackballs, Keyboards
Microvitec	01274 390011	Monitors
Mitsumi	01276 29029	CD-ROM drives
NEC Computer Products	0181 993 8111	PCs, CD-ROM drives
Nikon	0181 541 4440	Scanners
Olivetti	0800 447799	PCs, Notebook PCs, Printers
Orchid Europe	01256 844899	Display adapters
Packard Bell	0800 314314	PCs
Panasonic	01344 853508	Monitors, Printers, CD-ROM drives
Pioneer	01753 789731	CD-ROM drives
Plasmon Data	01763 262963	Recordable CD drives
Primax	01235 536374	Scanners
Psion	0171 258 7376	Palmtop computers

Company	Telephone	Products
Roland UK	01792 702701	Soundcards, MIDI hardware
Seagate	01628 474532	Hard drives
Sony UK	0181 784 1144	CD-ROM drives, Monitors
Star Micronics	01494 471111	Printers
Toshiba	01932 785666	CD-ROM drives, Printers, Notebook PCs
Trust Peripherals	01376 500770	Scanners, Modems, Multimedia peripherals
US Robotics	01734 228200	Modems
VideoLogic	01923 271300	Display adapters
Visioneer	0181 358 5850	Scanners
Western Digital UK	01372 360055	Hard drives

6: UK retailers

Company	Telephone	Products
Byte Direct	0121 7665559	PCs/Peripherals
Choice Peripherals	01909 530242	Peripherals/Components/Software
Currys	01442 888000	PCs/Peripherals
Dabs Direct	0800 674467	PCs/Peripherals/Software/Components/Consumables
Dan Technology	0181 830 1100	PCs
Dart Computers	01794 511505	PCs
Dell	01344 724872	PCs
Dixons	01442 888000	PCs, Peripherals/Software/Consumables
Elonex	0800 524444	PCs, Notebook PCs
Fox Computers	01621 744500	PCs/Peripherals/Components
Gateway 2000	0800 362000	PCs, Notebook PCs
Memory Bank	0181 956 7000	Memory/Peripherals/Software/Components
Mesh Computers	0181 452 1111	PCs
Novatech	0800 666500	PCs/Peripherals/Software/Consumables
PC World	0990 464464	PCs/Peripherals/Software/Consumables
Pico Direct	01483 202022	Notebook PCs/Notebook peripherals

Company	Telephone	Products
Plug & Play Technology	0181 341 3336	PC Cards/Notebook peripherals
Roldec	01902 456464	Peripherals/Components
Simply Computers	0181 498 2130	PCs/Peripherals/Components
SMC Computers	01753 550333	PCs/Peripherals/Components
Software Warehouse	01675 466467	Software/ Peripherals/Components/Consumables
Stak Trading	01788 577497	PCs/Peripherals/Components
Taurus Component Shop	01978 312372	Components/Peripherals
Tech Direct	0181 286 2222	Notebook PCs/Printers/Peripherals/Consumables
Technomatic	0990 559944	PCs/Peripherals/Software/Components
The Link	01442 888000	PCs/Peripherals
Time Computer Systems	01282 777111	PCs
Tiny Computers	01293 821333	PCs
Viglen	0181 758 7080	PCs, Notebook PCs
Virgin Megastore	0171 631 1234	Software
Watford Electronics	01582 745555	PCs/Software/Peripherals/Components

7: UK general services

Data Transfer, Conversion, Duplication	
A.L.Downloading Services	0181 994 5471
Mapej	01961 778659

Data Recovery (Disk failure, corruption, viruses)	
Authentic Data Recovery	0800 581263
Ontrack Data Recovery	0800 243996
Vogon International	01869 355255

PC Rental	
MC Rentals	01952 604411
Micro-Rent	0171 700 4848
Skylake Rentals	0800 373118

PC Security/Anti-theft	
Datamark Security	01494 434757
Secure PC	0171 610 3646

PC Memory	
AW Computer Memory Bargains	01382 807000
Click	0800 666500
Mem Com	0161 427 2222
Mr Memory	01483 799410
Offtek	0121 722 3993
Richnight	0800 318298

Printer Consumables	
Cartridge Care	0800 252410
Cartridge Express	0800 026 7023
Inkwell Direct	01344 843444
Jetica	0800 074 0587
Mannink	01462 627770
MX2	01481 43965
Owl Associates	01543 250377
Selectafont	01702 202835
Squire International	0181 345 7474
Themis	01883 333 0333
Vectorjet	01763 273115

Floppy Disks	
Owl Associates	01543 250377
Product Trade & Services	0800 136502
Squire International	0181 345 7474

Specialist Suppliers		
BBD Dust Covers	01257 425839	Computer dust-covers
C&T	0171 637 1767	Storage hardware

Capital Litho	01386 40321	Personalised mouse mats
Clove Technology	01202 302796	Palmtop computers & software
Linefeed	0171 474 1765	CD writers & media
MJ Communications	0800 526376	Modems
Monitor Man	01453 885599	Monitors
Semaphore Systems	0171 625 7744	Components
The Keyboard Company	07000 102105	Keyboards
The Monitor Shop	0115 911 0366	Monitors

Shareware

A1 Shareware	0181 806 5769
AWH Computer Services	01563 850645
Demon Shareware	01325 301849
Ferrari Software	01843 865083
Hornesoft PD	01142 967825
Islander Software	0345 660429
MicroWorld	01425 610699
Telescan	01253 829292

8: Useful Internet sites

The following is an alphabetical list of computer and Internet related companies with a presence on the World Wide Web, together with a few additional sites to help you track down the information or software you need.

Software companies

Adobe Systems Inc.	http://www.adobe.com
Asymetrix	http://munin.asymetrix.com
Berkeley Systems	http://www.berksys.com
Borland International Inc.	http://www.borland.com
Brooklyn North	http://www.brooknorth.com
Claris Corporation Software Works	http://www.claris.com

Corel Corporation	http://www.corel.com
Gold Disk Inc.	http://www.golddisk.com
JASC Inc.	http://www.jasc.com
Lotus Development	http://www.lotus.com
Macromedia	http://www.macromedia.com
McAfee	http://www.mcafee.com
Micrografx	http://www.micrografx.com
Microsoft Corp.	http://www.microsoft.com
Nico Mak	http://www.winzip.com
Plasmon Data Computing Inc.	http://www.plasmon.com
Quark Inc.	http://www.quark.com
Quarterdeck	http://www.qdeck.com
SoftQuad	http://www.sq.com
Steinberg	http://www.steinberg-us.com
Symantec	http://www.symantec.com

Hardware companies

AMD	http://www.amd.com
Award	http://www.award.com
Aztech	http://www.aztech.com.sg
Canon	http://www.canon.com
Casio	http://www.casio.com
Cirrus Logic	http://cirrus.com
Compaq	http://www.compaq.com
Creative Labs	http://www.creaf.com
Dell	http://www.us.dell.com
Diamond Multimedia Systems	http://www.diamondmm.com
Gateway 2000	http://gw2k.com
Gravis	http://www.gravis.com
Hayes	http://www.hayes.com
Hewlett-Packard	http://www.hp.com
IBM	http://www.ibm.com

Intel	http://www.intel.com
Iomega	http://www.careermosaic.com/cm/iomega
Logitech	http://www.logitech.com
Mitsumi	http://www.mitsumi.com
NEC	http://www.nec.com
Olivetti	http://www.olivetti.com
Panasonic	http://www.panasonic.com
Primax	http://www.primax.net
Seagate Technology	http://www.seagate.com
Sony Corporation	http://www.sony.com
Toshiba	http://www.toshiba.com
US Robotics	http://www.usr.com
VideoLogic	http://www.videologic.com

Internet software & general sites

Jumbo Software Archive	http://www.jumbo.com
No-Nags Internet Software	http://ded.com/nonags/main.html
Shareware.com	http://www.shareware.com
Software Warehouse Store	http://www.software-warehouse.co.uk
Tucows Internet Software	http://tucows.cableinet.net
Virtual Software Library	http://abyss.idirect.com/cgi-bin/vsl-front
Windows95.com	http://www.windows95.com

Index

Becoming a Prentice Hall Author

Getting Published with Prentice Hall

1. Can I Do It?

It is easy to think of the publishing process as a series of hurdles designed to weed out would-be authors. That may be true of some publishing houses, but not Prentice Hall.

- We do all we can to encourage new talent.

- We welcome unsolicited manuscripts.

- We carefully examine every proposal we receive, and we always write back to let the authors know what we think of it.

Although many of our authors have professional or educational experience, we look first for a passion for your chosen subject area. some of our most successful books are. written by first time authors. If you have built up expertise in any business, finance or computing topic, please get in touch. You'll be surprised how easy it is to get through to a commissioning editor.

2. Is Prentice Hall a Successful Company?

Prentice Hall is a highly respected brand in technical, financial and scientific publishing, a status reflected in our relationships with the book trade and various professional bodies. We're part of Simon & Schuster, a $2 billion dollar global publishing company. Simon and Schuster is host to Macmillan General Reference, The Free Press, Frommers, Macmillan Computer Publishing (home of renowned computer imprints such as Sams, Que, Waite Group Press, ZiffDavis Publishing, Hayden and New Riders Press). Simon & Schuster is itself owned by Viacom Inc, one of the world's largest entertainment and publishing companies. Viacom owns film and tv studios (Paramount Pictures), worldwide cable networks (MTV, Nickelodeon) and retail outlets (Blockbuster Video).

3. What Sort of Books Does Prentice Hall Publish?

We are happy to consider book proposals on absolutely any topic, although we have a special interest in business, computing and finance. Our progressive editorial policy encourages new authors and gives us the flexibility necessary in a rapidly changing technological environment.

4. What are the Rewards of Writing a Book?

Prentice Hall royalty rates are among the most competitive in the industry, and many of our authors earn considerable sums through royalties.

Payments are calculated along industry-standard guidelines, i.e. the author receives a percentage of the publisher's net sales revenue. The amount you receive depends on the selling price of the book, so talk to your editor about your likely income. We always offer preferential royalty rates for senior figures within any industry, or for books on hot topics written by experts. For the right book at the right time, the financial reward to the author can be extremely generous.

If you are an academic or a member of a profession, your livelihood may depend upon your intellectual reputation. Successful Prentice Hall authors enjoy a constant stream of business and vocational opportunities as a direct result of getting published. A book works like a business card, advertising the author's talent across a vast network of potential contacts.

5. How Do I Know my Ideas are Good Enough to Publish?

In assessing the market readiness of book proposals or finished manuscripts, Prentice Hall editors draw upon a huge database of technical advisors. All of our reviewers are senior figures within their field, and their role is to offer free advice to potential authors, highlighting both the strengths and weaknesses of proposals and manuscripts. The aim of the review process is to add value to your ideas, rather than just approving or rejecting them.

Many of our authors have not written a book before, so we are there to help them with advice on grammar and style.

6. How Much Control Would I Have Over My Book?

We understand that a book is a highly personal statement from the author, so we invite your participation at all stages of the publishing process, from the cover design through to the final marketing plans. A Prentice Hall book is a co-operative venture between author and publisher.

7. Will, I Get any Help with the Technical Aspects of Book Production?

Our highly professional staff will ensure that the book you envisaged is the book that makes it to the shelves. Once you hand over your manuscript to us, we will take care of all the technical details of printing and binding. Beyond the advice and guidance from your own editor, our 64-page author guide is there to help you shape your manuscript into a first-class book. Our large and efficient production department is among the quickest in the industry.

We are experts at turning raw manuscripts into polished books, irrespective of the technical complexity of your work. Technical queries can be answered by your production contact, assigned, where relevant, to you at contract stage. Our production staff fully understand the individual requirements of every project, and will work with you to produce a manuscript format that best complements your skills - hard copy manuscripts, electronic files or cameraready copy, where we pay the author to set the text out on the page.

8. How Quickly Can You Turn My Manuscript into a Book?

The production department at Prentice Hall is widely acknowledged to be among the quickest in the industry. Our turnaround times vary according to the nature of the manuscript supplied to us, but the average is about three months for camera-ready copy and four months for. a manuscript delivered on disk. For time-sensitive topics, we can turn out books in under twelve weeks.

9. Where Would my Book be Sold?

Prentice Hall has one of the largest sales forces of any technical publisher. Our highly experienced sales staff have developed firm business partnerships with all the major retail bookstores in Europe, America, Asia, the Middle East and South Africa, ensuring that your book receives maximum retail exposure. Prentice Hall's marketing department is responsible for ensuring the widest possible review coverage in magazines and journals.

Our books are usually present at major trade shows and exhibitions, either on our own stands or those belonging to major retail bookshops. Our presence at trade shows ensures that your work can be inspected by the most senior figures within any given field. We also have a very successful corporate and institutional sales team, dedicated to selling our books into large companies, user groups, book clubs, training seminars and professional bodies.

Local language translations can provide not only a significant boost to an author's royalty income, but also will allow your research/findings to reach a wider audience, thus furthering your professional prospects. To maintain both the author's and Prentice Hall's reputation, we license foreign language deals only with publishing houses of the highest repute.

10.I Don't have Time to Write a Book!

To enjoy all the advantages of being a published author, it is not always necessary for you to write an entire book. Prentice Hall welcomes books written by multiple authors. If you feel that your skills lie in a very specific area, or that you do not have the time to write an entire book, please get in touch regardless. Prentice Hall may have a book in progress that would benefit from your ideas. You may know individuals or teams in your field who could act as co-author(s). If not, Prentice Hall can probably put you in touch with the right people. Royalties for shared-author books are distributed according to respective participation.

11. Could my Company Benefit?

Many Prentice Hall authors use their book to lever their commercial interests, and we like to do all we can to help. If a well-written book is an excellent marketing tool for an author, then it can also be an excellent marketing tool for the author's company. A book is its own highly focused marketing channel, a respected medium that takes your company name to all the right people. Previous examples of marketing opportunities with our books include:

- Free advertising in the back pages

- Packaging in suitable corporate livery (book covers, flyers etc.)

- Mounting software demos in the back page on disk or CD-ROM

Although Prentice Hall has to keep its publications free of undue corporate or institutional bias, in general the options for cross-marketing are varied and completely open to discussion.

12.I Have an Idea for a Book. What Next?

We invite you to submit a book proposal. We need proposals to be formatted in a specific way, so please contact us at the address below for our free proposal guidelines.

The Acquisition Editor
Professional and Consumer Publishing
Prentice Hall
Campus 400, Maylands Avenue
Hemel Hempstead, Hertfordshire
HP2 7EZ
England

Tel: +44 (0)1442 881900
Fax: +44 (0)1442 252544
e-mail: jdunne@prenhall.co.uk

Now you've read all about the Internet you'll want to get online...

Try it FREE for a month

Internet Service Provider of the Year
Internet Magazine, 1997

"Best value for money"
Which Consumer Guide, July 1998

"Excellent for price and service"
Practical Internet June, 1997

Welcome to Virgin Net

We're here to give you the best Internet service there is. That's it. Once you've tried it we hope you will stay with us for a long time. Exploring the **Internet** can be a confusing experience at first. Virgin Net is here to provide a helping hand. We will guide you through the pitfalls and help you get the best from the Internet. Once you get online you'll find that we've provided you with a guide to some of the best things on the Internet, and a number of features of our own. Please feel free to contact us if you have any comments on how we might improve our service or if there are any new things you would like to see included.

If you feel yourself getting into trouble, please call our local call rate helpline.

24-hour helpline: 0845 650 0000

Your calls may be monitored for training purposes.

Internet

Millions of computers storing billions of files accessed by tens of millions of people. But don't panic: we'll show you around the basics before turning you loose.

AND WE'LL ALWAYS BE CLOSE AT HAND TO HELP.

Virgin Net is simple to use. You don't need to know anything about the Internet

This section contains simple step-by-step instructions for getting

on to the Internet, and will guide you through to a successful

connection within a few minutes.

All you need is a personal computer, a **modem**, an

ordinary telephone line and the installation pack on the CD.

Within minutes, you'll have access to the world's biggest reference

library, CD collection, department store and news-stand. You'll be

able to search for information, communicate with people all over

the world, discuss your interests and share ideas.

All for the price of a local rate phone call
24-hour helpline: 0845 650 0000

modem

A box of electronics that allows your computer to communicate through a telephone line. It's like a TV aerial tuned to Virgin Net, receiving all the things that you see on your screen. But unlike an aerial, your modem also sends your commands back.

ordinary telephone line

Your computer is connected to Virgin Net by telephone. No matter where your computer is getting information from, you only pay for a local rate call. Remember: while you're connected, you can't use that line to make or receive calls.

What you will need

1. A **personal computer**. You will need a PC running Windows 3.1 or **Windows 95** or an Apple Mac running MacOS 7.1 or better.

2. A modem. Plug its phone lead into a working telephone socket, and, unless your computer has an internal modem built inside it, plug the other lead into the appropriate socket in the side or back of your computer.

3. The CD included with this book.

4. The following information:

• Your name, address and postcode.

• The make and model of your modem.

• Your **payment details** for your subscription (Credit Card or **Direct Debit**).

personal computer

Detailed hardware requirements are provided at the back of this section.

Windows 95

If you are running Windows 95, you may also need your original Windows 95 CD or floppy disks.

payment details

This information will only be used if you choose to remain with us once your free trial period has expired.

Direct Debit

Due to the amount of time it takes to set up a Direct Debit, we will need to have your first payment via Credit or Debit Card.

Software pack

The Virgin Net software pack contains all the programs you need to connect to and use the Internet. Most of the information and entertainment you'll find on the Internet is linked by the **World Wide Web**. You navigate through the World Wide Web using a browser. A browser is a program which knows how to play and display the many different types of pictures, sounds, movies or text files that you will find on the 'Web'. The browser is also your tool for moving around the Web, just using clicks of your mouse. It will also let you send and receive **e-mail** and read and send messages to **newsgroups**. The Virgin Net software pack includes both Microsoft Internet Explorer and Netscape Navigator. During this installation we will recommend which browser is appropriate for your computer.

World Wide Web

An easy way of finding most of the information on the Internet. The Web is made up of millions of linked pages of text and pictures, which you can display on your computer.

e-mail

Keep in touch with your friends and colleagues by sending electronic messages. It's cheaper than a phone call.

newsgroups

Whatever your interest or hobby, you'll find people talking (in writing) about it in a newsgroup. Anyone can post messages to a newsgroup, and anyone can read them.

In addition to the browser

We will also install the following Virgin Net programs.

These are:

Global Chat

Lets you talk live to other people on the Net by typing messages.

Real Audio

Allows your browser to play sound files without downloading them first.

We also provide two optional extras, Cybersitter and Shockwave.

Full instructions can be found on the Help service once you are online.

Cybersitter

This program allows you to control your childrens access to the Internet.

Shockwave

This program allows your browser to place animated graphics and movies.

How to install Virgin Net

First, make sure that you have shut down any other programs and
applications that are running on your computer, except **Windows**
95 or Windows 3.1 or MacOS. Next, put the CD into your CD drive
The Installation program will do some tests on your computer, to
see if you have disk space for the Virgin Net programs and test
whether your machine can run them. If there's a problem, the
Installation program will tell you exactly what it is. Some problems
you can solve easily by following the on-screen instructions. If the
problem is more serious, call our 24-hour helpline on 0845 650
0000. Before you call, take a note of the problem message from the
Installation program it will help our team guide you through the
solution.

24-hour helpline: 0845 650 0000

Windows 95

During installation, you may be asked to insert your Windows 95 CD or floppy disks, so keep them handy. Virgin Net
uses certain Windows 95 programs to connect your computer and modem to the Internet.
These files may not have already been installed.
Remember: if you have any problems, simply call the 24-hour Virgin Net helpline on 0845 650 0000 for advice.

Window 95 and 98 users only

(If the installation starts automatically, you can skip straight to step 4.)

1. Select start on the Taskbar.

2. Select run in the Start menu.

3. If you are using a CD, type D:/virgin.net/setup

4. Click OK and follow the on-screen instructions.

Window 3.1 users only

1. Open Program Manager.

2. Select file from the Menubar.

3. Select Run.

4. Type D:/virgin.net/setup.

5. Click OK and follow the on-screen instructions.

Mac users only

1. Double-click on the 'Virgin Net' icon in the desktop.

2. In the 'Virgin Net' folder, click the 'Installer' icon.

3. Follow the on-screen instructions.

Registration

Once installation is complete you are ready to register with Virgin Net. Before you start, be sure to check that your modem, telephone line and computer are all properly linked up and that the modem is switched on. Then just follow the simple on-screen registration instructions. The Registration program will make a local rate telephone call to Virgin Net using your modem, and then will ask you for your **personal and payment detail** . The information you provide is used to set up your account. As soon as you have done this, Virgin Net will send you a unique Username and Password. Your Username will tell us who you are when you go online with Virgin Net. Your Password allows us to confirm that you are who you say you are. Please make a note of both your Username and your Password as you will need them every time you want to connect to Virgin Net. In addition, your Username will be used to set up your e-mail address on Virgin Net. For example, if your Username is "joe.bloggs" your e-mail address would be "joe.bloggs@virgin.net".

personal and payment details

This information is confidential and secure. Your details are sent by a direct link to our private computer, which is not connected to the Internet. The information you send cannot be intercepted or read by any other Internet user.

Problems with registration

If the Installation procedure has been successful, it should have taken you directly to our online registration screen. But if it hasn't, don't worry. First try this:

1. Check that your modem is turned on and plugged in correctly.

2. Check that your **telephone line** is working properly. Do this by plugging in an ordinary telephone and dialling the special Virgin Net Registration number, **0645 50 54 40**. You should first hear the line ringing and then something that sounds a bit like a fax machine or static on the radio.

If after these checks you still cannot register, call:

24-hour helpline on: 0845 650 0000.

telephone line

Make sure that no one is on the phone before you try to connect to Virgin Net. It won't work and they're likely to hear a horrible screeching.

Whenever you want to connect to Virgin Net

All you need to do is:

1. First, make sure that your modem, telephone line and computer are properly connected.

2. Then turn your modem and computer on and **double-click** the Virgin Net icon on your Windows 95/MacOS desktop or in the Virgin Net Program Group if you are using Windows 3.1.

3. If you are using Windows 95, you will need to confirm your Username and Password.

4. Finally, click the connect button. Your modem will connect you to Virgin Net by making a **local rate phone call** .

Remember, your Virgin Net subscription does not include the price of this call. The charges for this will appear on your next phone bill.

double-click

Tap the left-hand mouse button twice, quickly. Usually used to start a program. Remember: once you're using your browser, you only need to click ONCE to jump to a new link.

local rate phone call

Wherever you are in the country, your telephone connection to Virgin Net's computers is always charged as if you were making a local call.

Once the connection has successfully been made

The browser will **download** on to your screen the Virgin Net **home page**. Your home page is always the first thing you see each time you connect to the Internet, and the Virgin Net home page is designed clearly and simply to:

1. Help you to search for useful, entertaining or important information.

2. Give you direct links to the places we recommend.

3. Bring you up-to-the-minute news, sport and entertainment.

4. Let you download and play games or use your computer to connect to **websites** containing recorded and even live sounds, such as **Virgin Radio**.

That's it. The rest is up to you. Remember, you're in charge. From now on, we're just here to help.

download

Get information or files from a computer on the Internet and copy it on to your own computer.

home page

The place you'll begin your exploration of the Internet from. And don't worry if you ever get lost one click of the HOME button on your browser will take you straight back there.

websites

What a programme is to TV and a book is to a library, a website is to the Internet.

Virgin Radio

1215AM & 105.8FM. The world's greatest radio station, of course.

Help - and where to find it

We have made Virgin Net as simple and easy to use as possible.

Even so, we know that for newcomers the Internet can be a strange

and confusing place. That's why we've created a Help service that

will answer the **questions** you're most likely to ask.

And don't forget, if you still have a problem or have any

suggestions to make, call:

24-hour helpline on 0845 650 0000.

questions

There are some questions that come up again and again. They're referred to as "Frequently Asked Questions" or FAQs. Before asking a question – either in Virgin Net or a newsgroup it's a good idea to check to see if the answer is already in the relevant FAQ.

Electronic mail

Electronic mail, better known as e-mail, is so useful that many people get on to the Net just to use it. It's that good. Unlike old-fashioned 'snail mail', you don't need a stamp and it travels at the speed of light. Once you start using e-mail, you will be able to send messages and documents quickly, cheaply and at any time of the day or night to anyone in the world with an e-mail address.

To start using e-mail, press on the mail button on **the browser**. This will open Outlook Express the e-mail program. To receive e-mail, click on the send & receive button. Outlook Express will go to the **Virgin Net computers**, check to see if you have new mail waiting for you there and download any new messages on to your computer.

24-hour helpline on: 0845 650 0000

the browser

If you are using Netscape click GET MAIL to recieve an e-mail, TO MAIL to send one and RE: MAIL to reply.

Virgin Net computers

Giant, mysterious black cabinets covered in thousands of flashing lights and quietly leaking white coolant fumes. No? Actually they look pretty much like your machine, except a bit faster. Probably.

Electronic mail

New messages will appear in bold and you can read them by double-clicking on them. To send e-mail, click on the compose message button and an empty message window will appear. Type in the e-mail address of the person you want to write to, and then type your message. Send it by clicking on the send button. To reply directly to an e-mail that you have received, the simplest way is by clicking on the reply to author button. A window will open showing the original message with the sender's return e-mail address already filled in. Just type your reply and press the send button. To learn more about using e-mail, use the Virgin Net **Help service**, where we have prepared a full guide to using and getting the best out of e-mail.

Help service

We want to make using the Internet as easy as possible. And that means having the best help service you'll find anywhere. As well as our 24-hour helpline, we've prepared an online tutorial to take you through the basics, step by step. We've written reference pages that answer the most commonly asked questions. You can find the Help service in Virgin Net services.

Detailed hardware requirements

PC requirements:

- Windows 95, Windows 98 or Windows 3.1

- 486dx processor or better (100MHz for IE4)

- 6Mb free hard disk space (75Mb for Internet Explorer)

- 14.4Kbps or faster modem

- 256 colour display monitor

Apple Mac requirements:

- MacOS System 7.1 or above

- 68040 processor or better

- 16Mb free hard disk space (24Mb recommended)

- 14.4Kbps or faster modem

- 256 colour display monitor

"Richard Branson's crew have taken the market by storm with their keen prices and top quality support"

PC Answers, July 1997

"Internet Service Provider of the Year"

Internet Magazine, 1997

"Excellent for price and service"

Practical Internet, June 1997

"Best value for money"

Which? Consumer Guide, July 1998